BASICS OF COMPUTER NETWORKS

A STUDENT-FRIENDLY GUIDE TO NETWORKING FUNDAMENTALS

VAISHALI AMOL UJAGARE
DR. PREMANAND K. KADBE
DR. VANDANA MILIND ROHOKALE

Made with ♥ on the Notion Press Platform
www.notionpress.com

Contents

Preface

In the rapidly evolving landscape of science and technology, the need for clear understanding, practical knowledge, and conceptual clarity has never been more important. This book is an earnest effort to bridge the gap between theoretical concepts and their real-world applications, providing readers with a structured and meaningful learning experience.

Authored by Asst. Prof. Vaishali Ujagare, Dr. Premanand K. Kadbe, and Dr. Vandana Rohokal, this work reflects a blend of academic depth, teaching experience, and a strong commitment to student-centric learning. Each chapter has been carefully designed to simplify complex ideas, present them in an organized manner, and make the subject accessible to learners from diverse backgrounds.

The primary objective of this book is not only to cover the prescribed syllabus but also to develop analytical thinking and problem-solving skills among students. Special attention has been given to clarity of explanation, use of relevant examples, and logical flow of topics so that learners can build a strong conceptual foundation. Wherever necessary, practical insights and real-world perspectives have been incorporated to enhance understanding and application.

This book is intended to serve as a valuable resource for students, educators, and professionals alike. It can be used as a textbook for academic courses as well as a reference guide for self-study. The authors sincerely hope that this work will inspire curiosity, encourage continuous learning, and contribute positively to the academic journey of its readers.

The authors would like to express their gratitude to all those who directly and indirectly supported the development of this book. Constructive feedback and suggestions from readers will always be welcomed for further improvement in future editions.

Asst. Prof. Vaishali Ujagare
Dr. Premanand K. Kadbe
Dr. Vandana Rohokale

Vaishali Amol Ujagare (author)

Asst. Prof. Vaishali Amol Ujagare is a dedicated academician with a strong foundation in Information Technology and Computer Networks. She completed her Bachelor of Engineering (B.E.) in Information Technology from Bharati Vidyapeeth and pursued her Master of Engineering (M.E.) in Computer Networks from KJ College of Engineering. Her academic background has enabled her to develop a deep understanding of networking concepts and their practical applications.

She began her professional journey in the software testing domain, gaining valuable industry experience and practical exposure to real-world applications. This early experience played a crucial role in shaping her analytical thinking and problem-solving approach, which she later carried into her academic career.

Following her industry experience, she worked as a Technical Editor at TechMax Publications. During this tenure, she contributed significantly to the development and refinement of academic content, gaining expertise in presenting complex technical concepts in a clear, structured, and student-friendly manner.

She then transitioned into academics and served as a Lecturer at Swaraj College for three years. She is currently working as an Assistant Professor at Sinhgad Institute of Technology and Science, Narhe, Pune, where she continues to contribute to teaching and academic development. With over three years of teaching experience, she is committed to simplifying complex technical subjects and helping students build strong conceptual clarity.

Her areas of interest include Computer Networks, academic content development, and student-centric teaching methodologies. She believes in creating a learning environment that is both engaging and practical, enabling students to grasp fundamental concepts with confidence and clarity.

Dr. Premanand K. Kadbe (author)

Dr. Premanand K. Kadbe is an experienced academician and researcher in the field of Electronics and Communication Engineering. He received his Bachelor's degree in Electronics and Telecommunication Engineering from Amravati University in 2003 and his Master's degree in Electronics from RTM Nagpur University in 2007. He completed his Ph.D. from Savitribai Phule Pune University in 2025.

Currently, he is serving as an Assistant Professor at Savitribai Phule Pune University, Pune. He brings over 19 years of teaching experience along with 2 years of industry experience. His areas of research include VLSI, Signal Processing, and Communication Engineering.

Dr. Kadbe is a Life Member of professional bodies such as ISTE and IETE. He has published more than 40 research papers in various international journals and conferences and has also contributed five book chapters. He has reviewed over 140 research papers for reputed international conferences, including IEEE conferences, and has served as an Editorial Board Member and Program Committee Member for various international conferences.

He has also guided more than 50 undergraduate and 10 postgraduate students, contributing significantly to academic and research development.

Dr. Vandana Baste Rohokale (author)

Dr. Vandana Baste Rohokale is a distinguished academician and researcher in the field of Electronics and Communication Engineering. She completed her Bachelor's degree in Electronics Engineering from Pune University in 1997 and her Master's degree in Electronics from Shivaji University, Kolhapur in 2007. She earned her Ph.D. in Wireless Communication in 2013 from CTIF, Aalborg University, Denmark. Further strengthening her research credentials, she completed her Post Doctorate from Aarhus University in 2023 under the guidance of Prof. Ramjee Prasad.

Currently, she is serving as a Professor and Vice Principal at Sinhgad Institute of Technology and Science, Pune, Maharashtra, India. With over 28 years of teaching experience, she has made significant contributions to academics, research, and student development.

Dr. Rohokale has authored six internationally published books and has published more than 90 research papers in reputed international journals and conferences. She has also been actively involved in guiding research and contributing to the academic community through her extensive work.

Her research interests include Cooperative Wireless Communications, Ad Hoc and Cognitive Networks, Physical Layer Security, Digital Signal Processing, Information Theoretic Security, Cyber Security, Artificial Intelligence and Machine Learning, and Quantum Computing.

CHAPTER ONE

Fundamentals of Data Communication

Communication Systems and Data Communication

In today's digital world, communication between devices has become a fundamental part of everyday life. Every time we send a message on WhatsApp, watch a video on YouTube, send an email, or download a file from the internet, a process called data communication is taking place behind the scenes. Understanding how this communication works is the first step toward learning computer networks.

A communication system is a system that allows information to be transferred from one place to another. This information may be in the form of text, images, audio, video, or any other type of digital data. In computer networking, communication systems are responsible for transferring data between computers, servers, mobile devices, and other digital equipment.

Before computers were connected through networks, each computer worked independently. If a user wanted to share data with another computer, they often had to physically transfer files using storage devices such as floppy disks or CDs. This process was slow and inefficient. As technology evolved, the need to connect computers together became very important, which led to the development of computer networks and modern communication systems.

A data communication system enables two or more devices to exchange data through a communication medium. The main goal of such a system is to deliver information accurately, efficiently, and quickly from one device to another.

BASIC DATA COMMUNICATION SYSTEM SHOWING SENDER, TRANSMISSION MEDIUM, AND RECEIVER

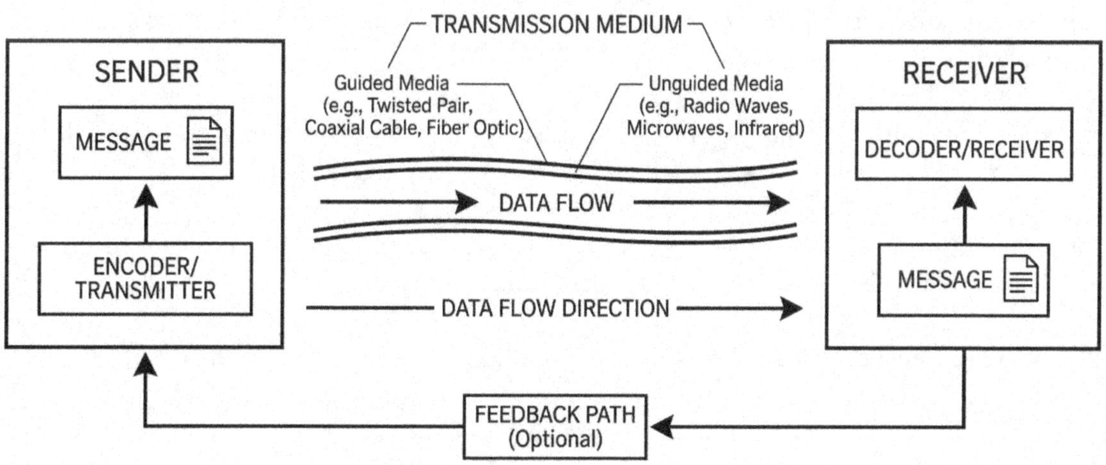

In a basic communication system, one device sends information and another device receives it. The data travels through a medium such as a cable, wireless signal, or optical fiber. The entire process must follow certain rules so that the devices can understand each other. These rules are known as protocols, which we will discuss in later sections.

To understand data communication clearly, let us consider a simple real-life example.

Imagine that you want to send a message to your friend using a messaging application on your mobile phone. When you type the message and press the send button, your phone acts as the sender. The message is converted into digital signals and transmitted through the internet network. These signals travel through different networking devices such as routers and switches until they reach your friend's mobile phone, which acts as the receiver. Your friend's phone then converts the signals back into readable text.

Although this process happens in just a few seconds, it involves several steps and technologies working together to make communication possible.

Data communication is not limited to mobile messaging. It is used in many real-world applications, including:

- Email communication
- Online banking transactions
- Video conferencing
- Cloud computing services
- Social media platforms
- Online education systems
- File sharing systems

All these applications rely on efficient communication systems that can transfer large amounts of data quickly and reliably.

For data communication to be effective, it must satisfy certain important characteristics.

The first characteristic is delivery. The data must reach the correct destination. If the data is delivered to the wrong device, the communication becomes useless.

The second characteristic is accuracy. The information that reaches the receiver must be exactly the same as the information that was sent. Errors during transmission can corrupt the data, which is why networks include error detection and correction mechanisms.

The third characteristic is timeliness. Some types of data must be delivered within a certain time limit. For example, during video calls or online gaming, delayed data can cause poor user experience.

The fourth characteristic is jitter, which refers to variation in the arrival time of data packets. In multimedia communication such as video streaming, consistent timing is important to maintain smooth playback.

A communication system must ensure that all these characteristics are maintained during data transmission.

Another important concept in data communication is the direction of communication. Communication between devices can occur in different ways depending on how data flows between them.

In some systems, communication occurs in only one direction. In other systems, communication can occur in both directions. The direction of communication is called the transmission mode, which will be discussed in detail in later chapters.

Data communication systems can also vary depending on the type of signals used. Some systems use analog signals, which are continuous electrical waves, while others use digital signals, which represent information using binary values such as 0 and 1. Modern computer networks mainly use digital signals because they are more reliable and easier to process.

Another important aspect of communication systems is the communication medium, which is the path through which data travels. Communication media can be classified into two main types:

Wired communication media.
Wireless communication media.

Wired communication media include cables such as twisted pair cables, coaxial cables, and optical fiber cables. These cables physically connect network devices and allow signals to travel through them.

Wireless communication media, on the other hand, use electromagnetic waves to transmit data through the air. Technologies such as Wi-Fi, Bluetooth, and mobile networks are examples of wireless communication systems.

Both wired and wireless communication systems have their advantages and limitations. Wired networks usually provide higher reliability and speed, while wireless networks offer flexibility and mobility.

Another important component of modern communication systems is network devices. Devices such as routers, switches, hubs, and gateways help manage and direct the flow of data through a network. These devices ensure that data reaches the correct destination efficiently.

In large networks such as the internet, data may travel through many intermediate devices before reaching the final destination. These intermediate devices analyze the data packets and determine the best path for them to follow.

The concept of dividing data into smaller units called packets is widely used in modern networks. Instead of sending a large block of data all at once, the data is divided into smaller packets that travel independently through the network. Once all packets reach the destination, they are reassembled into the original message.

This technique improves network efficiency and reliability because packets can take different routes if one path becomes congested or unavailable.

Data divided into packets traveling through a network

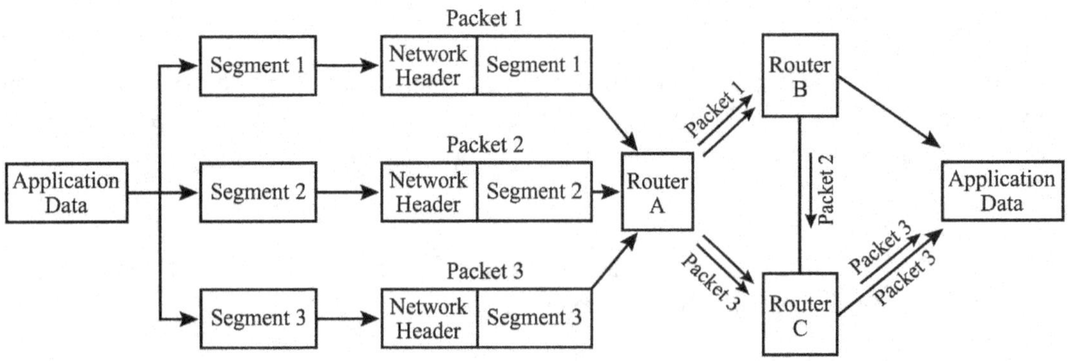

As computer networks continue to expand across the world, communication systems have become increasingly complex and sophisticated. Modern communication networks must support millions of users simultaneously while maintaining high speed and reliability.

Technologies such as fiber-optic communication, satellite communication, and high-speed wireless networks have made it possible to transmit enormous amounts of data across long distances within seconds.

Understanding the basic concepts of communication systems and data communication is essential for students studying computer networks. These concepts form the foundation for more advanced topics such as network protocols, transmission media, error control, routing, and internet technologies.

In the next section, we will explore the basic components of a data communication system in detail and understand how each component contributes to successful communication between devices.

Components of a Data Communication System

In the previous section, we learned that data communication is the process of transferring information from one device to another through a communication medium. However, for this communication to happen successfully, several important components must work together. Each component plays a specific role in ensuring that the data is transmitted correctly and reaches the intended destination.

A data communication system generally consists of five basic components:

Message.
Sender.
Receiver.
Transmission Medium.

Protocol.

All these components together form a complete communication system. If any one of these components is missing or fails to function properly, the communication process cannot be completed successfully.

COMPONENTS OF A DATA COMMUNICATION SYSTEM: SENDER → MEDIUM → RECEIVER WITH MESSAGE AND PROTOCOL

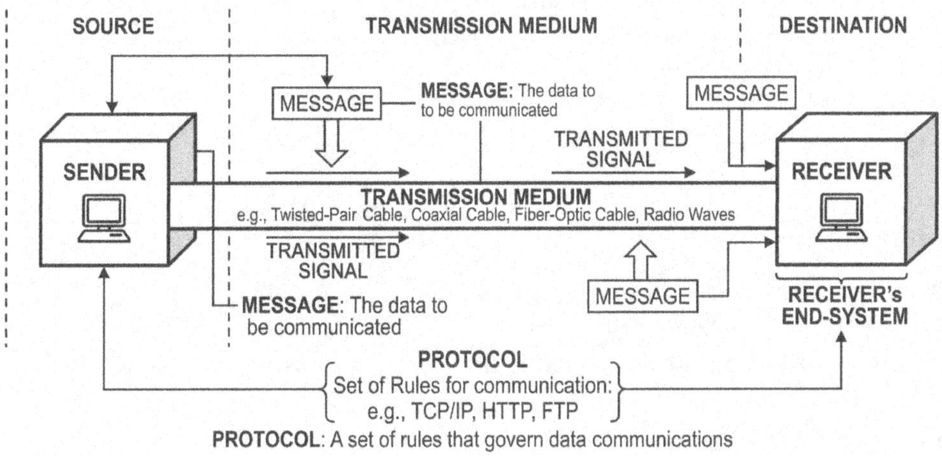

Let us now understand each of these components in detail.

Message

The message is the actual information that needs to be communicated from one device to another. It is the content or data that the sender wants to transmit to the receiver.

In computer networks, a message can take many different forms depending on the type of communication taking place. Some common examples of messages include:

Text messages sent through messaging applications.
Emails containing written content.
Images shared through social media platforms.
Audio files such as voice recordings.
Video files such as movies or video calls.
Documents such as PDF or Word files.

All these types of information are treated as data in computer networks. Before transmission, this data is converted into a format that computers and network devices can understand, usually in the form of digital signals consisting of binary values (0 and 1).

For example, when you send a photo through WhatsApp, the image file is converted into binary data. This binary data is then transmitted through the network until it reaches the receiver's device, where it is converted back into an image.

The message is therefore the core element of data communication because it represents the information being exchanged.

Sender

The sender is the device that originates or sends the message. It is responsible for generating the data that will be transmitted across the communication network.

In modern communication systems, the sender can be any device capable of sending digital information. Some common examples include:

A personal computer.
A smartphone.
A laptop.
A server.
A tablet.
A network printer.
An IoT device such as a smart sensor.

The sender performs several important functions before transmitting the message. These functions may include:

Preparing the data for transmission.
Converting the data into signals.
Dividing the data into packets if required.
Sending the data through the communication medium.

For example, when a user sends an email, the computer or smartphone used to compose and send the email acts as the sender. The device converts the message into digital signals and sends it through the internet.

In large networks such as the internet, a sender device may also communicate with other networking devices such as routers or switches before the data reaches its final destination.

Receiver

The receiver is the device that receives the transmitted message. It is the destination where the data sent by the sender finally arrives.

Just like the sender, the receiver can also be any type of digital device capable of receiving and processing information. Examples of receiver devices include:

Computers.
Smartphones.
Servers.
Tablets.
Smart televisions.
IoT devices.

The receiver performs the opposite operations of the sender. Once the data reaches the receiver, the device must:

Accept the incoming signals.
Convert the signals back into usable data.

Reassemble data packets if they were divided during transmission.
Present the information to the user in a readable format.

For instance, when someone sends you an email, your device acts as the receiver. The incoming data packets are received from the network, assembled in the correct order, and displayed as an email message.

Without a receiver, communication cannot be completed because there would be no device to accept the transmitted information.

Transmission Medium

The transmission medium is the physical or wireless path through which data travels from the sender to the receiver. It acts as the channel that carries the signals containing the data.

Transmission media can be broadly classified into two categories:

Wired (Guided) Media.
Wireless (Unguided) Media.
Wired Transmission Media.

In **wired communication**, signals travel through physical cables that connect network devices.

Common examples of wired media include:

Twisted Pair Cable – widely used in telephone lines and local area networks.
Coaxial Cable – used in cable television networks.
Optical Fiber Cable – used for high-speed internet and long-distance communication.

Optical fiber cables are especially important in modern communication systems because they can transmit data at extremely high speeds using light signals.

Wireless Transmission Media

Wireless communication does not require physical cables. Instead, it uses electromagnetic waves to transmit signals through the air.
Common examples include:

Wi-Fi networks.
Bluetooth communication.
Mobile networks (4G and 5G).
Satellite communication.

Wireless communication provides mobility and convenience because devices can communicate without being physically connected.

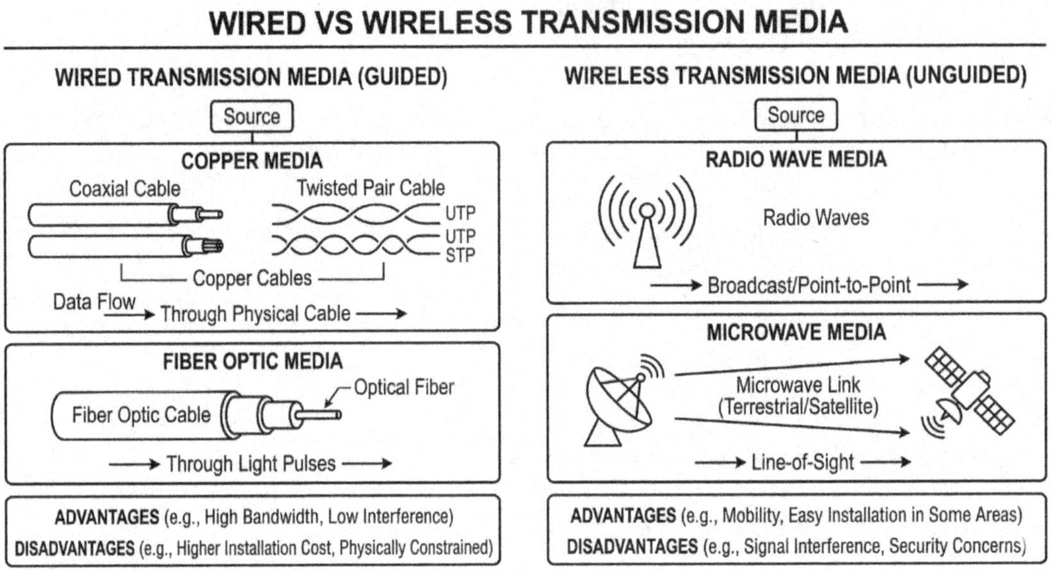

The transmission medium plays a very important role in determining the speed, reliability, and distance of communication.

Protocol

The final and one of the most important components of data communication is the protocol.

A protocol is a set of rules and standards that govern how data is transmitted between devices in a network. These rules ensure that the sender and receiver can understand each other during communication.

Without protocols, devices would not know how to interpret the incoming data, which would lead to confusion and communication failure.

Protocols define several important aspects of communication, such as:

The format of the data being transmitted.
The timing of data transmission.
Error detection and correction methods.
The way devices establish and terminate connections.

Some well-known network protocols include:

HTTP (HyperText Transfer Protocol) – used for web communication.
FTP (File Transfer Protocol) – used for file transfer.
SMTP (Simple Mail Transfer Protocol) – used for sending emails.
TCP/IP (Transmission Control Protocol / Internet Protocol) – used for internet communication.

For example, when you open a website in your web browser, your device uses the HTTP protocol to request the web page from the server.

Communication using protocols between two devices

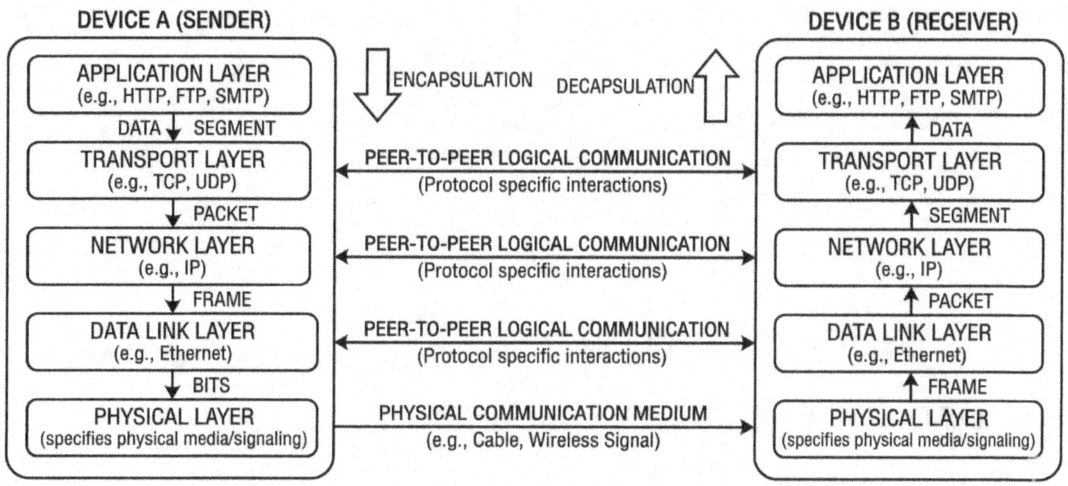

Protocols ensure that communication between devices is organized, reliable, and standardized.

Importance of These Components

All five components of a data communication system must work together to enable effective communication.

The message represents the data to be transmitted.
The sender generates the message.
The transmission medium carries the data signals.
The receiver accepts the transmitted data.
The protocol defines the rules for communication.

When all these components function correctly, communication becomes efficient, reliable, and fast.

Understanding these components is essential because they form the foundation of all computer networking technologies. Every communication process in a network, whether simple or complex, depends on these fundamental elements.

In the next section, we will explore the different types of communication systems and transmission methods used in computer networks.

Types of Data Communication Systems

In the previous section, we discussed the basic components of a data communication system, such as the sender, receiver, transmission medium, message, and protocol. These components work together to enable communication between devices.

However, communication between devices does not always happen in the same way. Depending on how data flows between the sender and receiver, different types of communication systems can be used. Understanding these types is important because different applications require different communication methods.

For example, the way a television broadcast system works is different from the way a telephone conversation works. Similarly, communication in a computer network can occur in multiple ways depending on how the data is transmitted.

Based on the direction of data flow, data communication systems can be classified into three main types:

Simplex Communication
Half-Duplex Communication
Full-Duplex Communication

These communication modes are also commonly referred to as transmission modes in computer networking.

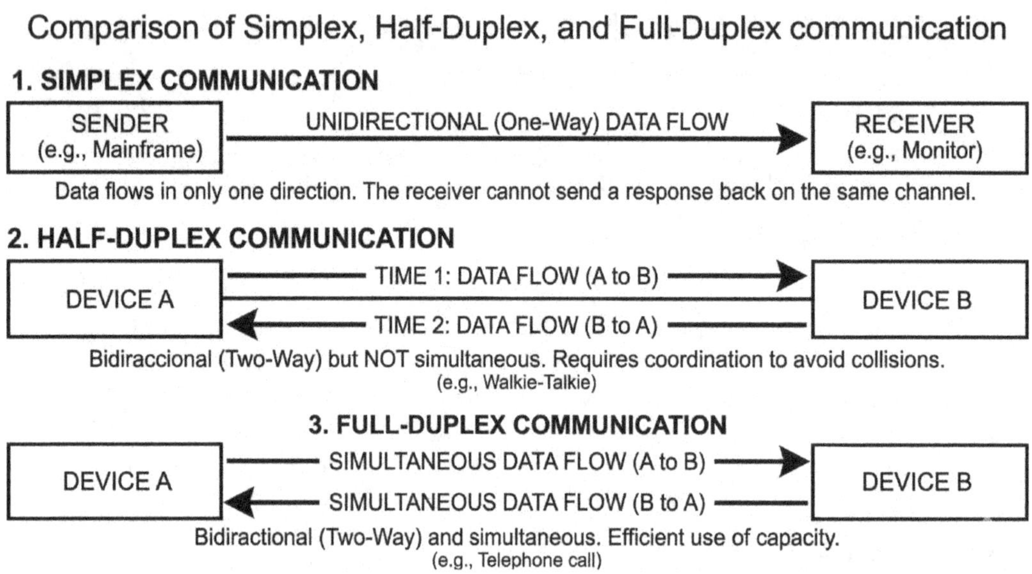

Let us understand each type in detail.

Simplex Communication

In simplex communication, data flows in only one direction. This means that one device can only send data while the other device can only receive data. Communication cannot occur in the opposite direction.

In this type of communication, the sender always acts as the transmitting device, and the receiver always acts as the receiving device.

Simplex communication showing one-way data flow

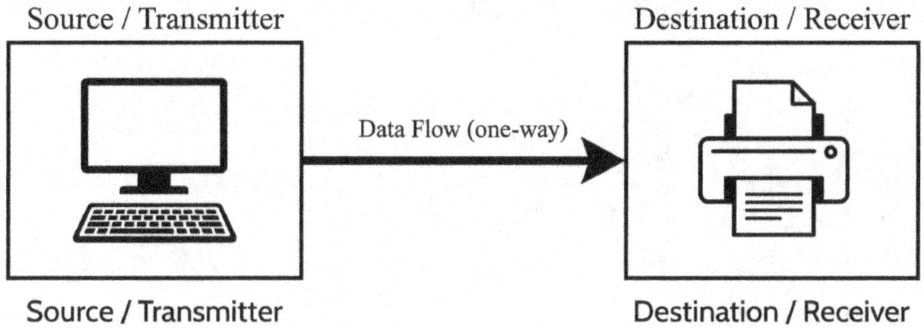

A good example of simplex communication is television broadcasting.

In television broadcasting:

The TV station sends signals to viewers.
Viewers receive the signals on their televisions.

However, the television cannot send information back to the TV station.

This means the communication is one-way only.

Another example is a keyboard connected to a computer. When a user presses keys on the keyboard, the keyboard sends input signals to the computer. The computer receives the signals but does not send signals back to the keyboard in the same way.

Some key characteristics of simplex communication include:

Data flows in only one direction.
The sender cannot receive data.
The receiver cannot send data.

It is mainly used in broadcast-type systems.

Although simplex communication is simple and efficient for one-way communication, it is not suitable for applications where two-way communication is required.

Half-Duplex Communication

In half-duplex communication, data can travel in both directions, but not at the same time.

This means that both devices can act as sender and receiver, but they must take turns when transmitting data. When one device is sending data, the other device must wait until the transmission is completed.

Half-duplex communication showing alternating data flow.

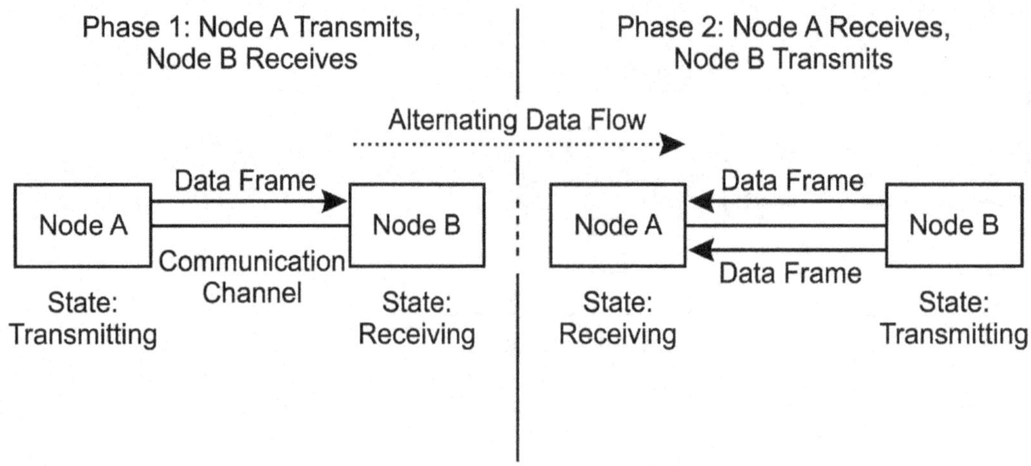

A common example of half-duplex communication is a walkie-talkie.

When using a walkie-talkie:

One person speaks while the other listens.
The other person must wait until the first person finishes speaking.
Then the second person presses the talk button and responds.

Because only one person can speak at a time, this system is considered half-duplex.

Another example can be found in certain wireless communication systems, where devices must take turns transmitting signals to avoid interference.

The main characteristics of half-duplex communication include:

Data can flow in both directions.
Communication cannot occur simultaneously.
Devices must take turns sending data.

It is more flexible than simplex communication.

Half-duplex communication is often used in systems where simultaneous communication is not necessary, but two-way communication is still required.

Full-Duplex Communication

In full-duplex communication, data can flow in both directions simultaneously. This means that both devices can send and receive data at the same time.

Full-duplex communication provides the most efficient form of communication because there is no need to wait for the other device to finish transmitting.

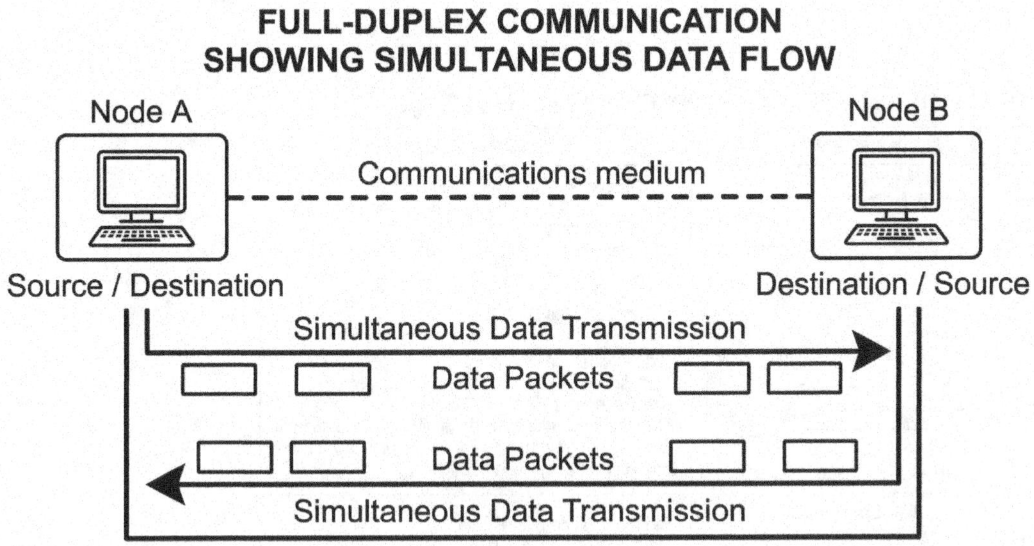

A common example of full-duplex communication is a telephone conversation.

When two people talk on the phone:

Both individuals can speak and listen at the same time.
The communication happens simultaneously in both directions.

Another example is modern computer networks, where devices can send and receive data simultaneously through network interfaces.

Full-duplex communication has several advantages:

Faster communication.
Higher efficiency.
Reduced waiting time.
Better user experience in real-time applications.

This type of communication is widely used in modern Ethernet networks, video conferencing systems, and internet communication technologies.

Comparison of Communication Types

Each communication mode has its own advantages and limitations. The choice of communication system depends on the requirements of the application.

Simplex communication is suitable for systems where data needs to flow in only one direction, such as broadcasting.

Half-duplex communication is useful when two-way communication is needed but simultaneous transmission is not necessary.

Full-duplex communication is ideal for systems that require fast and efficient two-way communication, such as internet-based applications.

TABLE COMPARISON OF SIMPLEX, HALF-DUPLEX, AND FULL-DUPLEX.

COMMUNICATION TYPE	DATA FLOW DIAGRAM	KEY CHARACTERISTICS
SIMPLEX	ONE-WAY DATA FLOW DEVICE A → DEVICE B (e.g., Radio Broadcasting, Keyboard)	- Unidirectional data transmission. - Only one device can transmit at any time; the other can only receive. - The entire channel capacity is dedicated to a single direction. - Most common in broadcasting or when input is strictly from one source.
HALF-DUPLEX	TWO-WAY, NOT SIMULTANEOUS TIME 1: A → B DEVICE A ⇄ DEVICE B TIME 2: B → A (e.g., Walkie-Talkies, Hub-based Ethernet)	- Bidirectional data transmission. - Data flow is possible in both directions, but not simultaneously. - Devices must take turns transmitting on the channel. - Sharing bandwidth; actual throughput is lower than physical capacity due to switching.
FULL-DUPLEX	TWO-WAY, SIMULTANEOUS A → B DEVICE A ⇄ DEVICE B B → A (e.g., Telephone Calls, Switch-based Ethernet)	- Bidirectional data transmission. - Data flow occurs in both directions simultaneously. - Devices can send and receive at the same time without needing to turn around. - Maximum utilization of channel capacity; independent paths for each direction.

Importance of Transmission Modes in Networking

Understanding these communication modes is important because they influence how data is transmitted in a network. Network designers must choose the appropriate transmission mode depending on the type of application and communication requirements.

For example:

Broadcasting systems use simplex communication.
Wireless communication devices may use half-duplex communication.
Modern computer networks and internet communication often use full-duplex communication.

Transmission modes also affect network performance, efficiency, and communication speed.

Role of Communication Systems in Modern Networks

Modern computer networks rely heavily on efficient communication systems to support a wide variety of applications. These include video streaming, online gaming, cloud computing, remote learning, and digital communication platforms.

To support these applications, networks must handle large amounts of data while ensuring fast, reliable, and accurate transmission.

Advances in communication technologies such as optical fiber networks, wireless communication systems, and high-speed internet protocols have significantly improved the performance of modern communication systems.

Understanding the different types of data communication systems helps students build a strong foundation in computer networking, which will be useful when studying advanced topics such as network protocols, transmission media, and routing techniques.

Importance of Computer Networks in Modern Communication

In the previous sections, we learned about data communication and the different ways in which data can flow between devices. Now we will understand why computer networks are so important in today's world.

A computer network is a system in which multiple computers and devices are connected together so that they can share information, resources, and services. Without computer networks, modern digital communication would not be possible.

Today almost every organization, business, educational institution, and government system depends on computer networks. Even in our daily lives, we constantly use networks through mobile phones, laptops, tablets, and other smart devices.

For example, when you send an email, stream a movie online, participate in a video call, or transfer money through online banking, computer networks are working in the background to make these activities possible.

The importance of computer networks can be understood through several key benefits they provide.

Resource Sharing

One of the most important advantages of computer networks is resource sharing. Resource sharing means that different devices connected to the network can share hardware, software, and data.

For example, in an office environment, several computers may be connected to a single network printer. Instead of purchasing a separate printer for each computer, all users can share the same printer through the network.

Similarly, a company may have a central server that stores important files and documents. Employees from different departments can access these files through the network without needing to store them individually on their computers.

Network showing multiple computers sharing a printer and server

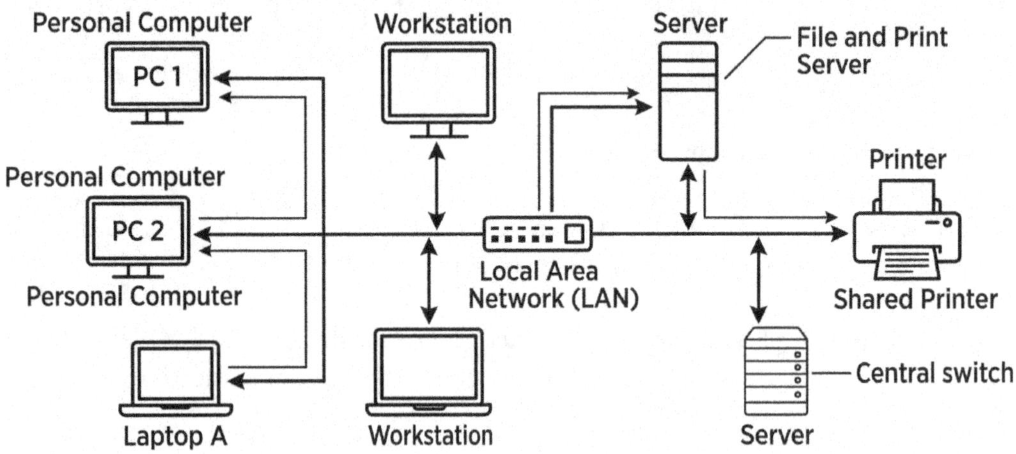

Network showing multiple computers sharing a printer and server

Resource sharing helps organizations reduce costs, improve efficiency, and make better use of available resources.

Data Sharing and Information Exchange

Computer networks allow users to easily share information and data with others. This is especially important in businesses, educational institutions, and research organizations.

For instance, students working on a group project can share documents through a network or cloud platform. Employees in a company can collaborate on files stored on a shared server.

The internet itself is the largest example of data sharing. Millions of websites provide information that users can access from anywhere in the world.

Because of computer networks, information can be distributed quickly and efficiently to a large number of users.

Communication and Collaboration

Computer networks have revolutionized communication. People can now communicate with others across the world instantly through various digital platforms.

Some common forms of network-based communication include:

Email communication.
Instant messaging.
Video conferencing.
Voice over Internet Protocol (VoIP) calls.
Social media platforms.

For example, applications like Zoom, Microsoft Teams, and Google Meet allow people to conduct meetings and attend classes remotely.

These communication technologies have become especially important in modern workplaces where employees may work from different locations.

Global network communication connecting multiple users

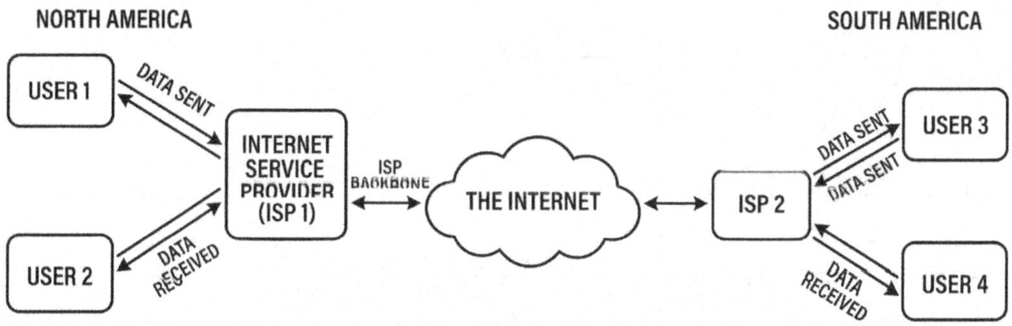

Computer networks make communication faster, easier, and more convenient compared to traditional communication methods.

Access to Remote Information

Another important benefit of computer networks is the ability to access information stored in remote locations.

With the help of networks, users can access data stored on servers located in different parts of the world. This is known as remote access.

For example:

Students can access online libraries and research databases.
Employees can access company servers from home.
Doctors can access patient records stored in hospital databases.
Businesses can access cloud-based applications.

Cloud computing services such as Google Drive, Dropbox, and Microsoft OneDrive are examples of remote data access systems.

These services allow users to store and retrieve files from anywhere using the internet.

Improved Reliability and Backup

Computer networks also improve reliability by providing backup systems and redundant communication paths.

In large organizations, important data is often stored on multiple servers so that if one server fails, another server can continue providing the service. This helps prevent data loss and system failures.

Network administrators also use backup systems to store copies of important data. If a computer crashes or a file is accidentally deleted, the data can be recovered from the backup.

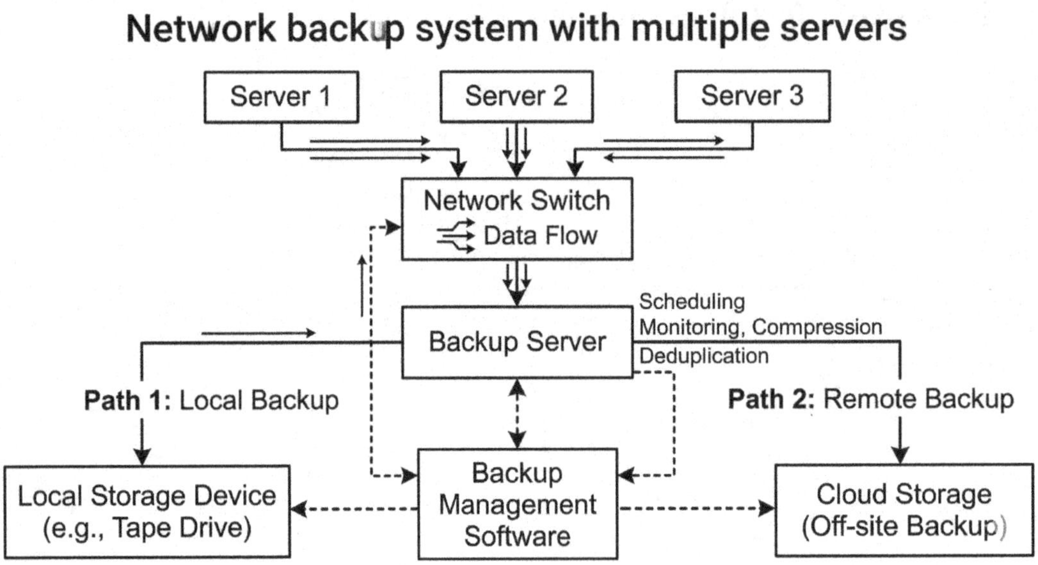

This improves the reliability and safety of data within the network.

Centralized Management

Computer networks allow organizations to manage their systems from a central location. This concept is known as centralized management.

For example, in a company network, a network administrator can control:

User access permissions.
Software installations.
Security settings.
System updates.

Instead of configuring each computer individually, the administrator can manage the entire network through a central server.

This makes network management more efficient and reduces maintenance time.

Cost Efficiency

Computer networks help organizations reduce operational costs by enabling efficient resource utilization.

For instance, instead of purchasing separate hardware for every employee, companies can share expensive equipment such as:

High-performance servers.

Network storage devices.
Printers.
Internet connections.

In addition, communication costs are reduced because employees can communicate through network-based systems rather than traditional phone systems.

Online meetings and remote collaboration also reduce travel expenses.

Support for Modern Technologies

Many modern technologies depend entirely on computer networks. Some of the most important examples include:

Cloud Computing
Cloud computing allows users to store data and run applications on remote servers rather than on local computers.

Internet of Things (IoT)
IoT devices such as smart home appliances, wearable devices, and sensors communicate through networks to share data and perform automated tasks.

Online Services
Many services such as e-commerce platforms, streaming services, and digital payment systems rely heavily on computer networks.

Artificial Intelligence Systems
AI systems often process large amounts of data stored in distributed networks and cloud platforms.
These technologies demonstrate how essential computer networks have become in modern digital infrastructure.

Global Connectivity
One of the most powerful aspects of computer networks is global connectivity. Through the internet, billions of devices around the world are connected to each other.

This global network allows users to communicate, share information, and access services from almost anywhere on the planet.

For example:

A student in India can attend an online course offered by a university in another country.
A business owner can sell products to customers across the world through an online store.
Researchers can collaborate on scientific projects even if they are located in different countries.

GLOBAL INTERNET CONNECTIVITY SHOWING MULTIPLE NETWORKS CONNECTED WORLDWIDE

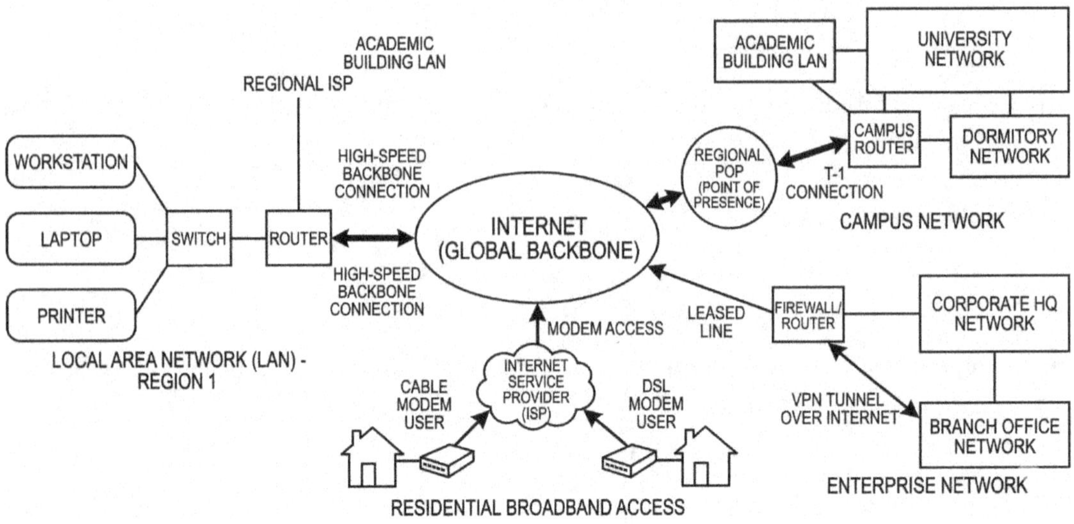

This global connectivity has transformed how people interact, learn, and conduct business.

Summary

Computer networks have become an essential part of modern life. They allow devices to communicate with each other, share resources, and exchange information quickly and efficiently.

Some of the major advantages of computer networks include resource sharing, communication, collaboration, remote data access, centralized management, improved reliability, and support for modern technologies.

Because of these benefits, computer networks are widely used in businesses, education systems, healthcare organizations, government institutions, and everyday personal communication.

Understanding the importance of computer networks helps students appreciate why networking technologies play such a critical role in today's digital world.

In the next chapter, we will explore the concept of computer networks in detail, including different types of networks and how they are structured.

CHAPTER TWO

Computer Networks and Topologies

Introduction to Computer Networks

In the modern digital world, computers rarely work alone. Most computers today are connected to other computers and devices through networks. These connections allow devices to share information, resources, and services with each other. The system that connects these devices together is known as a computer network.

A computer network is a collection of interconnected computers and other devices that communicate with each other to exchange data and share resources.

The devices connected in a network may include:

Desktop computers.
Laptops.
Smartphones.
Servers.
Printers.
Storage devices.
Networking equipment such as routers and switches.

When these devices are connected together, they can communicate with each other using communication protocols and networking technologies.

Figure 1.1: Multiple computers connected together forming a computer network

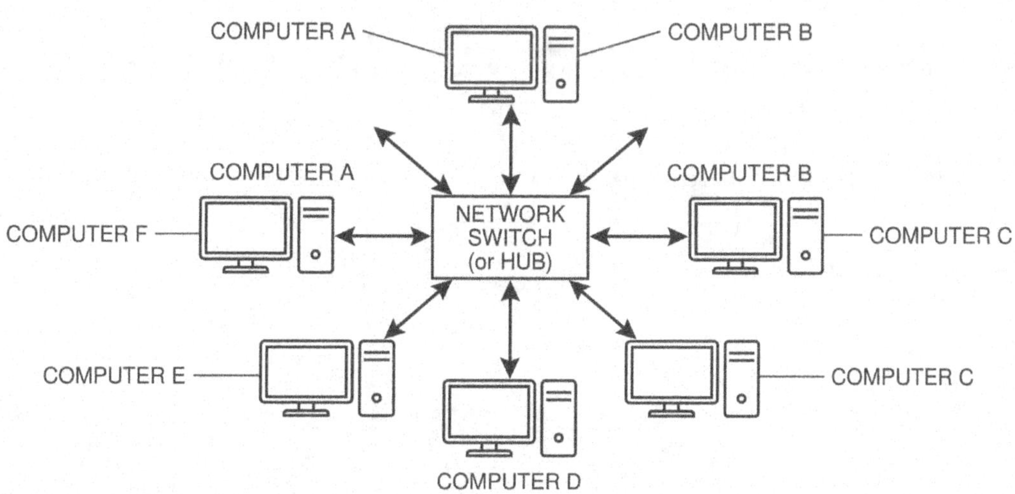

Computer networks are everywhere today. When you connect your mobile phone to Wi-Fi, your phone becomes part of a network. When employees in an office access files stored on a central server, they are using a network. Even the internet itself is a very large network that connects billions of devices across the world.

Why Computer Networks are Needed

Before networks were developed, computers worked as standalone systems. This meant that each computer operated independently and could not easily share information with other computers.

For example, if a user wanted to transfer a file from one computer to another, they had to use physical storage devices such as:

Floppy disks.
CDs or DVDs.
USB drives.

This method was slow, inconvenient, and inefficient. As organizations began using computers more frequently, the need to connect computers together became very important.

Computer networks solved this problem by allowing computers to exchange information electronically. This made communication faster and more efficient.

Characteristics of Computer Networks

A computer network has several important characteristics that make communication possible and efficient.

Connectivity

Connectivity refers to the ability of devices to connect with each other. A network allows multiple devices to be linked together so that they can communicate and share information.

For example, in a university network, hundreds of computers may be connected through switches and routers.

Resource Sharing

One of the main purposes of a network is to allow devices to share resources. These resources may include hardware devices, software applications, or data files.

For instance, several computers in an office may share a common printer connected to the network.

NETWORK SHOWING MULTIPLE COMPUTERS SHARING A PRINTER

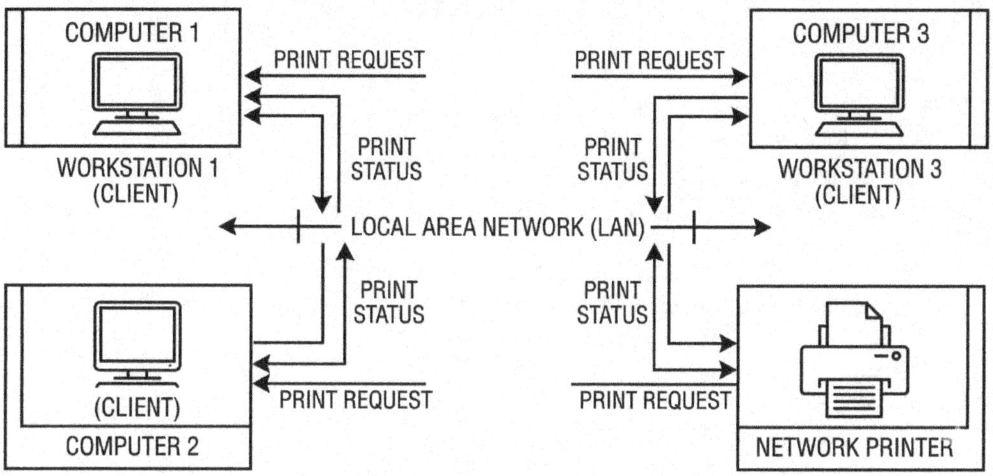

Communication

Computer networks allow users to communicate with each other easily. Through networks, people can send emails, messages, and files to other users located anywhere in the world.

Communication tools such as video conferencing and online collaboration platforms rely heavily on networks.

Reliability

Networks improve system reliability by providing backup and alternative communication paths. If one communication path fails, the network may use another path to deliver the data.

Scalability

Scalability refers to the ability of a network to grow and expand. New devices can be added to a network without significantly affecting the performance of existing devices.

For example, a small office network may initially connect only a few computers, but additional devices can be added as the organization grows.

Components of a Computer Network

A computer network consists of several important components that work together to enable communication.

End Devices

End devices are the devices that send and receive data in the network. These devices include computers, smartphones, tablets, and servers.

These devices are also sometimes referred to as hosts.

Networking Devices

Networking devices are responsible for directing data through the network. Some common networking devices include:

Switches, which connect multiple devices in a local network.
Routers, which connect different networks together.
Hubs, which broadcast data to all connected devices.
Gateways, which connect networks using different communication protocols.

Network showing computers connected through switch and router.

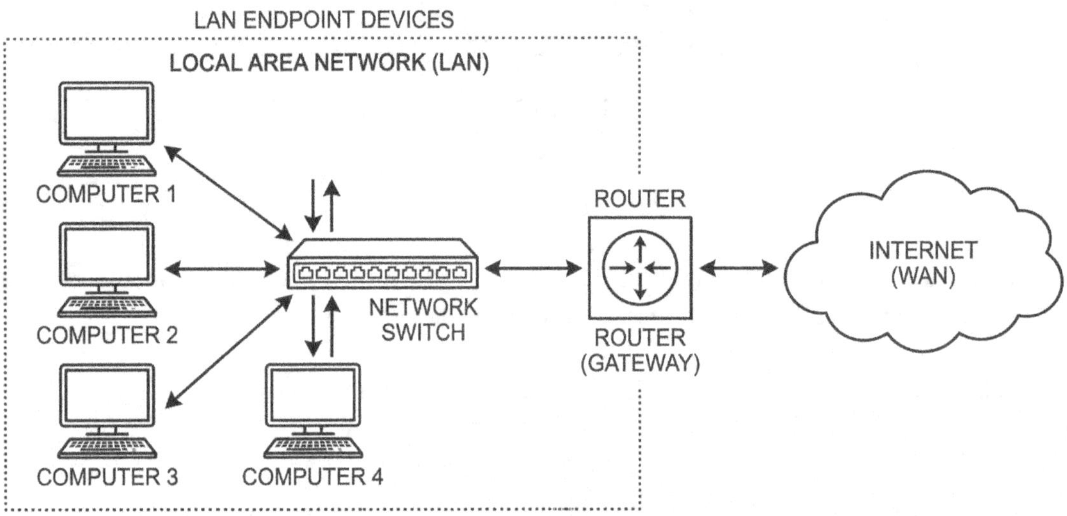

Transmission Media

Transmission media provide the physical or wireless pathway for data transmission.

Common examples include:

Twisted pair cables.
Coaxial cables.
Optical fiber cables.
Wireless signals.

These media carry the signals that contain the transmitted data.

Network Software and Protocols

Network software and communication protocols control how devices communicate with each other. These protocols define the rules for data transmission and ensure that devices understand each other's messages.

Examples of protocols include TCP, IP, HTTP, and FTP.

Real-Life Examples of Computer Networks

Computer networks are used in many real-world environments.

Home Networks

In many homes today, multiple devices such as smartphones, laptops, and smart televisions connect to the internet through a Wi-Fi router.

Office Networks

Businesses often connect all office computers to a central network so that employees can access shared resources and communicate with each other.

Educational Networks

Schools and universities use networks to connect computer laboratories, administrative offices, and libraries.

Internet

The internet is the largest computer network in the world. It connects billions of devices globally and allows users to access websites, online services, and communication platforms.

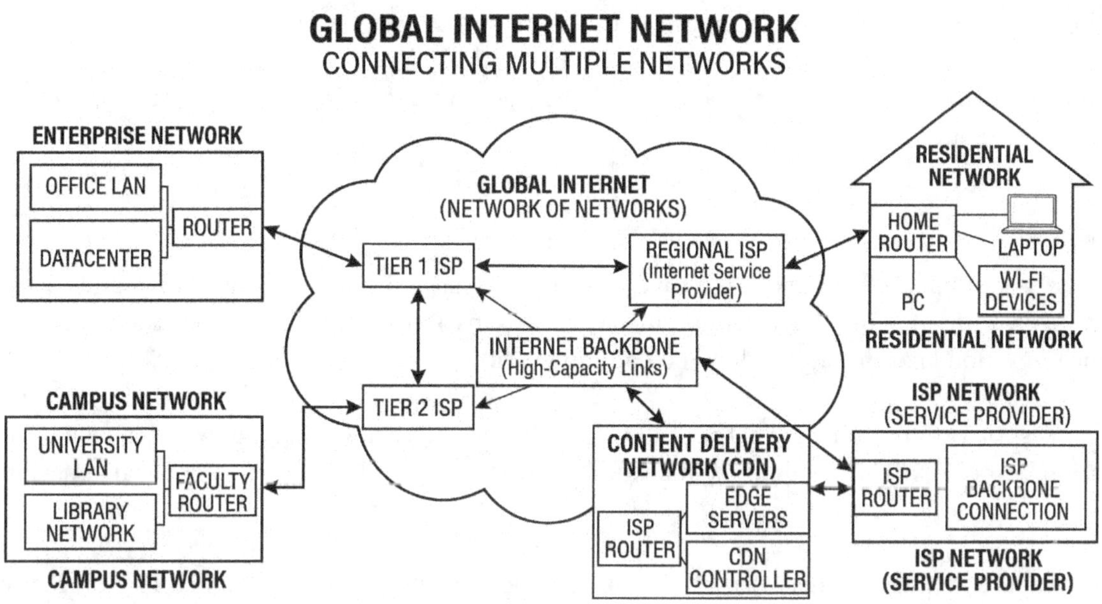

Advantages of Computer Networks

Computer networks provide several advantages that make them essential in modern organizations.

Efficient Communication

Networks enable fast communication between users through emails, messaging applications, and video conferencing.

Easy Data Sharing

Files and documents can be shared quickly between users connected to the network.

Cost Reduction

Sharing resources such as printers, storage devices, and internet connections helps reduce operational costs.

Remote Access
Users can access network resources from remote locations through the internet.

Centralized Control
Network administrators can manage and control network resources from a central location.

Challenges in Computer Networks

Although networks provide many advantages, they also present certain challenges.

Security Risks
Networks can be vulnerable to cyber attacks such as hacking, malware, and data theft.

Network Failures
Hardware failures or communication problems can interrupt network services.

Maintenance
Large networks require regular maintenance and monitoring to ensure smooth operation.

Network engineers and administrators work to solve these challenges by implementing security systems, backup solutions, and network management tools.

Summary

A computer network is a system that connects multiple devices so that they can communicate and share resources. Networks play an essential role in modern communication systems and support many important services such as email, online education, cloud computing, and digital communication.

Computer networks consist of various components including end devices, networking equipment, transmission media, and communication protocols. These components work together to enable efficient data transmission between devices.

Understanding the concept of computer networks is important because it forms the foundation for many advanced networking topics that will be discussed in later chapters.

In the next section, we will study different types of computer networks, such as Local Area Networks, Metropolitan Area Networks, and Wide Area Networks.

Types of Computer Networks (LAN, MAN, WAN)

In the previous section, we learned about the concept of computer networks and why they are important in modern communication systems. However, not all computer networks are the same. Networks can vary in size, coverage area, and purpose.

Some networks connect devices within a small room, while others connect devices across cities or even across the entire world. Because of this difference in size and coverage, computer networks are classified into different types.

Based on the geographical area they cover, computer networks are mainly divided into three types:

Local Area Network (LAN)
Metropolitan Area Network (MAN)
Wide Area Network (WAN)

Each type of network is designed to serve a specific purpose and operate within a particular geographical range.

Comparison of LAN, MAN, and WAN coverage areas

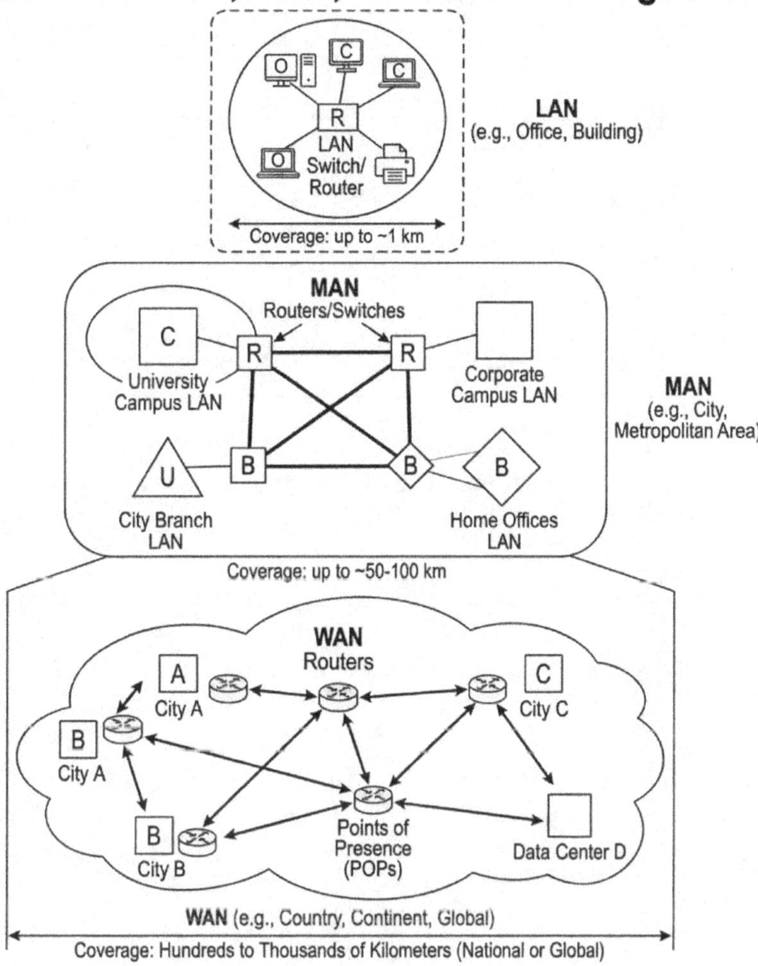

Let us now understand each type of network in detail.

Local Area Network (LAN)

A Local Area Network (LAN) is a network that connects computers and devices within a small geographical area. This area may include a single room, a building, a school campus, or a small office.

LANs are the most commonly used type of computer networks because they are easy to install and maintain. In a LAN, multiple computers are connected using networking devices such as switches and routers.

For example, in a school computer laboratory, all computers may be connected through a switch so that students and teachers can share files and access common resources.

Local Area Network connecting computers in a building.

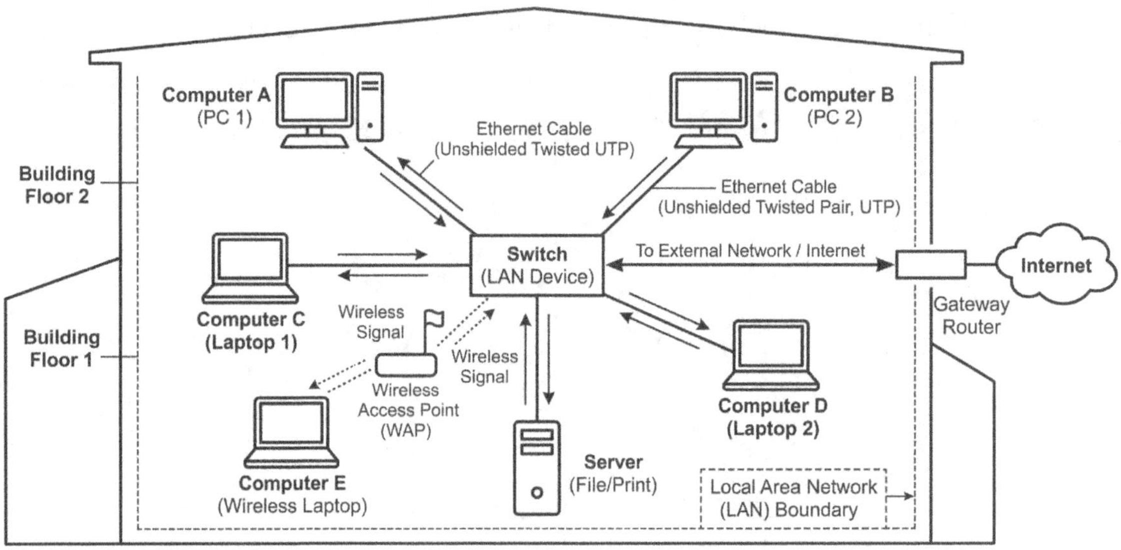

LAN networks usually use wired connections, such as Ethernet cables, although wireless LANs using Wi-Fi are also very common today.

Characteristics of LAN

Some important characteristics of Local Area Networks include:

Covers a small geographical area.
Provides high data transfer speed.
Usually owned and managed by a single organization.
Uses technologies such as Ethernet or Wi-Fi.
Easy to maintain and manage.

Advantages of LAN

LAN networks offer several advantages.

First, they allow fast data communication between devices because the network distance is short. This means data can be transmitted quickly.

Second, LAN networks allow resource sharing. For example, multiple computers can share printers, storage devices, and internet connections.

Third, LAN networks provide better control and security because they are usually managed by a single organization.

Example of LAN

Examples of LAN networks include:

School computer laboratories.
Office networks.
Home Wi-Fi networks.
University campus networks.

In all these examples, devices located within a limited area are connected together to form a network.

Metropolitan Area Network (MAN)

A Metropolitan Area Network (MAN) is a network that connects multiple LANs within a large geographical area such as a city or metropolitan region.

A MAN is larger than a LAN but smaller than a WAN. It is designed to connect different local networks across a city.

For example, a city's municipal offices, universities, and government departments may be connected through a metropolitan network that allows them to share information and services.

Metropolitan Area Network connecting multiple buildings across a city.

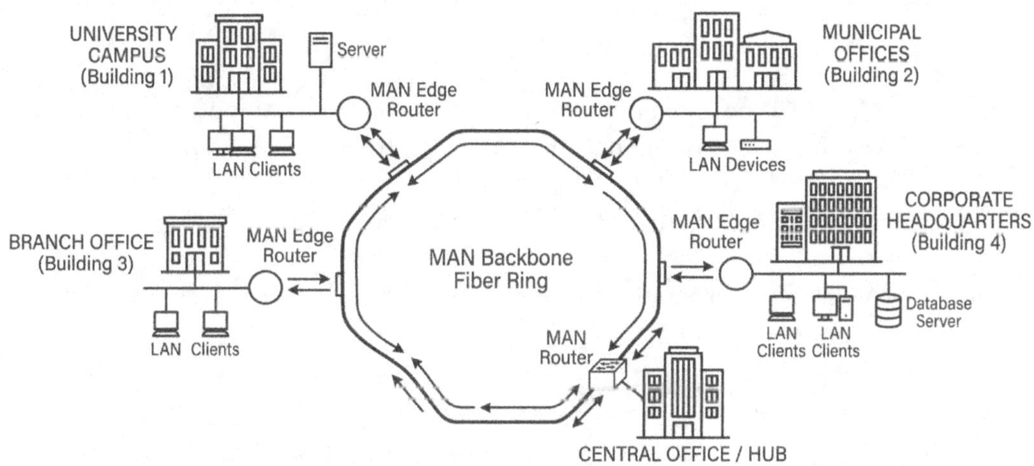

Diagram shows MAN connecting LANs in four locations across a metropolitan area using a fiber-optic ring and routers.

MAN networks often use high-speed communication technologies such as fiber-optic cables to transmit data across long distances within a city.

Characteristics of MAN

Some important characteristics of Metropolitan Area Networks include:

Covers an entire city or metropolitan region.
Connects multiple LAN networks together.

Provides high-speed communication using fiber networks.
Often operated by government agencies or service providers.

Advantages of MAN

MAN networks provide several benefits.

First, they allow organizations located in different parts of a city to communicate efficiently.

Second, they support high-speed data transmission, which is necessary for services such as video conferencing, cloud computing, and large data transfers.

Third, they help improve communication infrastructure within a city.

Example of MAN

Examples of MAN networks include:

City-wide internet service provider networks.
Cable television networks.
Government communication networks connecting different departments in a city.

These networks enable efficient communication between institutions located within a metropolitan area.

Wide Area Network (WAN)

A Wide Area Network (WAN) is the largest type of computer network. It connects computers and networks across very large geographical areas, such as countries, continents, or even the entire world.

WAN networks are designed to connect multiple LANs and MANs together.

The most well-known example of a WAN is the Internet, which connects billions of devices across the world.

Wide Area Network connecting networks across different countries.

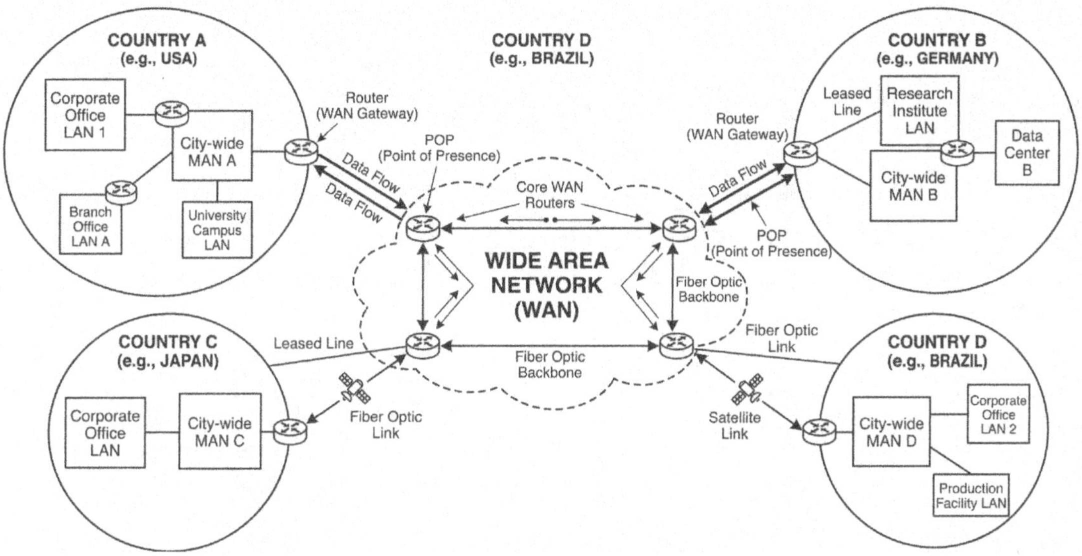

WAN networks often use communication technologies such as:

Optical fiber communication.
Satellite communication.
Microwave communication.
Undersea communication cables.

These technologies allow data to travel across very long distances.

Characteristics of WAN

Some key characteristics of Wide Area Networks include:

Covers very large geographical areas.
Connects multiple LAN and MAN networks.
Uses long-distance communication technologies.
Often operated by telecommunications companies.

Advantages of WAN

WAN networks provide several important advantages.

First, they allow communication between users located in different parts of the world.

Second, they support global connectivity for businesses, educational institutions, and governments.

Third, they enable services such as global email communication, international video conferencing, and worldwide data sharing.

Example of WAN

Examples of WAN networks include:

The Internet.
International banking networks.
Airline reservation systems.
Global corporate networks.

These networks allow organizations and individuals to communicate and share data on a global scale.

Comparison of LAN, MAN, and WAN

Although LAN, MAN, and WAN are all types of computer networks, they differ mainly in terms of their size, coverage area, and communication technologies.

LAN networks cover small areas and provide high-speed communication within organizations.

MAN networks connect multiple LANs within a city.

WAN networks connect networks across large geographical areas and enable global communication.

TABLE COMPARING LAN, MAN, AND WAN

Characteristic	LAN (Local Area Network)	MAN (Metropolitan Area Network)	WAN (Wide Area Network)	Comparative Visual	Key Use Case
Scale & Geographic Area	Small (e.g., Office, Building, Home).	Medium (e.g., City, Campus).	Large (e.g., Country, Continent, Global).	LAN → MAN → WAN	Corporate office network.
Ownership	Private (single individual or organization).	Mixed (private or provider-owned).	Mixed (often service provider, public, or state-owned)		Interconnecting distant company branches.
Data Rate	High (Gbps-Tbps).	Moderate (Mbps-Gbps).	Lower (Kbps-Mbps)		Linking different branches in a city.
Transmission Media	Ethernet, Wi-Fi, Twisted Pair, Fiber (short-range)	Fiber, Leased Lines, Coaxial Cable, Microwave	Fiber, Satellite, Coaxial Cable, Leased Lines, Radio (long-range).		A city's emergency service network.
Data Transfer Cost	Low (capital, maintenance).	Moderate (recurring costs)	High (recurring usage and provider fees)		The entire global Internet.
Traffic Type	High data volume, real-time internal services.	High data volume, real-time within city/campus.	Inter-city, national, international traffic, mixed data	Internal office communication flow. City-wide data flow. Long-range connection points flow.	Home network with smart devices.
Example Implementation Connection	The LAN connection connects locally (short connections).	The MAN connection connects across larger city distances.	The WAN connects between distant LANs LANs or MANs.	A visual flow across all three.	A University campus-wide network.

Importance of Network Classification

Understanding different types of networks is important for network design and management. Network engineers must select the appropriate type of network depending on the communication requirements and geographical coverage.

For example:
A school may use a LAN to connect computers within the campus.

A city administration may use a MAN to connect different government offices.

International companies may use WAN networks to connect their offices around the world.

By combining different types of networks, it is possible to create large and complex communication systems such as the internet.

Summary

Computer networks can be classified into different types based on the geographical area they cover. The three main types of networks are Local Area Networks, Metropolitan Area Networks, and Wide Area Networks.

LAN networks connect devices within a small area, such as an office or school. MAN networks connect multiple local networks across a city. WAN networks connect networks across large geographical areas and enable global communication.

Understanding these types of networks helps students learn how communication systems are structured and how different networking technologies are used in real-world environments.

In the next section, we will explore network topologies, which describe the physical and logical arrangement of devices in a computer network.

Network Topologies

In the previous section, we studied different types of computer networks such as LAN, MAN, and WAN. Now we will learn about another very important concept in networking known as network topology.

When multiple devices are connected to form a network, the way these devices are arranged and connected to each other is called network topology.

In simple words, network topology describes the layout or structure of a network. It shows how computers, cables, and networking devices are connected together.

Network topology plays a very important role in determining how data flows through the network. It also affects the network's performance, reliability, and scalability.

For example, in some networks all devices may be connected to a central device such as a switch, while in other networks devices may be connected in a circular pattern or directly with each other.

Basic concept of network topology showing multiple devices connected in different layouts.

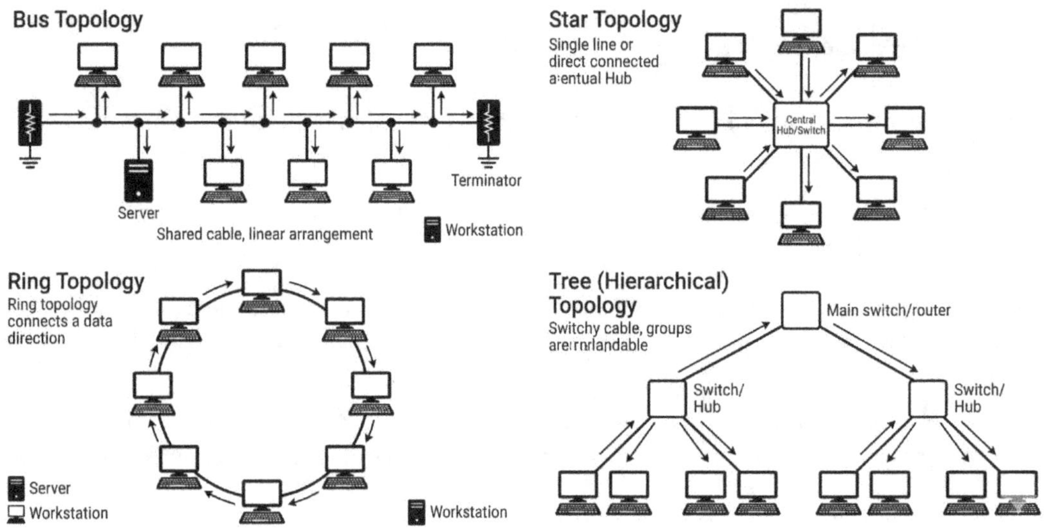

Network topology can be categorized in different ways depending on how devices are arranged. The most common types of network topologies are:

Bus Topology.
Star Topology.
Ring Topology.
Mesh Topology.
Hybrid Topology.

Each topology has its own advantages, disadvantages, and suitable use cases.

Bus Topology

In bus topology, all devices in the network are connected to a single communication cable called the bus or backbone cable.

This main cable acts as the central communication channel through which all data travels. When a device sends data, the data is transmitted along the bus cable and can be received by other devices connected to the network.

Bus Topology showing multiple computers connected to a single backbone cable

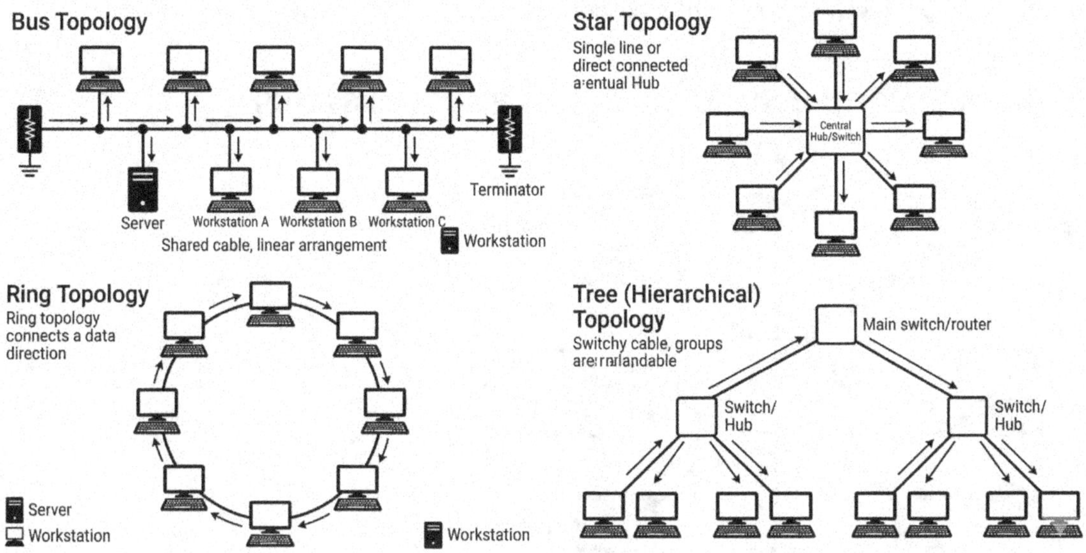

In this topology, each device is connected to the main cable through connectors or taps. The ends of the main cable usually contain devices called terminators, which prevent signals from bouncing back along the cable.

Advantages of Bus Topology

Bus topology offers several advantages.

First, it is simple and easy to install because it requires a smaller amount of cable compared to some other topologies.

Second, it is cost-effective for small networks because fewer networking components are required.

Third, adding a new device to the network is relatively easy because the device can simply be connected to the main cable.

Disadvantages of Bus Topology

Despite its simplicity, bus topology has several limitations.

One major disadvantage is that if the main cable fails, the entire network stops working because all devices depend on that cable for communication.

Another problem is that as more devices are added, network performance can decrease because all devices share the same communication channel.

For these reasons, bus topology is rarely used in modern large networks.

Star Topology

In star topology, all devices in the network are connected to a central device, such as a hub or switch.

Instead of connecting directly to each other, each computer communicates through this central device.

Star topiology showing conputers connected to a central switch

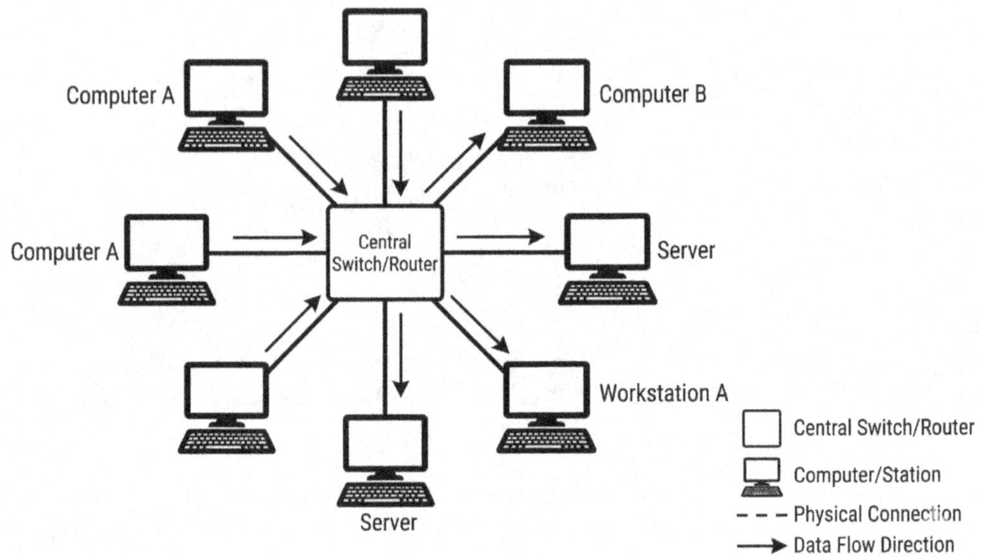

When a device sends data, the data first travels to the central device. The central device then forwards the data to the intended destination device.

Star topology is one of the most widely used network structures in modern computer networks, especially in Ethernet-based LANs.

Advantages of Star Topology

Star topology provides several important benefits.

One major advantage is that if one cable fails, only the device connected to that cable is affected. The rest of the network continues to function normally.

Another advantage is that the central device helps manage network communication efficiently, which improves overall performance.

It is also easy to add or remove devices from a star network without affecting other devices.

Disadvantages of Star Topology

The main disadvantage of star topology is that the entire network depends on the central device.

If the hub or switch fails, the entire network will stop functioning.

Additionally, star topology requires more cables compared to bus topology because each device needs its own connection to the central device.

Ring Topology

In ring topology, devices are connected in a circular structure where each device is connected to two neighboring devices.

Data travels around the network in a circular direction until it reaches its destination.

Ring topoogy showing computers connected in a cir:ular loop.

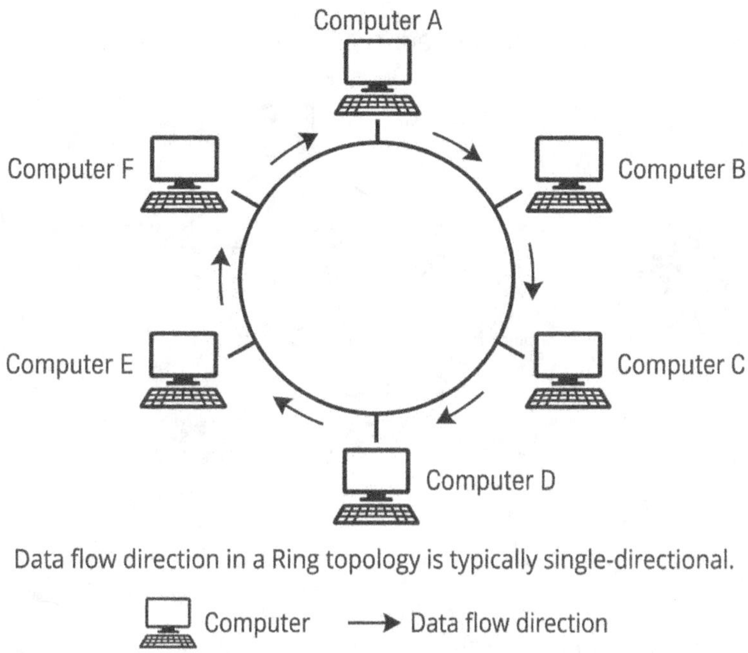

In many ring networks, data travels in only one direction. Each device receives the data, checks whether it is the intended recipient, and if not, forwards it to the next device in the ring.

This process continues until the data reaches the correct device.

Advantages of Ring Topology

One advantage of ring topology is that data flows in an organized manner through the network, reducing the chances of data collisions.

Another advantage is that each device has equal access to the network.

Disadvantages of Ring Topology

However, ring topology also has some disadvantages.

If one device or cable in the ring fails, the entire network may be disrupted because the communication path is broken.

In addition, adding or removing devices from the ring can be difficult because it may require temporarily shutting down the network.

For these reasons, ring topology is less commonly used in modern networks.

Mesh Topology

In mesh topology, every device in the network is connected directly to every other device.

This means that each device has a dedicated communication link with every other device in the network.

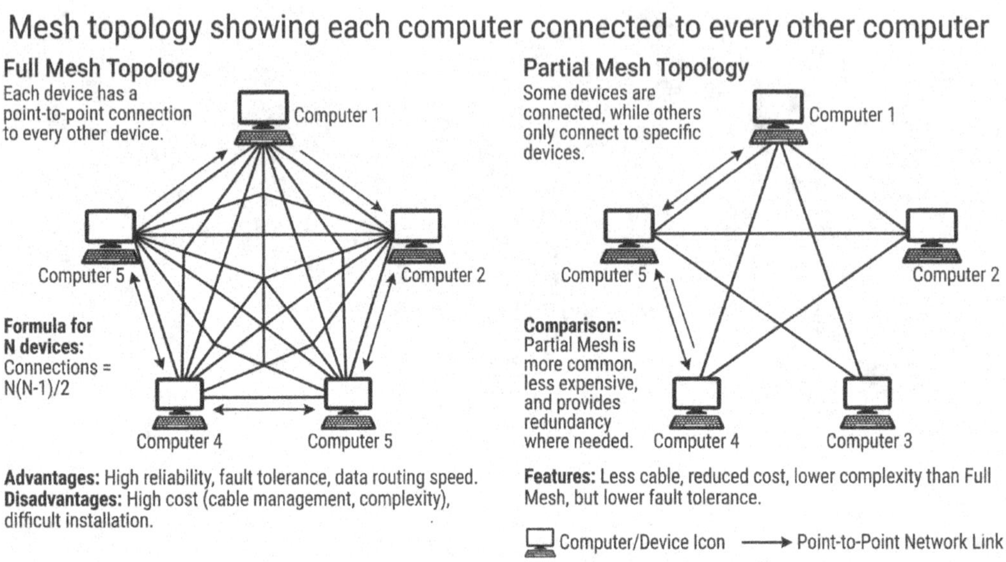

Mesh topology provides very high reliability because multiple communication paths exist between devices.

If one connection fails, data can still travel through another path to reach the destination.

Advantages of Mesh Topology

Mesh topology offers several important advantages.

First, it provides excellent reliability because there are multiple paths between devices.

Second, it improves security because data can travel through dedicated communication links.

Third, network failures can be easily detected and isolated.

Disadvantages of Mesh Topology

Despite its advantages, mesh topology has some significant drawbacks.

The biggest disadvantage is the large number of cables and connections required. As the number of devices increases, the number of connections increases rapidly.

This makes mesh topology expensive and complex to implement.

Because of these reasons, mesh topology is mainly used in specialized networks where reliability is extremely important.

Hybrid Topology

A hybrid topology is created by combining two or more different network topologies into a single network.

For example, a network may use star topology in one section and bus topology in another section.

Hybrid topology combining **star** and **bus** networks

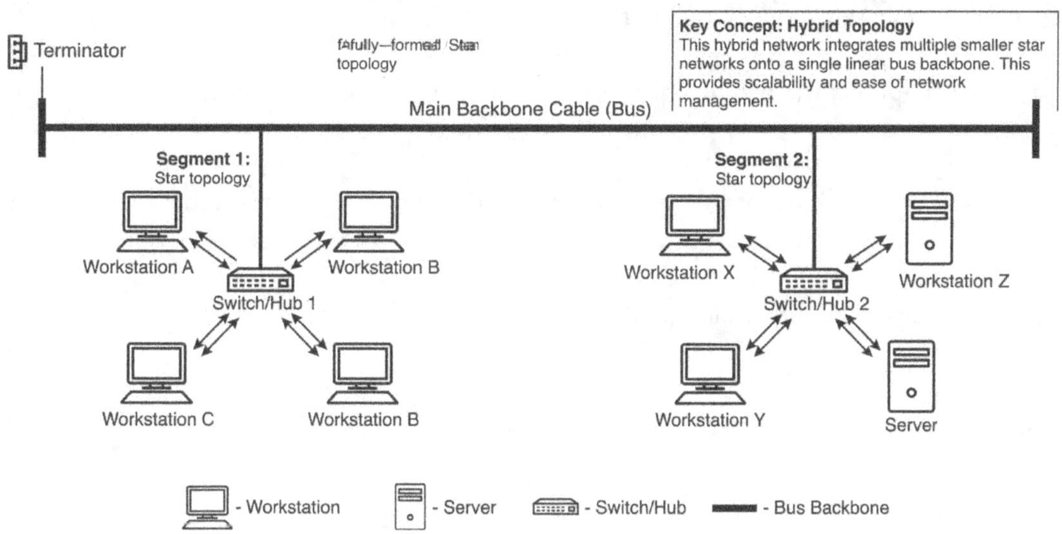

Hybrid topologies are commonly used in large organizations where different types of network structures are required to meet different communication needs.

Advantages of Hybrid Topology

Hybrid topology offers flexibility because network designers can choose the best topology for each section of the network.

It also improves scalability because new network segments can be added easily.

Disadvantages of Hybrid Topology

The main disadvantage of hybrid topology is that it can be complex to design and manage.

It may also require more networking equipment and careful planning.

Importance of Network Topology

Choosing the correct network topology is very important when designing a computer network.

The topology affects several factors, including:

Network performance.

Reliability.
Scalability.
Cost of installation.
Ease of maintenance.

Network engineers must carefully evaluate these factors before selecting a topology for a particular network.

Summary

Network topology refers to the arrangement of devices and connections in a computer network. Different topologies provide different ways of connecting devices and managing communication.

The most common types of network topologies include bus topology, star topology, ring topology, mesh topology, and hybrid topology.

Each topology has its own advantages and disadvantages, and the choice of topology depends on the requirements of the network.

Understanding network topology helps students understand how networks are structured and how data travels between devices.

In the next section, we will study network protocols, which define the rules that allow devices to communicate with each other.

Network Protocols

In the previous section, we learned about network topologies, which describe how devices are physically or logically arranged in a network. However, simply connecting devices together is not enough for communication to occur successfully. The devices must also follow a common set of rules so that they can understand each other during communication.

These rules are known as network protocols.

A network protocol is a set of rules and standards that define how data is transmitted, received, and interpreted between devices in a computer network.

In simple words, protocols are like a common language used by computers to communicate with each other. Without protocols, devices would not know how to send data, how to interpret incoming data, or how to respond to communication requests.

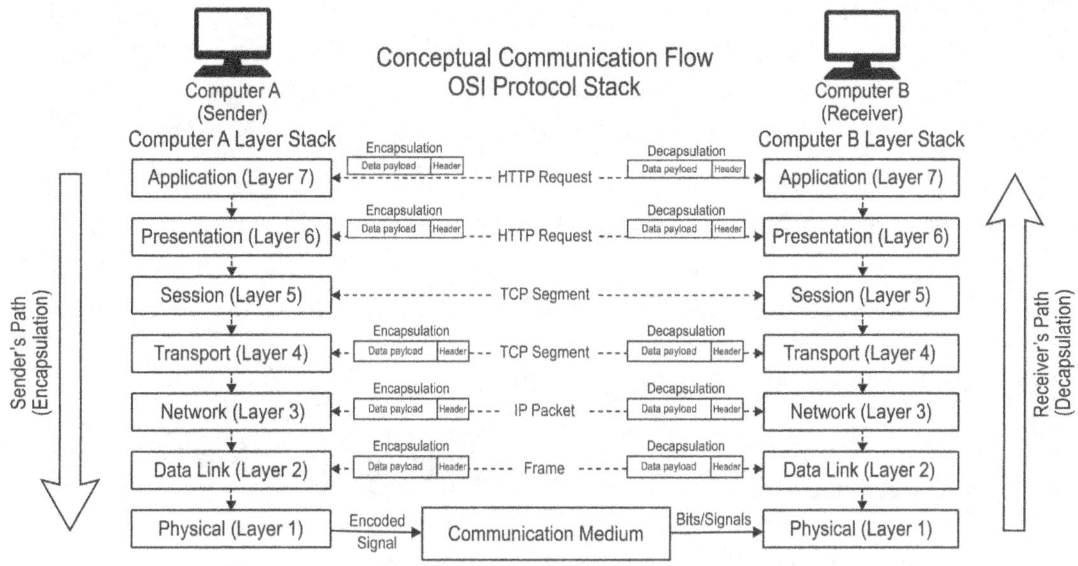

To better understand this concept, consider a real-life example of human communication. When two people communicate, they must follow a common language and certain rules of conversation. If one person speaks English and the other only understands Japanese, communication will not be effective.

Similarly, computers must follow agreed communication rules so that data can be exchanged correctly. These rules are defined by protocols.

Why Network Protocols Are Necessary

Network protocols are essential for several reasons. They ensure that communication between devices is organized, reliable, and efficient.

One of the main reasons protocols are needed is standardization. Computers and networking devices are manufactured by different companies and may use different hardware and software systems. Protocols provide standard communication rules so that devices from different manufacturers can communicate with each other.

Another important reason is data organization. Protocols define how data should be structured during transmission. For example, they determine how data should be divided into smaller units called packets and how these packets should be reassembled at the destination.

Protocols also help manage error detection and correction. During data transmission, errors may occur due to noise or interference in the communication medium. Protocols include mechanisms to detect these errors and request retransmission if necessary.

Additionally, protocols define how devices establish, maintain, and terminate communication sessions. This ensures that data is transmitted in an organized and controlled manner.

Elements of a Network Protocol

Every network protocol consists of several important elements that define how communication takes place.

The three main elements of a protocol are:

Syntax.
Semantics.
Timing.

Let us understand each of these elements.

Syntax

Syntax refers to the structure or format of the data being transmitted.

It defines how the bits and bytes are arranged within a message. For example, syntax determines the order in which different parts of the data are placed in a packet.

If the structure of the message is not correctly followed, the receiving device may not be able to understand the data.

For example, in many network protocols, data packets contain fields such as:

Source address.
Destination address.
Data payload.
Error-checking information.

The syntax specifies how these fields are organized within the packet.

Structure of a datε packet showing header, data, and error-checking fields.

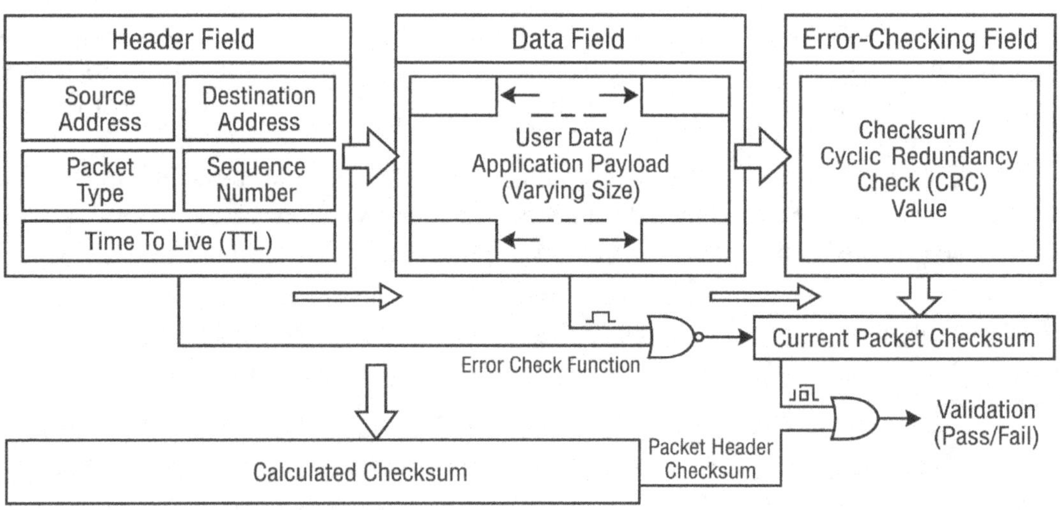

Semantics

Semantics refers to the meaning of each part of the message.

While syntax describes how the message is structured, semantics explains what the information in the message represents.

For example, if a data packet contains a field indicating the destination address, semantics defines what that address represents and how the receiving device should interpret it.

Semantics also defines how devices should respond to different types of messages. For instance, if an error is detected during transmission, semantics may specify that the receiver should send an error notification back to the sender.

Timing

Timing refers to when data should be transmitted and how fast it should be sent.

Timing ensures that the sender and receiver are synchronized during communication. If data is sent too quickly, the receiver may not be able to process it properly. If data is sent too slowly, communication may become inefficient.

Timing rules also determine how long a device should wait for a response before retransmitting data.

In many protocols, timing mechanisms help control the flow of data between devices so that communication remains stable and efficient.

Types of Network Protocols

There are many different network protocols used in computer networks. Each protocol is designed to perform specific communication tasks.

Some protocols are responsible for transferring files, while others manage web communication or email transmission.

Let us look at some commonly used network protocols.

HTTP (HyperText Transfer Protocol)

HTTP is a protocol used for communication between web browsers and web servers. When you open a website, your browser sends an HTTP request to the server hosting the website.

The server then sends the requested web page back to the browser using HTTP.

HTTP communication between client and web server

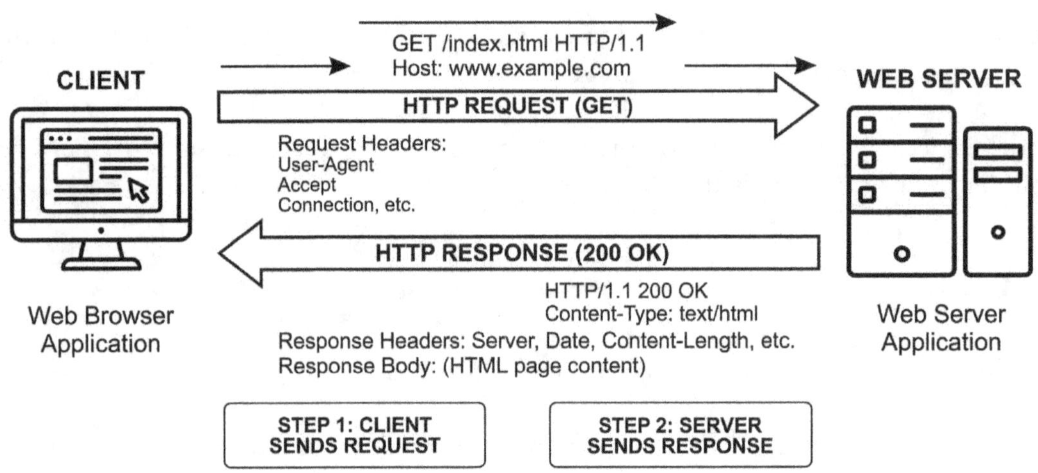

FTP (File Transfer Protocol)

FTP is used to transfer files between computers over a network. It allows users to upload or download files from remote servers.

FTP is commonly used by web developers to upload website files to hosting servers.

SMTP (Simple Mail Transfer Protocol)

SMTP is a protocol used for sending emails across networks. When you send an email, your email client uses SMTP to transfer the message to the mail server.

The server then forwards the email to the recipient's mail server.

TCP/IP (Transmission Control Protocol / Internet Protocol)

TCP/IP is the most important protocol suite used in the internet. It defines how data packets are transmitted across networks.

TCP is responsible for ensuring reliable data transmission, while IP handles addressing and routing of packets.

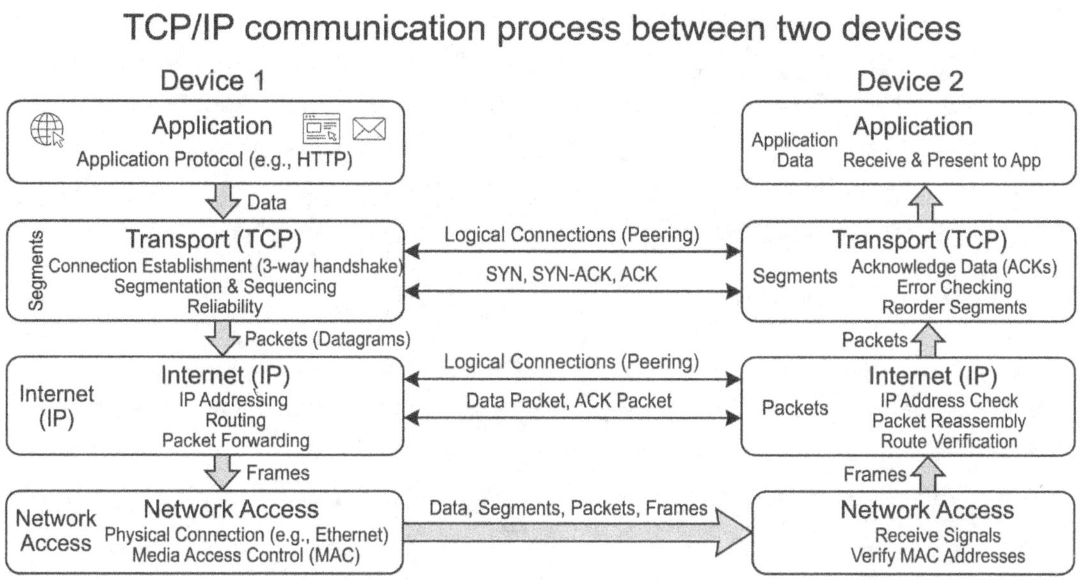

TCP/IP allows computers located in different parts of the world to communicate through the internet.

Importance of Protocol Standardization

Because computer networks connect devices from different manufacturers, it is important to establish universal communication standards.

Standardization ensures that devices developed by different companies can work together without compatibility issues.

International organizations responsible for developing networking standards include:

ISO (International Organization for Standardization)
IEEE (Institute of Electrical and Electronics Engineers)
IETF (Internet Engineering Task Force)
ITU (International Telecommunication Union)

These organizations develop protocols and standards that define how communication systems operate globally.

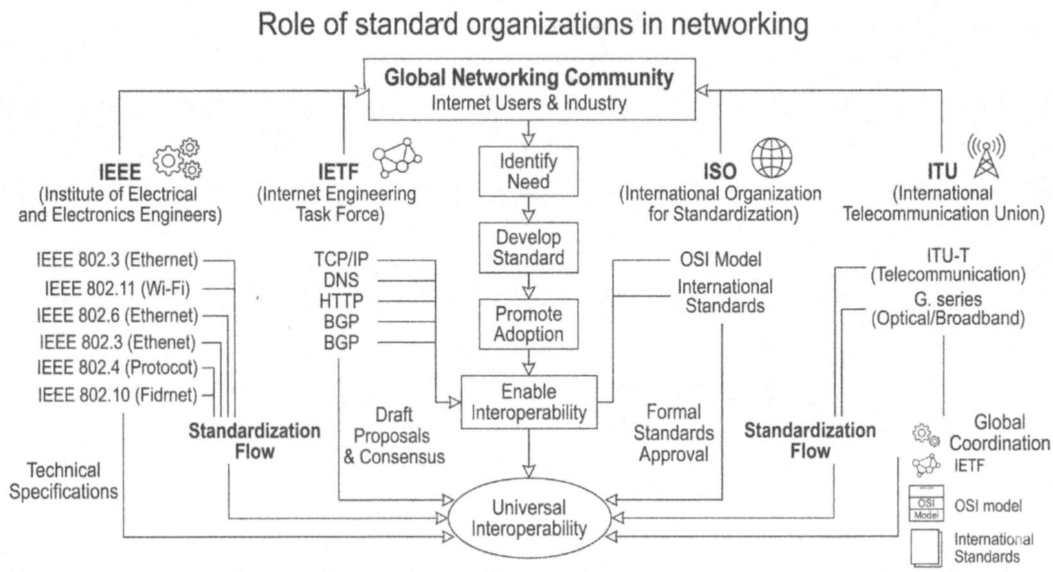

Protocols in Everyday Applications

Network protocols are used in many everyday technologies.

For example:

When you browse a website, your browser uses HTTP to communicate with web servers.
When you send an email, SMTP is used to transfer the message.
When you download files from a server, FTP may be used.
When data travels across the internet, TCP/IP ensures that the packets reach their destination correctly.

Although users may not see these protocols directly, they operate continuously behind the scenes to support digital communication.

Summary

Network protocols are essential for communication in computer networks. They define the rules that devices must follow to transmit and receive data correctly.

Protocols control important aspects of communication such as message format, data interpretation, and timing of transmissions.

Some of the most commonly used protocols include HTTP, FTP, SMTP, and TCP/IP. These protocols allow devices across the world to communicate and exchange information efficiently.

Understanding network protocols is an important step toward learning advanced networking concepts such as network architecture and layered communication models.

In the next chapter, we will begin studying network architecture and layered models, which explain how communication processes are organized in modern computer networks.

CHAPTER THREE

Network Architecture and OSI Model

Need for Network Architecture

As computer networks became larger and more complex, communication between devices also became more complicated. In the early days of networking, there were no clear standards for how devices should communicate. Different manufacturers developed their own networking technologies, which often made it difficult for devices from different companies to work together.

For example, a computer built by one company might not be able to communicate properly with a network device manufactured by another company because they followed different communication methods. This lack of standardization created many problems in network communication.

To solve these issues, networking experts introduced the concept of network architecture.

Network architecture refers to the structured design and organization of a computer network. It defines how different networking components, protocols, and communication processes are arranged to ensure efficient and reliable data transmission.

In simple words, network architecture provides a framework or blueprint that explains how data communication should take place in a network.

Basic concept of network architecture showing layered communication between two computers

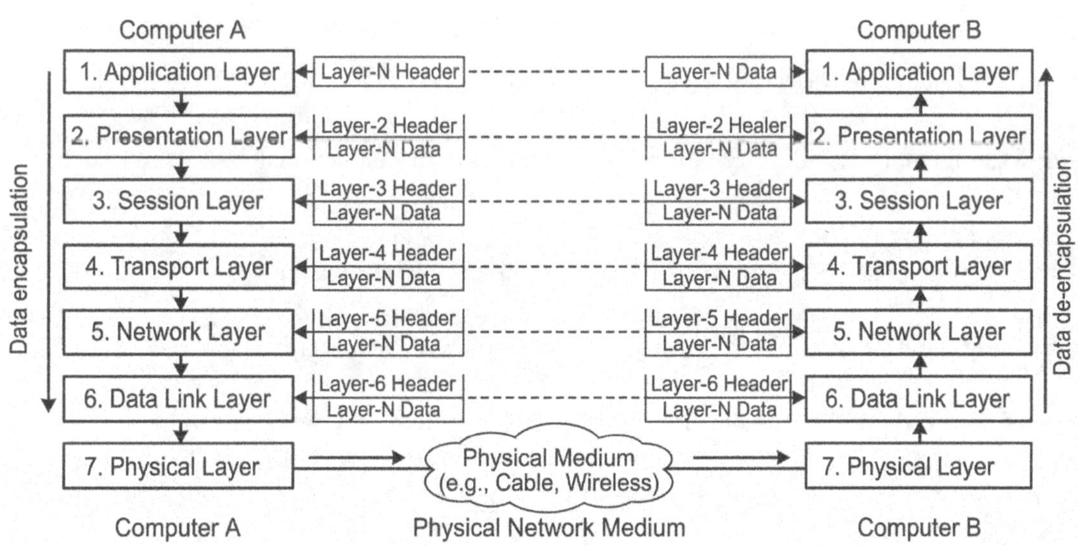

Network architecture ensures that all devices in a network follow a common structure for communication. This allows different hardware and software systems to work together smoothly.

Why Network Architecture is Necessary

Modern networks support millions or even billions of connected devices. Without a proper communication structure, managing such large networks would be extremely difficult.

Network architecture helps solve this problem by organizing communication into smaller and manageable parts.

There are several reasons why network architecture is necessary.

Standardization
One of the main reasons for network architecture is standardization. Networking devices are produced by many different companies around the world. Standard architectures ensure that devices from different manufacturers can communicate with each other.

For example, a laptop manufactured by one company should be able to connect to a router manufactured by another company without any compatibility problems.

Standardized network architecture makes this possible.

Simplified Network Design

Network architecture divides communication tasks into smaller layers. This layered approach makes it easier for engineers to design and develop network systems.

Instead of building the entire communication system as a single complex structure, developers can focus on designing individual layers.

Each layer performs a specific function, which simplifies network design and development.

Easier Troubleshooting

Another important benefit of network architecture is easier troubleshooting.

If a network problem occurs, engineers can identify which layer of the network is responsible for the issue.

For example:
If there is a problem with data transmission signals, the issue may be in the physical layer.

If data packets are not reaching their destination, the problem may be in the network layer.

Because communication is organized into layers, identifying and fixing problems becomes easier.

Flexibility and Scalability

Network architecture also provides flexibility when networks need to expand.

New devices and technologies can be added to a network without completely redesigning the entire communication system.

For example, new communication technologies such as wireless networks, cloud services, and Internet of Things devices can be integrated into existing networks because they follow standard architectural models.

Layered Approach in Networking

To manage complex communication tasks, network architecture uses a layered approach. In this approach, the entire communication process is divided into multiple layers.

Each layer performs a specific function and communicates with the layer above and below it.

For example:
One layer may be responsible for transmitting electrical signals.

Another layer may handle addressing and routing.

Another layer may manage error detection.

This layered structure makes network communication more organized and efficient.

Layered network architecture showing multiple communication layers

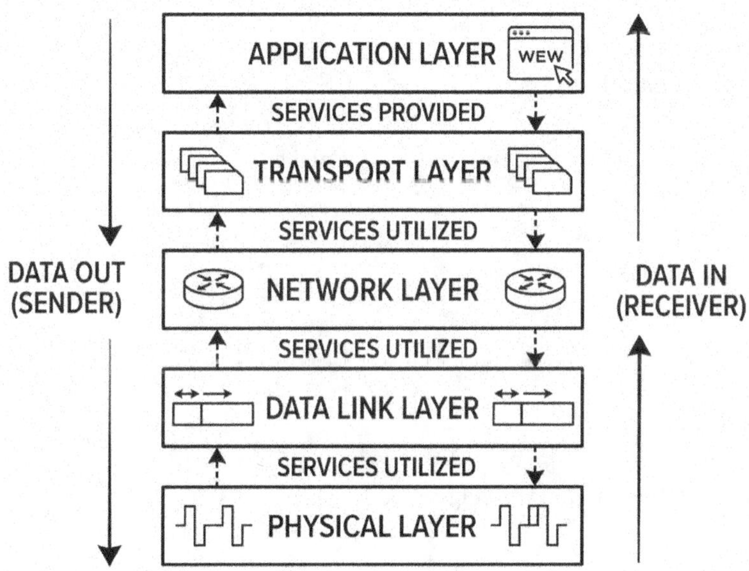

In this layered system, data moves from the top layer of the sender device down to the bottom layer before being transmitted through the network. At the receiving end, the data moves upward through the layers until it reaches the application used by the receiver.

This process ensures that each layer performs its task without interfering with other layers.

Benefits of Layered Network Architecture

The layered architecture used in networking provides several important benefits.

Modular Design

Each layer of the network architecture performs a specific function. This modular design allows engineers to modify one layer without affecting the entire system.

For example, improvements in wireless communication technology may only affect the physical layer, while higher layers remain unchanged.

Interoperability

Because network architectures follow standard protocols, devices developed by different manufacturers can communicate with each other easily.

This interoperability is essential for the functioning of global networks such as the internet.

Simplified Learning

From an educational perspective, layered architecture makes networking concepts easier to understand.

Students can study each layer individually rather than trying to understand the entire communication system at once.

Example of Network Architecture in Real Life
Consider the process of sending an email.

When a user sends an email, several networking functions take place:
The email application prepares the message.

The message is converted into data packets.

The packets are given addresses.

The packets travel through multiple networks.

The receiving system reconstructs the original message.

All these tasks are handled by different layers of network architecture working together.

This layered approach ensures that communication occurs smoothly and efficiently.

Introduction to Networking Models

To standardize network architecture, experts developed formal models that define how communication layers should operate.

Two of the most important networking models are:

OSI Reference Model
TCP/IP Model

These models describe how data communication should be organized into layers and how different networking functions should interact.

The OSI model is mainly used as a conceptual framework for understanding networking principles, while the TCP/IP model forms the foundation of modern internet communication.

In the next section, we will study the OSI Reference Model, which divides network communication into seven different layers.

OSI Reference Model

As computer networks became larger and more complex, it became necessary to develop a standard model that could describe how communication takes place between different devices. To solve this problem, the International Organization for Standardization (ISO) developed a conceptual model called the OSI Reference Model.

OSI stands for Open Systems Interconnection.

The OSI model provides a structured framework that explains how data travels from one device to another in a network. Instead of treating communication as one complex process, the OSI model divides the entire communication process into seven different layers, where each layer performs a specific function.

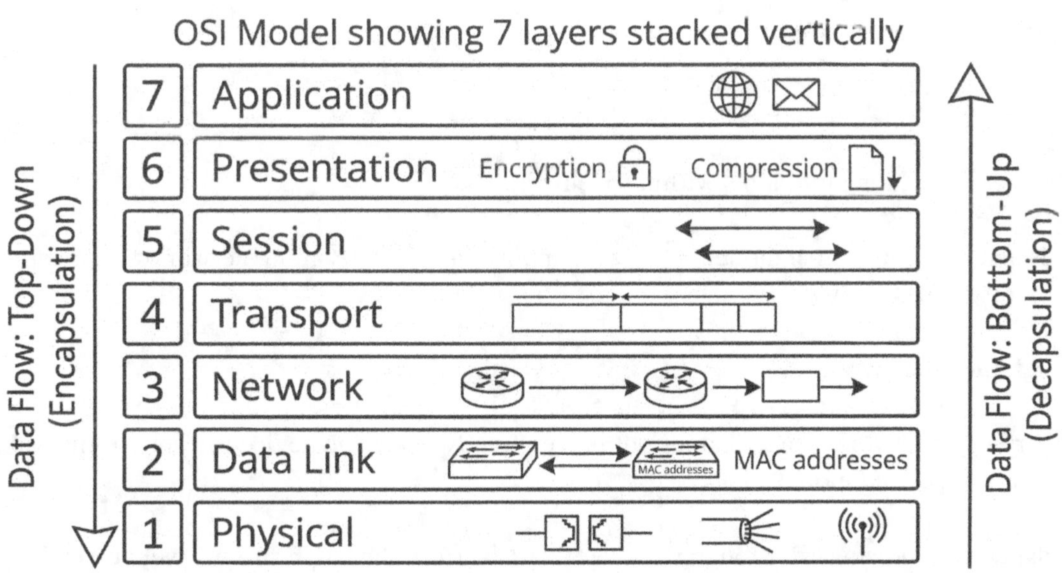

These seven layers work together to ensure that data is transmitted correctly from the sender to the receiver.

The seven layers of the OSI model are:

Physical Layer

Data Link Layer

Network Layer

Transport Layer

Session Layer

Presentation Layer

Application Layer

Each layer communicates with the layer above it and the layer below it. This layered structure helps organize communication tasks and makes network design easier.

Purpose of the OSI Model

The OSI model was created mainly to standardize network communication. By defining clear layers and functions, the model helps different systems communicate with each other even if they are developed by different manufacturers.

Some important purposes of the OSI model include:

Providing a standard framework for network communication.

Simplifying network design and implementation.

Helping engineers understand networking processes.

Making troubleshooting easier by isolating problems within specific layers.

Although the OSI model is mainly a conceptual model, it plays an important role in teaching networking concepts and designing communication protocols.

How Data Travels Through the OSI Layers

When a user sends data through a network, the data does not move directly from one device to another. Instead, it passes through the seven layers of the OSI model.

At the sender's side, the data moves downward through the layers starting from the Application Layer and ending at the Physical Layer. The Physical Layer then transmits the data through the communication medium.

At the receiver's side, the data moves upward through the layers starting from the Physical Layer and ending at the Application Layer.

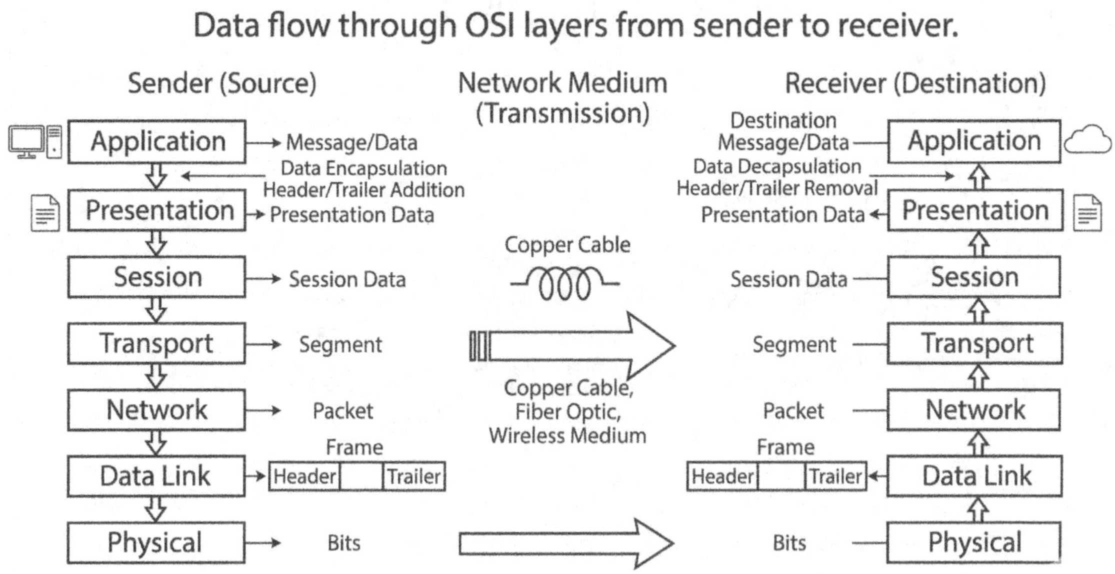

This process ensures that each layer performs its own specific task during communication.

Overview of the Seven Layers

Let us briefly understand the role of each layer in the OSI model.

Physical Layer

The Physical Layer is the lowest layer of the OSI model. It is responsible for transmitting raw bits of data over the physical communication medium.

This layer deals with the electrical, mechanical, and physical aspects of data transmission.

Some responsibilities of the physical layer include:

Converting data into electrical or optical signals.

Defining cable types and connectors.

Managing data transmission speeds.

Handling physical connections between devices.

Devices such as network cables, connectors, and network interface cards operate at this layer.

PHYSICAL LAYER: TRANSMITTING BITS THROUGH CABLE

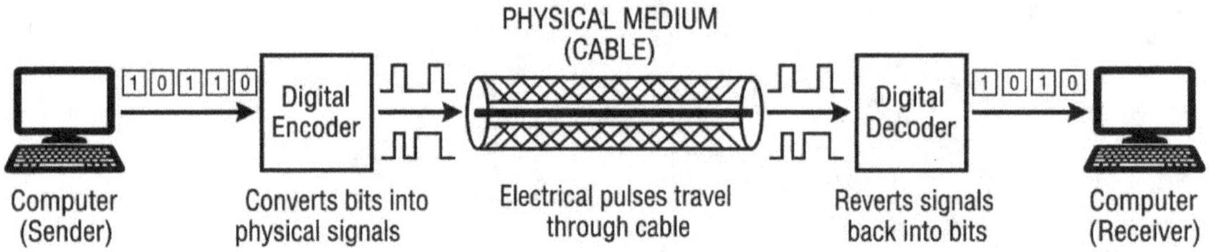

Data Link Layer

The Data Link Layer is responsible for ensuring reliable communication between two directly connected devices.

It organizes data into units called frames and manages error detection and correction during transmission.

Some important functions of the data link layer include:

Framing data packets.

Error detection using techniques such as CRC.

Flow control.

Managing access to the communication medium.

Network devices such as switches and network interface cards often operate at this layer.

FRAME STRUCTURE IN DATA LINK LAYER

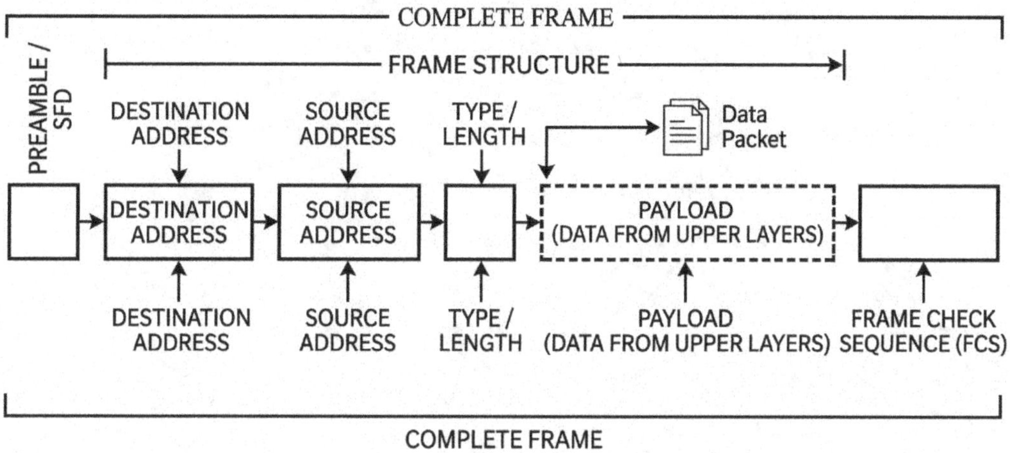

Network Layer

The Network Layer is responsible for determining the best path for data to travel from the sender to the receiver.

This process is known as routing.

The network layer assigns logical addresses to devices and manages the movement of data packets across multiple networks.

Some functions of this layer include:

Logical addressing using IP addresses.

Routing data packets through different networks.

Managing packet forwarding.

Devices such as routers operate mainly at the network layer.

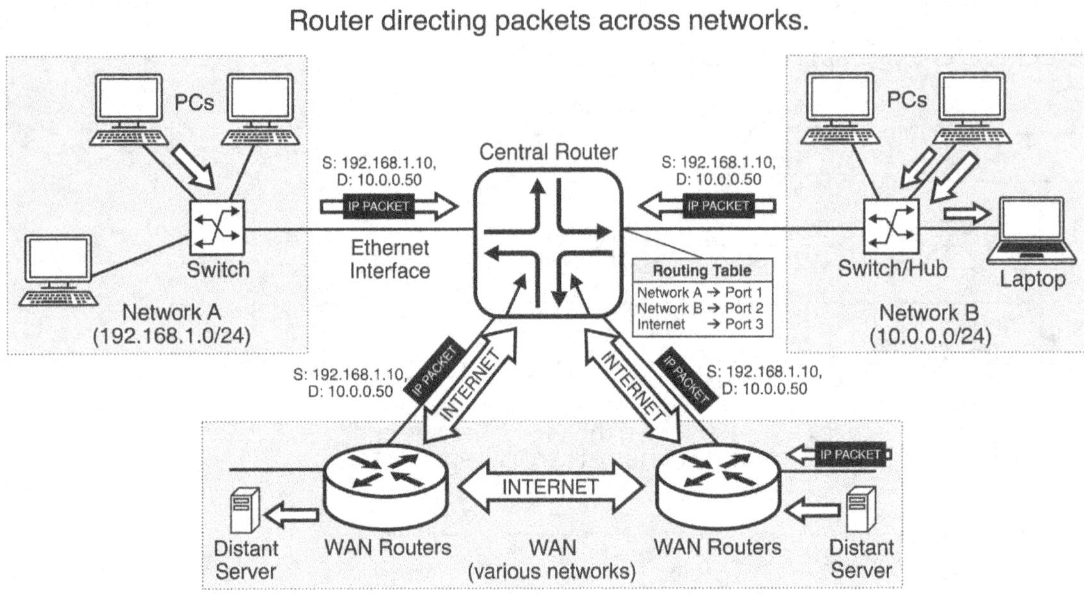

Transport Layer

The Transport Layer ensures that data is delivered reliably and in the correct order from the sender to the receiver.

It divides large data messages into smaller segments and reassembles them at the destination.

Key functions of the transport layer include:

End-to-end communication.

Error recovery.

Flow control.

Data segmentation and reassembly.

Protocols such as TCP and UDP operate at this layer.

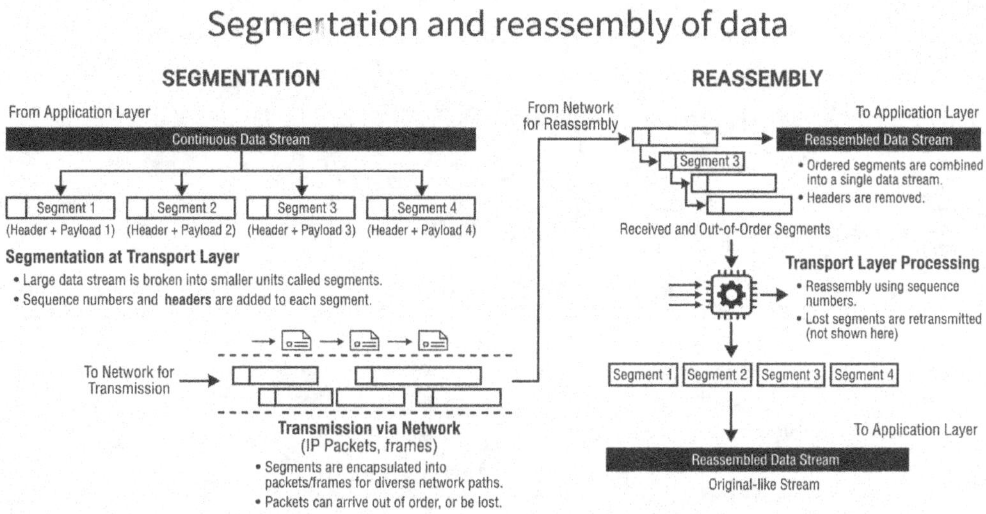

Session Layer

The Session Layer manages communication sessions between devices.

A session refers to a continuous exchange of data between two devices.

The session layer is responsible for:

Establishing communication sessions.

Maintaining active connections.

Terminating sessions when communication ends.

This layer ensures that communication between devices occurs in an organized manner.

Presentation Layer

The Presentation Layer is responsible for formatting and translating data so that it can be understood by the receiving system.

Different systems may use different data formats. The presentation layer converts the data into a standard format during transmission.

This layer also handles:

Data encryption and decryption.

Data compression.

Character encoding.

For example, if a file is encrypted before transmission, the presentation layer handles the encryption and decryption processes.

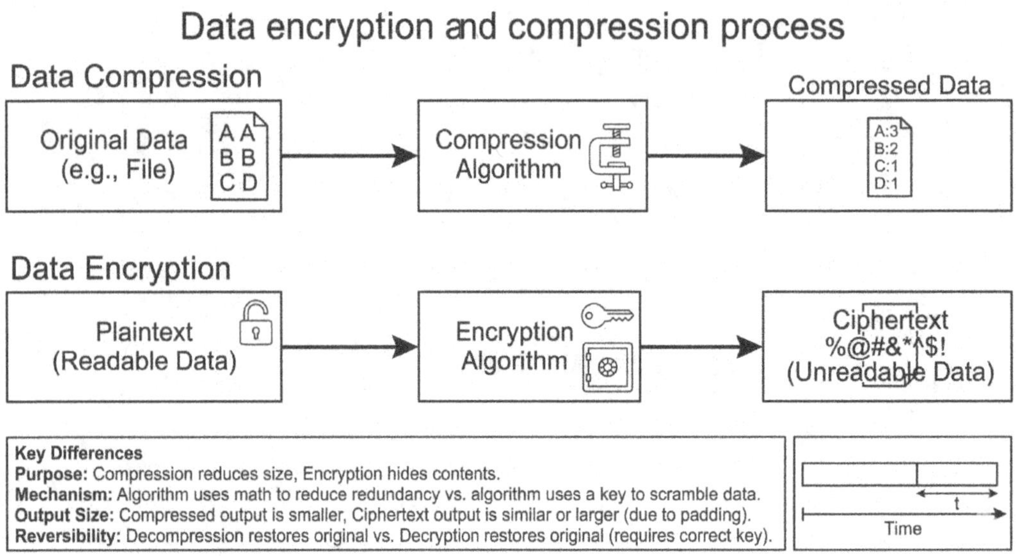

Application Layer

The Application Layer is the top layer of the OSI model. It provides network services directly to user applications.

This layer allows software applications to interact with the network.

Examples of services provided by the application layer include:

Web browsing.

Email communication.

File transfer.

Remote login.

Protocols such as HTTP, FTP, SMTP, and DNS operate at this layer.

Application layer interacting with user applications

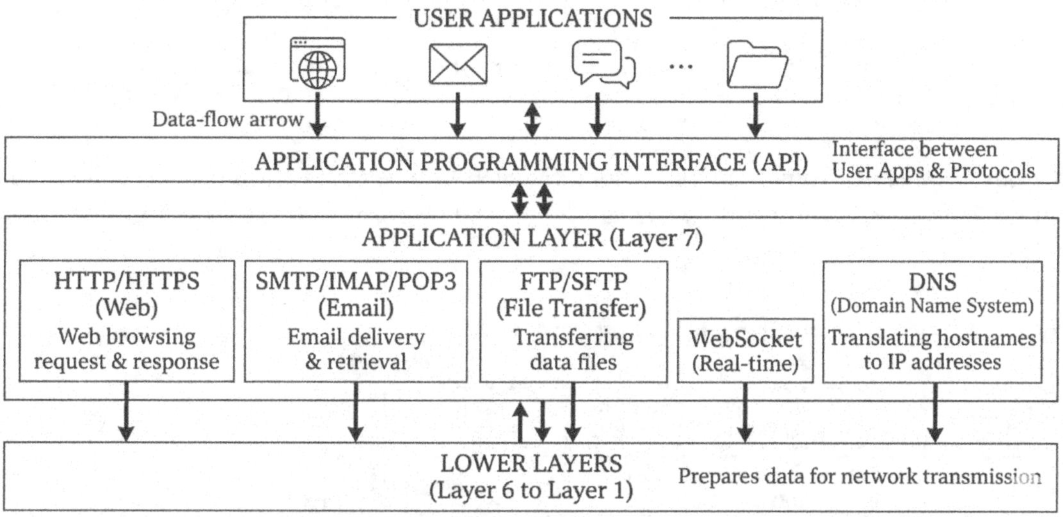

Importance of the OSI Model

The OSI model is extremely important for understanding how networks operate.

Even though modern networks mainly use the TCP/IP model, the OSI model is widely used for teaching networking concepts because it clearly explains how communication is organized.

Network engineers and administrators often use the OSI model to troubleshoot network problems. By analyzing each layer separately, they can quickly identify where the problem is occurring.

For example, if a network cable is damaged, the problem occurs at the Physical Layer. If a routing issue occurs, the problem may be at the Network Layer.

Summary

The OSI Reference Model is a conceptual framework that divides network communication into seven layers. Each layer performs specific functions that help ensure reliable and efficient data transmission.

The seven layers of the OSI model are Physical, Data Link, Network, Transport, Session, Presentation, and Application.

By organizing communication tasks into layers, the OSI model simplifies network design, improves interoperability, and helps engineers troubleshoot network problems more effectively.

Understanding the OSI model is essential for students studying computer networks because it provides the foundation for learning advanced networking technologies.

Functions of OSI Layers

In the previous section, we introduced the OSI Reference Model and learned that it consists of seven layers. Each layer in the OSI model performs specific tasks that help in successful communication between two devices.

Although the layers work independently, they cooperate with each other to ensure that data is transmitted correctly from the sender to the receiver.

In this section, we will study the detailed functions performed by each layer of the OSI model. Understanding these functions is very important because it helps students clearly understand how network communication works step by step.

OS model layers with their major functions.

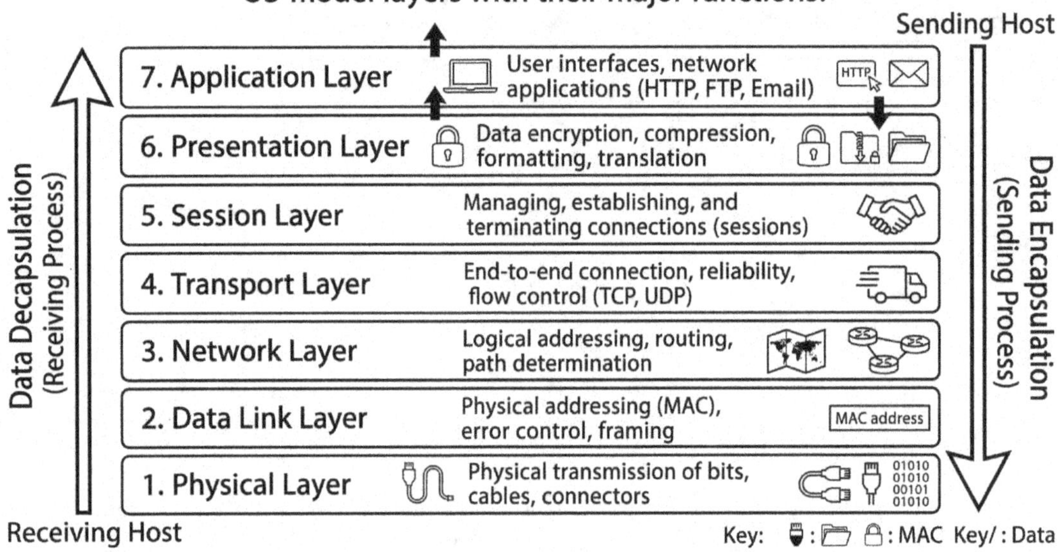

1. Physical Layer – Transmission of Raw Bits

The Physical Layer is the lowest layer in the OSI model. It is responsible for transmitting raw bits (0s and 1s) over the physical communication medium.

This layer does not interpret the meaning of data. Instead, it simply focuses on how bits are transmitted through cables, optical fibers, or wireless signals.

Some of the major functions of the Physical Layer include:

Bit Transmission

The physical layer converts digital data into electrical signals, light signals, or radio signals depending on the type of transmission medium used.

For example, when data is sent through an Ethernet cable, it is converted into electrical signals. When data is transmitted through optical fiber, it is converted into light signals.

Physical Connections

This layer defines how devices are physically connected to the network. It includes specifications for cables, connectors, voltage levels, and signal transmission methods.

For instance, Ethernet cables such as Cat5e or Cat6 follow certain physical layer standards.

Data Transmission Rate

The physical layer also determines the speed at which data is transmitted. This includes transmission rates such as 100 Mbps, 1 Gbps, or higher speeds.

Signal Encoding

It defines how digital bits are converted into signals that can travel through the communication medium.

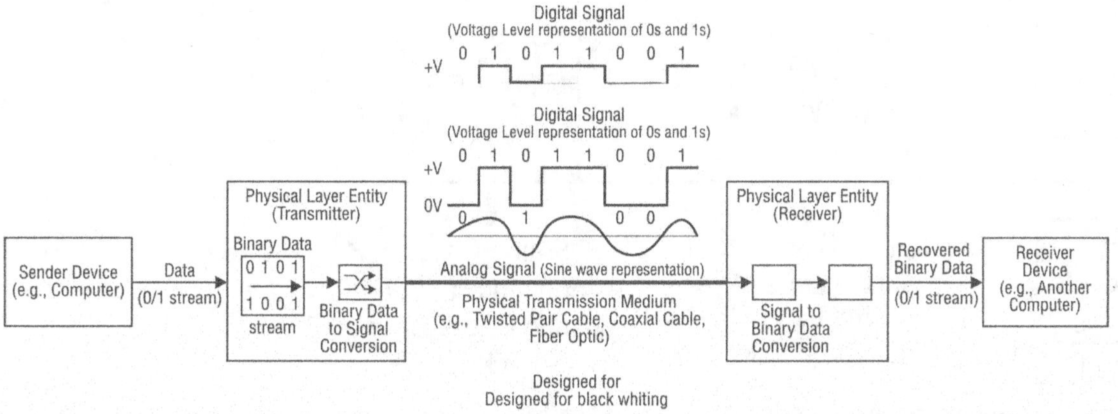

Devices that operate at the physical layer include:

Network cables.
Hubs.
Repeaters.
Network interface cards (NIC).

2. Data Link Layer – Reliable Node-to-Node Communication

The Data Link Layer is responsible for ensuring reliable communication between two directly connected devices.

It receives raw data from the physical layer and organizes it into structured units called frames.

Framing

One of the most important functions of the data link layer is framing. Data received from the network layer is divided into frames before transmission.

Each frame contains:
Source address.

Destination address.

Data.

Error checking information.

Frame structure showing header, data, and trailer.

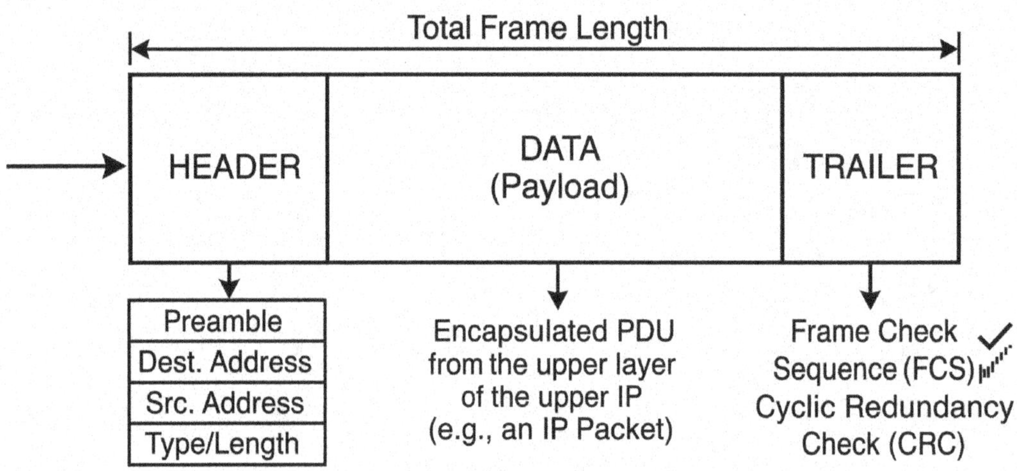

Frame structure showing header, data, and trailer.

Error Detection

During transmission, errors may occur due to noise or interference in the communication medium. The data link layer detects these errors using techniques such as Cyclic Redundancy Check (CRC).

If an error is detected, the receiver may request retransmission of the corrupted frame.

Flow Control

Flow control ensures that the sender does not transmit data faster than the receiver can process it.

For example, if a fast computer sends data to a slower device, the data link layer helps regulate the speed of transmission.

Media Access Control

In networks where multiple devices share the same communication medium (such as Ethernet), the data link layer controls which device is allowed to transmit data at a particular time.

Devices that commonly operate at this layer include:

Switches.

Bridges.

Network Interface Cards.

3. Network Layer – Logical Addressing and Routing

The Network Layer is responsible for delivering data from the source device to the destination device across multiple networks.

The most important task of this layer is routing, which means determining the best path for data packets to travel through the network.

Logical Addressing

Every device in a network must have a unique logical address so that it can be identified. The network layer uses IP addresses to identify devices.

For example, a device may have an address such as 192.168.1.10.

These addresses help routers determine where data packets should be sent.

Routing

When data needs to travel through multiple networks, routers analyze the destination address and determine the best path for the packet to reach its destination.

This process is known as routing.

Router forwarding packets between networks.

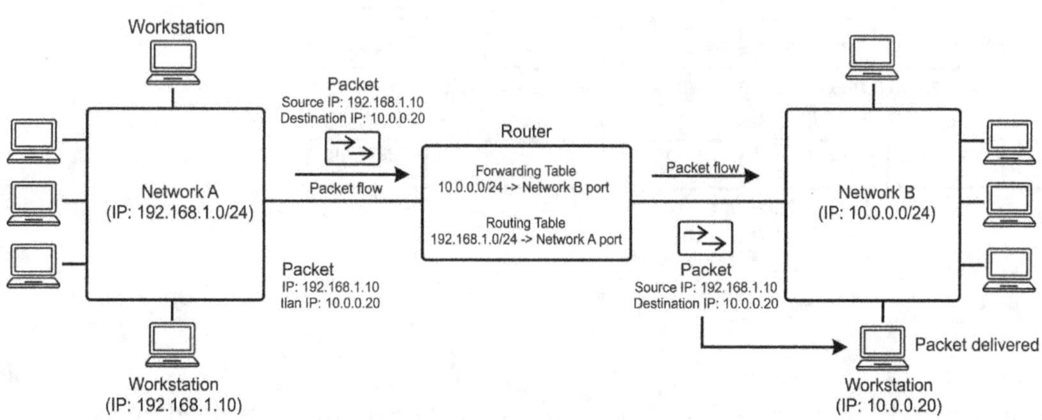

Packet Forwarding

The network layer is responsible for forwarding packets from one network to another until they reach the final destination.

Devices operating at the network layer include:

Routers.

Layer-3 switches.

4. Transport Layer – End-to-End Communication

The Transport Layer ensures reliable delivery of data between the sender and the receiver.

While the network layer focuses on routing packets across networks, the transport layer focuses on ensuring that the entire message arrives correctly.

Segmentation

Large data messages are divided into smaller units called segments before transmission. This makes data transmission more efficient.

At the receiving side, these segments are reassembled to form the original message.

Segmertation of data into smaller segments

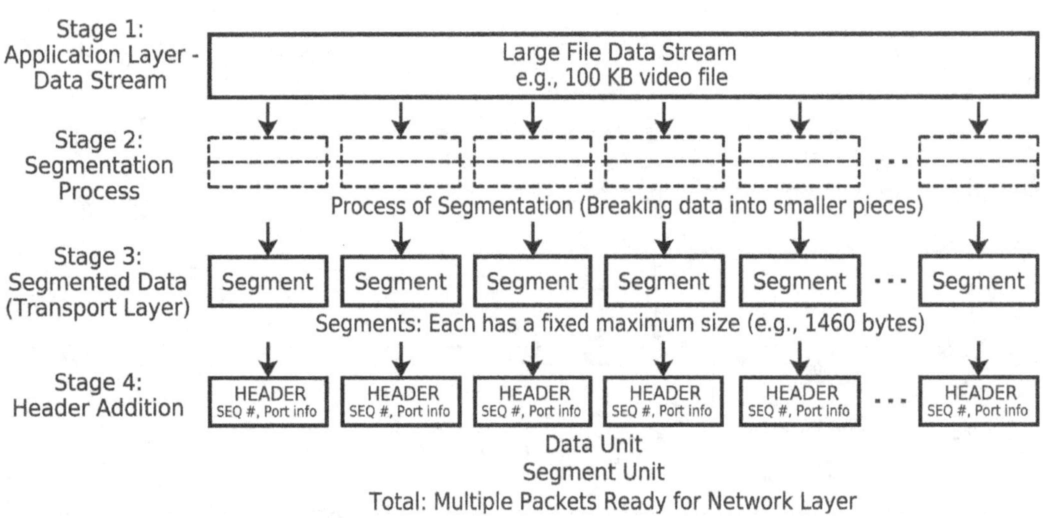

Error Control

The transport layer ensures that data arrives without errors. If a segment is lost or corrupted, the sender may retransmit it.

Flow Control

This layer also controls the rate of data transmission so that the receiver is not overwhelmed.

Reliable Communication

Protocols such as TCP (Transmission Control Protocol) ensure reliable communication by confirming the successful delivery of data.

Another protocol called UDP (User Datagram Protocol) provides faster but less reliable communication.

5. Session Layer – Managing Communication Sessions

The Session Layer is responsible for establishing, maintaining, and terminating communication sessions between devices.

A session is a logical connection that allows two devices to communicate with each other.

For example, when two users participate in a video conference, a communication session is established between their systems.

Functions of the session layer include:

Establishing communication sessions.

Maintaining active connections.

Synchronizing data transmission.

Terminating sessions when communication ends.

This layer ensures that communication occurs smoothly and continuously.

6. Presentation Layer – Data Translation and Formatting

The Presentation Layer is responsible for translating data into a format that both the sender and receiver can understand.

Different computer systems may use different data formats. The presentation layer converts the data into a standard format during transmission.

Data Translation

It converts data from one format to another.

For example, text data may be converted between ASCII and Unicode formats.

Data Encryption

To ensure security, the presentation layer may encrypt data before transmission.

At the receiver's side, the encrypted data is decrypted.

Data Compression

This layer may also compress data to reduce the amount of data transmitted over the network.

Data compression and encryption process.

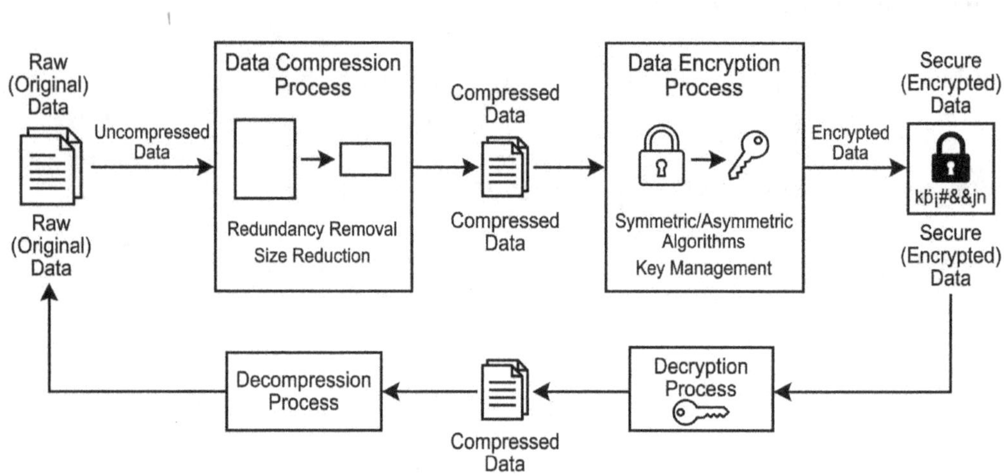

7. Application Layer – Interface for User Applications

The Application Layer is the topmost layer of the OSI model. It provides network services directly to user applications.

This layer acts as an interface between software applications and the network.

Common services provided by the application layer include:

Web browsing.

Email communication.

File transfer.

Remote login.

For example:

When you open a website in a browser, the HTTP protocol at the application layer sends requests to the web server.

Similarly, when sending emails, protocols such as SMTP are used.

How All OSI Layers Work Together

Although each layer performs its own specific functions, they work together as a complete system.

When a user sends data:

The application layer prepares the data.

The presentation layer formats and encrypts it.

The session layer establishes communication.

The transport layer segments the data.

The network layer assigns addresses and routes packets.

The data link layer frames the data.

The physical layer transmits the bits through the medium.

At the receiver's side, the process happens in reverse order.

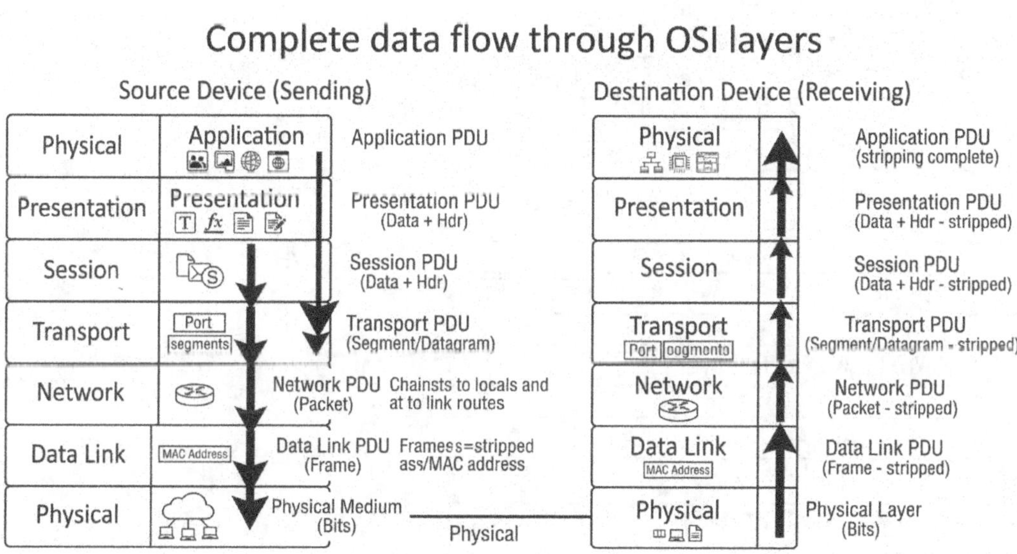

Summary

The OSI model consists of seven layers, each responsible for specific communication tasks.

The physical layer handles signal transmission, the data link layer ensures reliable node-to-node communication, the network layer manages routing, and the transport layer ensures reliable data delivery.

The session, presentation, and application layers handle communication management, data formatting, and user interaction.

By dividing network communication into layers, the OSI model makes networking systems easier to design, implement, and troubleshoot.

Understanding the functions of each OSI layer helps students gain a deeper understanding of how computer networks operate.

Data Encapsulation Process

In the previous sections, we learned about the OSI model and the functions of its layers. Each layer of the OSI model performs a specific task in the communication process. However, an important question arises: how does the data actually move through these layers when it travels from one device to another?

The answer lies in a process called data encapsulation.

Data encapsulation is the process in which data is wrapped with additional information as it moves through the different layers of the OSI model before being transmitted over the network.

In simple words, encapsulation means adding control information to the original data so that it can travel safely through the network and reach the correct destination.

OSI layers showing encapsulation from Application Layer to Physical Layer

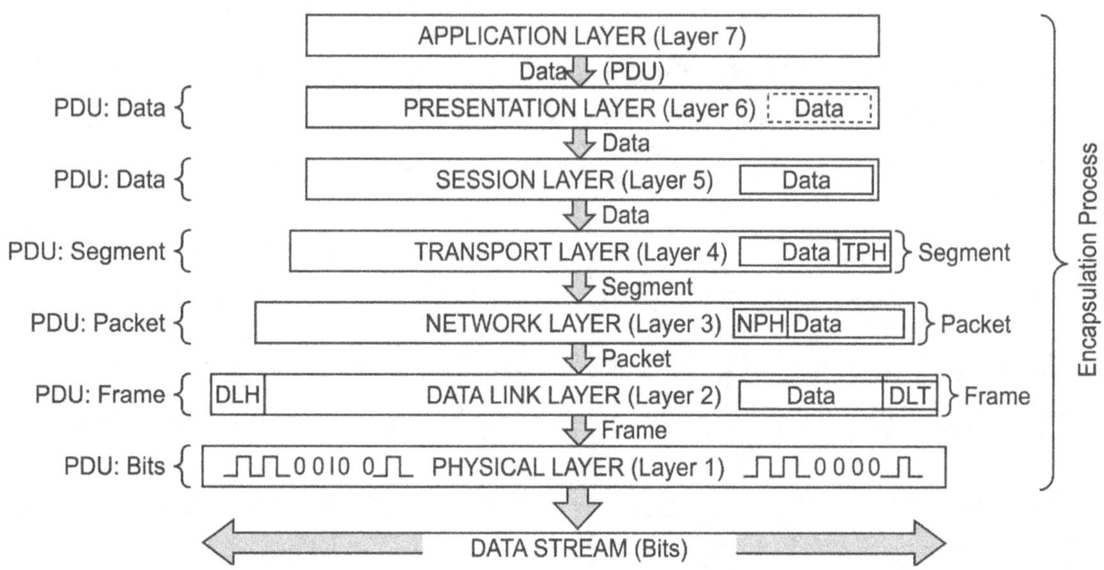

Understanding Encapsulation with a Simple Example

To understand encapsulation easily, let us take an example from daily life.

Imagine that you want to send a letter to your friend through postal service.

The process usually happens like this:

First, you write the message on a piece of paper.
Then you place the paper inside an envelope.
The envelope contains important information such as the sender's address and receiver's address.
After that, the postal service adds further routing information so the letter can travel through different post offices.

Finally, the letter is delivered to the destination.

Similarly, when data is sent through a computer network, it is not transmitted directly. Instead, each layer of the OSI model adds its own information to the data so that it can be transmitted properly through the network.

This process of wrapping the data with additional information at each layer is known as encapsulation.

How Encapsulation Happens in the OSI Model

When a user sends data through a network, the data starts at the Application Layer and moves downward through the OSI layers until it reaches the Physical Layer.

At every layer, additional information known as a header is added to the data. Sometimes, a trailer is also added.

These headers contain important information such as:

Source address.

Destination address.

Error detection information.

Port numbers.

Sequence numbers.

This extra information helps networking devices understand how the data should be handled and where it should be delivered.

Encapsulation Process showing headers added at each layer.

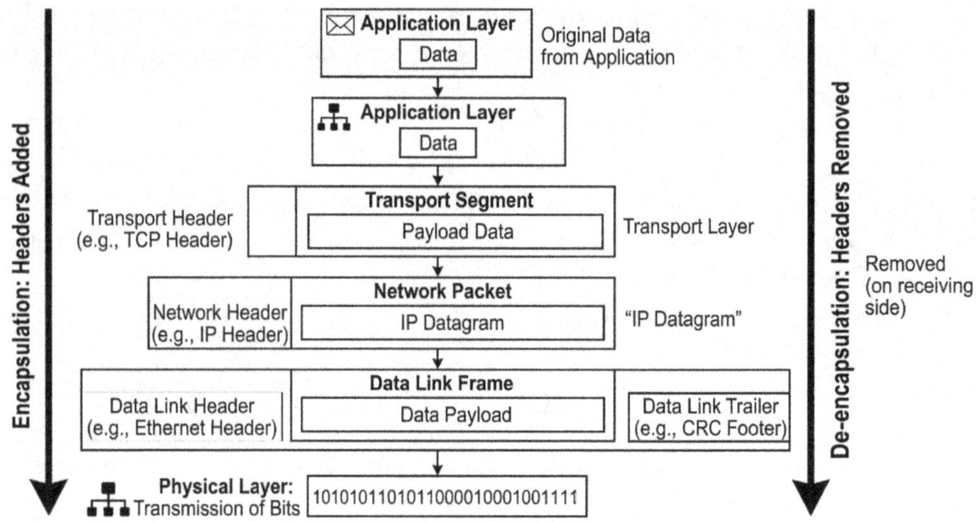

Step-by-Step Process of Data Encapsulation

Let us understand how encapsulation works step by step as data moves through the layers.

Data at the Application Layer

The process begins at the Application Layer, where the user generates data.

For example, a user may:

send an email.

upload a file.

browse a website.

send a message through an application.

At this stage, the information is simply called data or message.

The application layer prepares the data for transmission and passes it to the next layer.

Processing at the Presentation Layer

The Presentation Layer is responsible for preparing the data so that the receiving system can understand it.

At this layer, the data may undergo several processes such as:

Data formatting.

Data compression.

Data encryption.

For example, if confidential information is being sent, it may be encrypted to protect it from unauthorized access.

Once the data is formatted properly, it moves to the session layer.

Session Layer – Managing the Communication Session

The Session Layer establishes and manages the communication session between two devices.

A session refers to a logical connection between the sender and the receiver.

This layer ensures that communication begins properly and remains active during the data transfer process.

For example, when two computers are exchanging files or participating in a video conference, a session is established between them.

After managing the session information, the data is passed to the transport layer.

Transport Layer – Segmentation of Data

When the data reaches the Transport Layer, it may be divided into smaller units called segments.

Large messages are broken into smaller segments because smaller units are easier to transmit and manage within the network.

The transport layer also adds its own header containing important information such as:

Port numbers.

Sequence numbers.

Error control information.

These details help ensure that the segments arrive at the destination in the correct order and without errors.

Large message divided into smaller segments

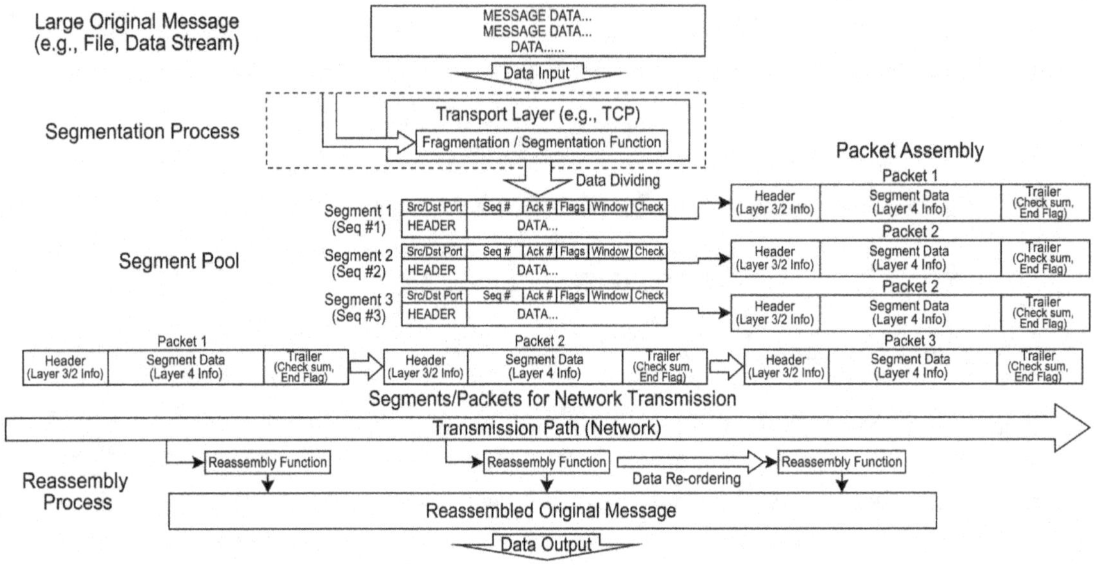

Network Layer – Packet Creation and Addressing

After segmentation, the data moves to the Network Layer.

At this layer, logical addressing information is added to each segment. This information includes the source IP address and destination IP address.

Once this addressing information is added, the segment becomes a packet.

The network layer is responsible for determining the best path through which the packet should travel across multiple networks.

Devices called routers use this addressing information to forward packets toward their destination.

Packet with IP addressing information

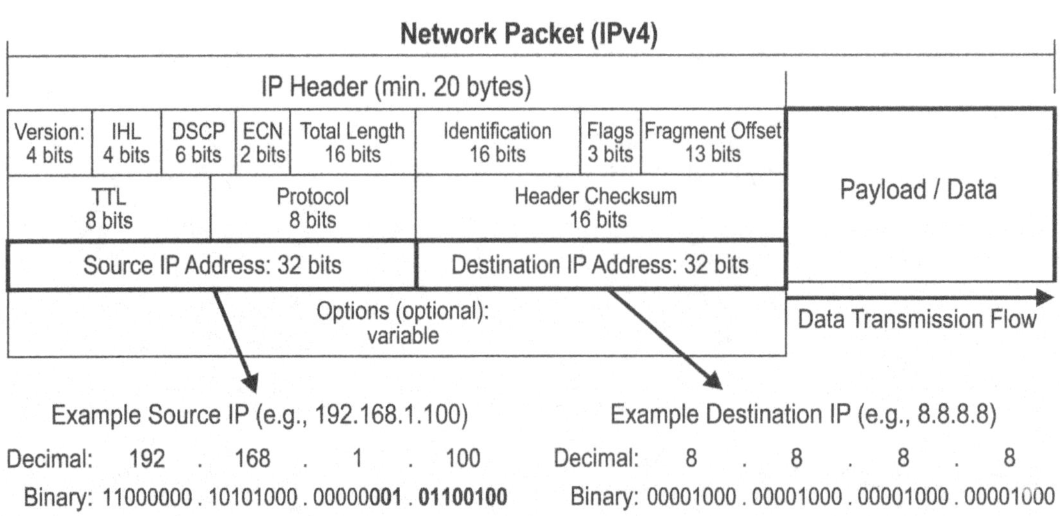

Data Link Layer – Frame Formation

Next, the packet reaches the Data Link Layer.

Here, the packet is enclosed within another structure called a frame.

The data link layer adds two types of information:

A header, which contains physical addressing information such as the source and destination MAC addresses.

A trailer, which usually contains error detection information.

This frame structure helps ensure that communication between directly connected devices occurs reliably.

Frame structure showing header, data, and trailer.

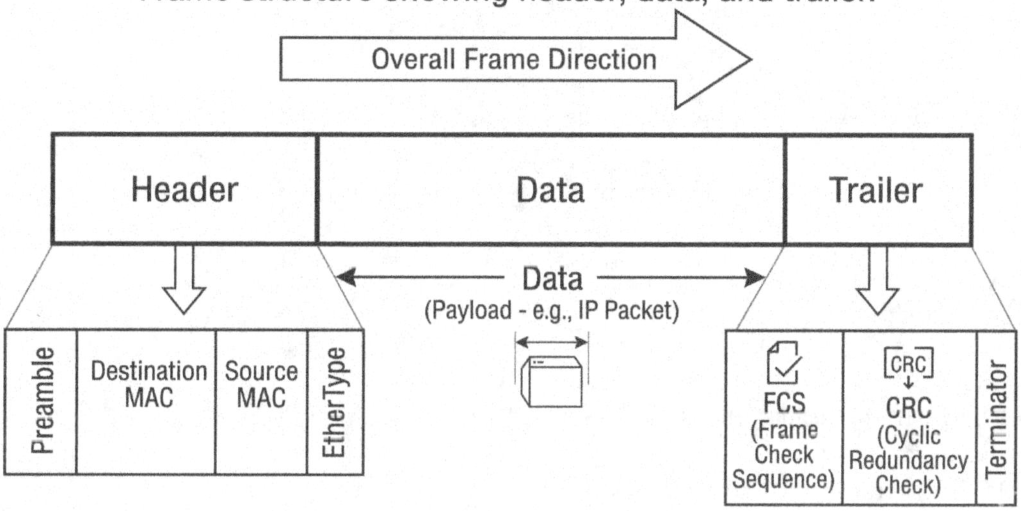

Physical Layer – Transmission of Bits

Finally, the frame reaches the Physical Layer.

At this layer, the frame is converted into a stream of binary bits (0s and 1s).

These bits are then transmitted through the communication medium, which may include:

Ethernet cables.

Optical fiber cables.

Wireless signals.

The physical layer sends these signals through the network toward the destination device.

Binary bits transmitted through communication medium.

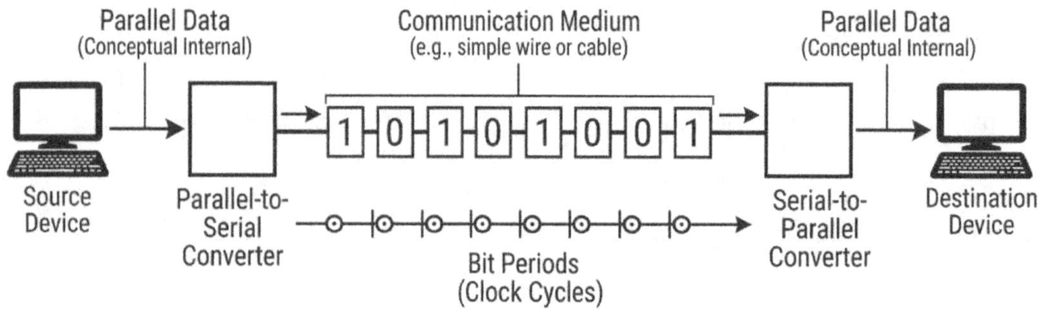

Decapsulation Process

When the data reaches the receiving device, the opposite process occurs. This process is called decapsulation.

During decapsulation, each layer removes the header that was added by the corresponding layer at the sender's side.

The process occurs in reverse order:

First, the physical layer receives the bits.
Then the data link layer removes the frame header and trailer.
The network layer processes the packet.
The transport layer reassembles the segments into the original data.
Finally, the application layer delivers the message to the user application.

Decapsulation process from Physical Layer to Application Layer

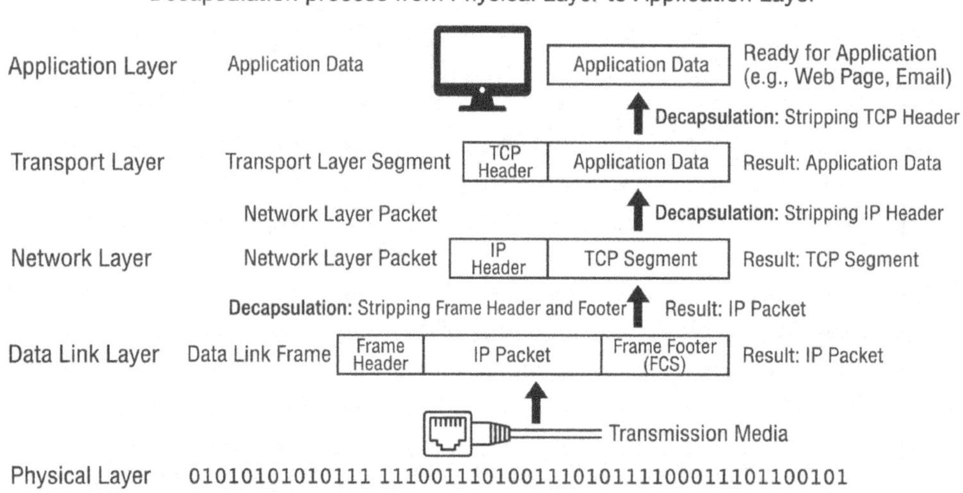

Data Units at Different Layers

During the encapsulation process, the data is referred to by different names at different layers of the OSI model.

At the Application Layer, Presentation Layer, and Session Layer, the information is simply called data.

When the information reaches the Transport Layer, it is divided into smaller units known as segments.

At the Network Layer, addressing information is added, and the segment becomes a packet.

At the Data Link Layer, the packet is enclosed inside a frame.

Finally, at the Physical Layer, the frame is converted into a stream of bits that travel through the communication medium.

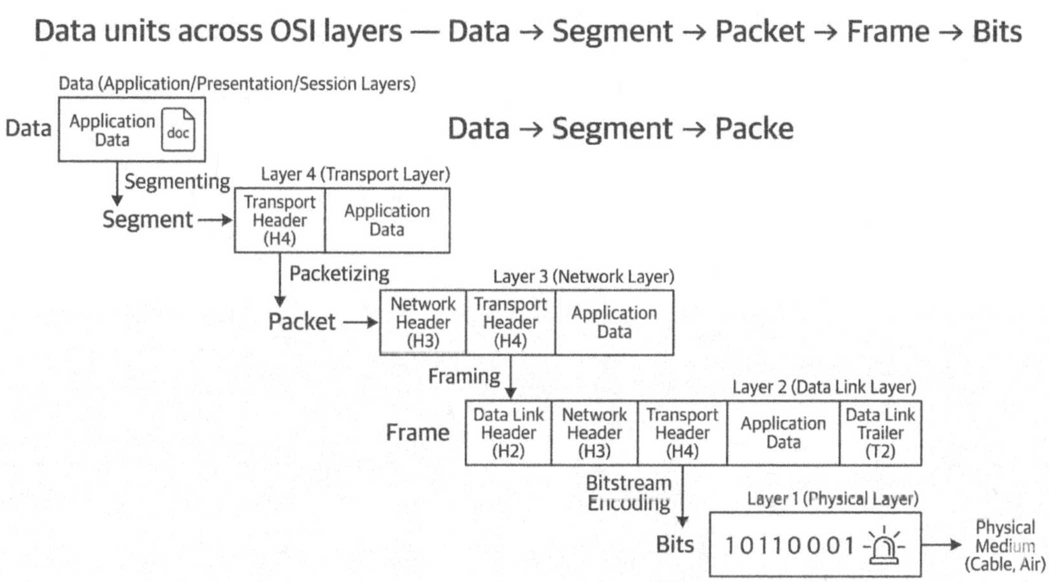

Importance of Data Encapsulation

Data encapsulation plays an important role in network communication.

First, it organizes communication in a structured manner so that complex network processes can be handled efficiently.

Second, the headers added during encapsulation contain addressing and control information that help data reach the correct destination.

Third, encapsulation allows different networking layers to perform their tasks independently without interfering with each other.

Finally, it improves reliability by enabling error detection, sequencing, and proper routing of data.

Summary

Data encapsulation is a fundamental process in computer networking in which data is wrapped with additional control information as it moves through the layers of the OSI model.

Each layer adds its own header or trailer that helps manage communication tasks such as addressing, routing, segmentation, and error detection.

At the receiver's side, the reverse process called decapsulation removes these headers and delivers the original data to the user.

Encapsulation ensures that data communication across networks is organized, reliable, and efficient.

CHAPTER FOUR

TCP/IP Model and Internet Architecture

Introduction to TCP/IP Model

In the previous chapter, we studied the OSI Reference Model, which explains network communication using seven layers. The OSI model is very useful for understanding networking concepts. However, in real-world networking and especially on the Internet, another model is widely used. This model is known as the TCP/IP Model.

The TCP/IP Model is the practical networking architecture used on the Internet. It was developed as part of the ARPANET project by the United States Department of Defense in the 1970s. The goal was to create a communication system that could allow different computer networks to communicate with each other reliably.

TCP/IP stands for Transmission Control Protocol / Internet Protocol.

It is not just a single protocol but a set of communication protocols that work together to enable data communication across networks.

Basic TCP/IP communication between two computers over the Internet.

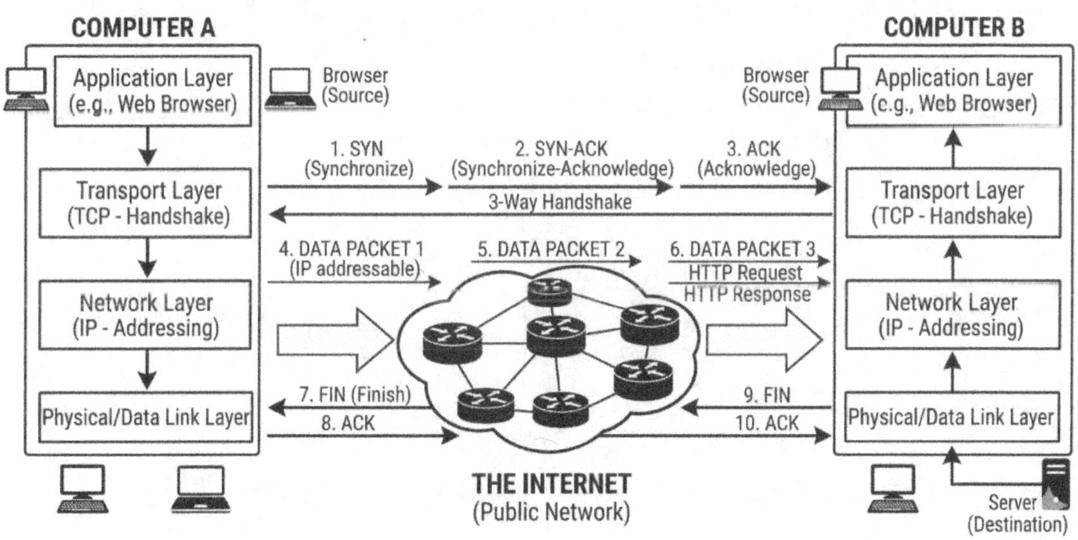

Today, the TCP/IP model forms the foundation of the global Internet, allowing millions of devices such as computers, smartphones, servers, and IoT devices to communicate with each other.

Why the TCP/IP Model Was Developed

Before the development of standardized network models, many organizations used their own networking technologies. These technologies were often incompatible with each other, making communication between different networks very difficult.

The TCP/IP model was developed to solve these problems. It introduced a standard framework that allowed multiple networks to interconnect and communicate effectively.

Some important objectives behind the development of TCP/IP include:

Enabling communication between different types of networks.

Providing reliable data transmission.

Supporting large-scale networks such as the Internet.

Ensuring fault tolerance and data reliability.

Because of these capabilities, TCP/IP became the standard communication architecture used worldwide.

Layers of the TCP/IP Model

Unlike the OSI model, which contains seven layers, the TCP/IP model consists of four layers. These layers perform similar functions but are organized differently.

The four layers of the TCP/IP model are:

Application Layer.

Transport Layer.

Internet Layer.

Network Access Layer.

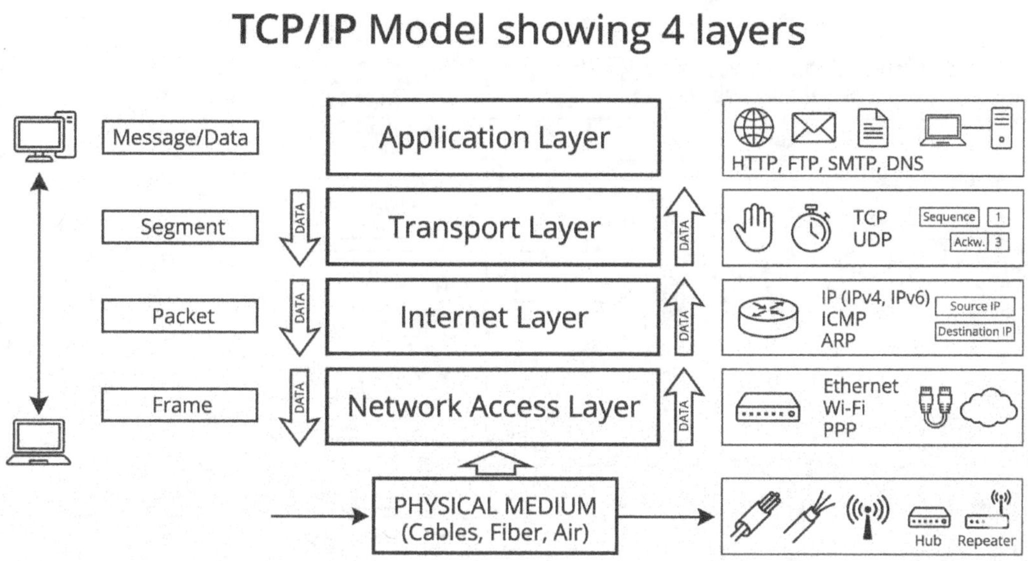

Each of these layers performs a specific role in the communication process.

1. Application Layer

The Application Layer is the top layer of the TCP/IP model. It provides network services directly to user applications.

This layer allows software programs to interact with the network and exchange information with other systems.

Examples of applications that use this layer include:

Web browsers.

Email applications.

File transfer programs.

Remote login systems.

Some common protocols operating at the application layer include:

HTTP (HyperText Transfer Protocol) for web browsing.

FTP (File Transfer Protocol) for file transfers.

SMTP (Simple Mail Transfer Protocol) for email transmission.

DNS (Domain Name System) for resolving domain names.

When a user accesses a website, the browser uses HTTP to send a request to the web server through the application layer.

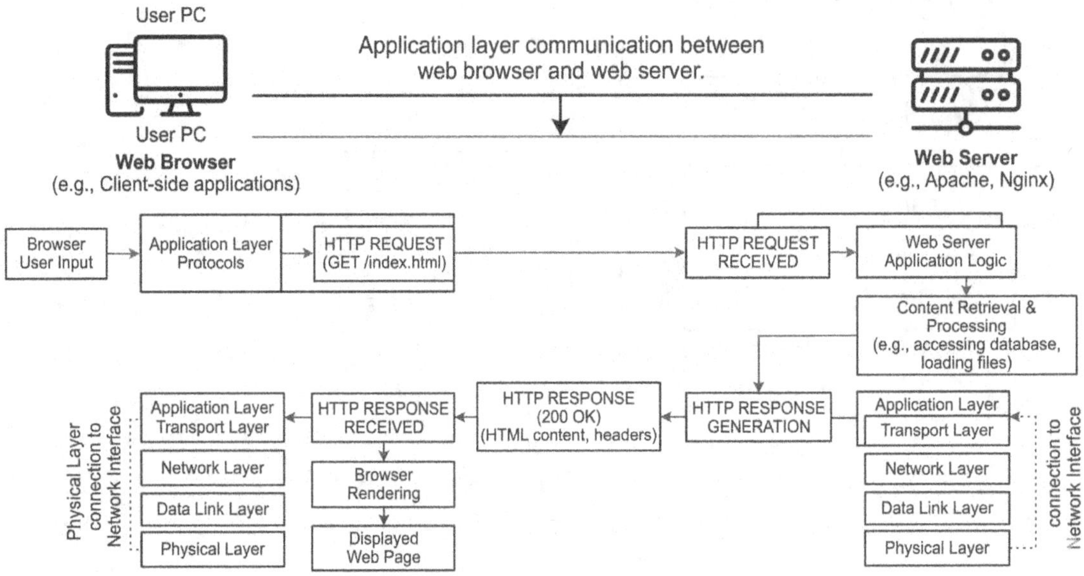

2. Transport Layer

The Transport Layer is responsible for providing reliable communication between the source and destination devices.

This layer ensures that data is delivered correctly, completely, and in the proper order.

The transport layer performs several important functions, including:

Segmenting large messages into smaller units.

Ensuring reliable delivery of data.

Controlling the flow of data between sender and receiver.

Detecting and correcting transmission errors.

Two important protocols operate at this layer:

TCP (Transmission Control Protocol)

TCP provides reliable communication. It ensures that data packets are delivered correctly and in the correct sequence.

TCP is commonly used in applications where reliability is very important, such as web browsing and file transfers.

UDP (User Datagram Protocol)

UDP provides faster communication but with less reliability. It does not guarantee packet delivery or order.

UDP is often used in applications where speed is more important than reliability, such as video streaming and online gaming.

TCP reliab le cor munication vs UDP fast communication.

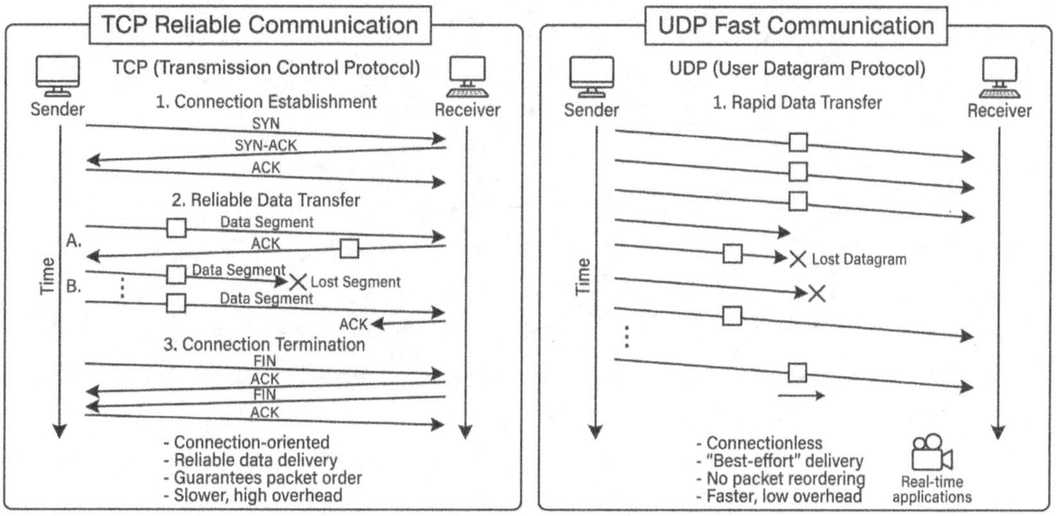

3. Internet Layer

The Internet Layer is responsible for addressing and routing data packets across networks.

Its main function is to ensure that data travels from the source device to the destination device through multiple networks.

The Internet Layer uses logical addressing, which is commonly known as the IP address.

Each device connected to the Internet has a unique IP address that identifies it in the network.

The main protocol operating at this layer is the Internet Protocol (IP).

Functions of the Internet Layer include:

Assigning IP addresses.

Routing data packets through networks.

Handling packet forwarding.

Managing packet fragmentation if required.

Devices such as routers operate mainly at this layer.

Router forwarding packets using IP addresses

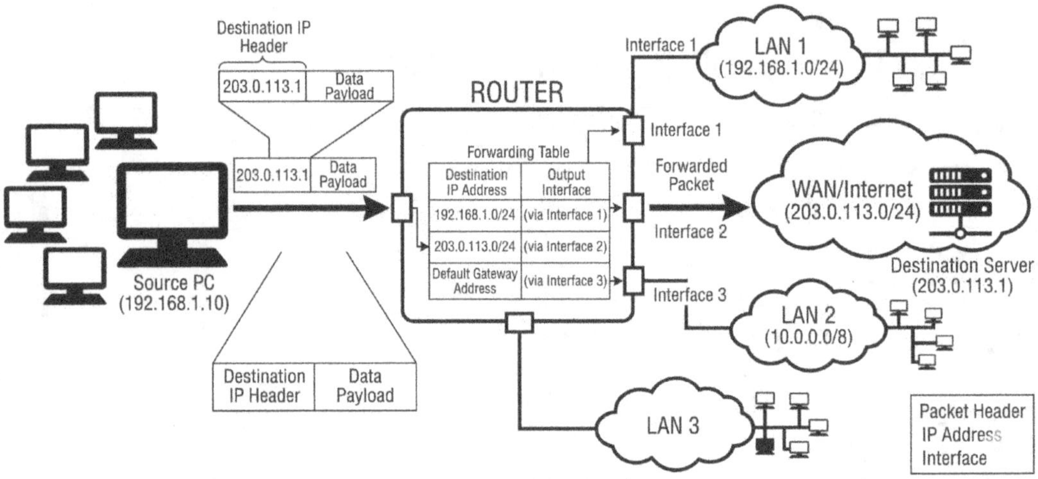

4. Network Access Layer

The Network Access Layer is the lowest layer of the TCP/IP model. It is responsible for the physical transmission of data over the network.

This layer combines the functions of the Physical Layer and Data Link Layer of the OSI model.

The network access layer deals with:

Physical transmission of data.

Framing of data packets.

Error detection.

Access to the communication medium.

Examples of technologies operating at this layer include:

Ethernet.

Wi-Fi.

Fiber optic communication.

Network devices such as switches, network interface cards, and cables operate at this layer.

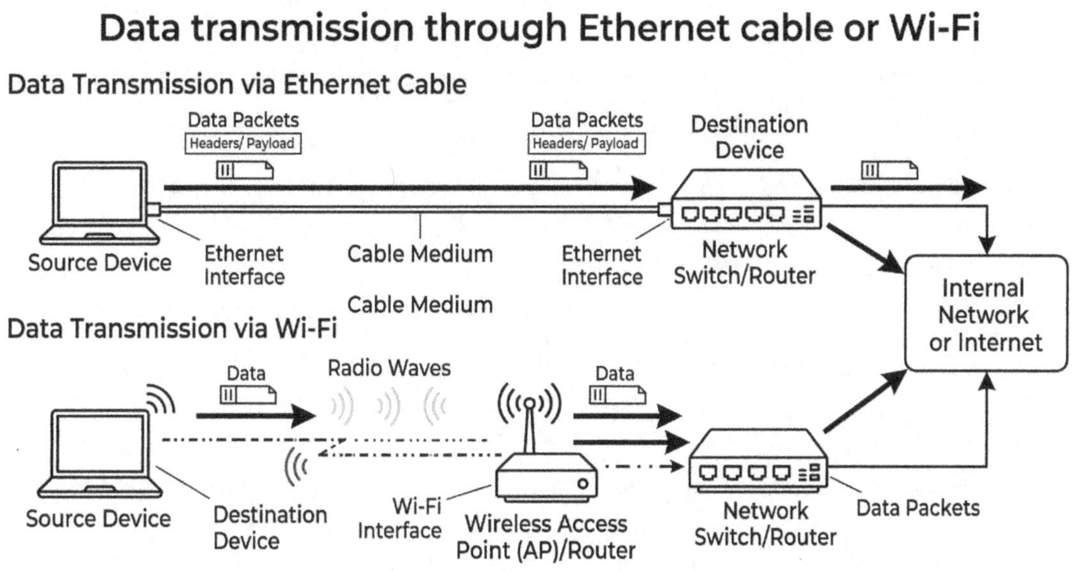

Data Flow in the TCP/IP Model

When a user sends data through a network using the TCP/IP model, the data moves through the layers of the model.

First, the application layer prepares the data.
Next, the transport layer divides the data into segments and ensures reliable delivery.
Then the Internet layer adds IP addressing information and converts the data into packets.
Finally, the network access layer transmits the packets as frames and bits through the communication medium.

At the receiving device, the reverse process takes place and the original data is reconstructed.

Data flow through TCP/IP layers.

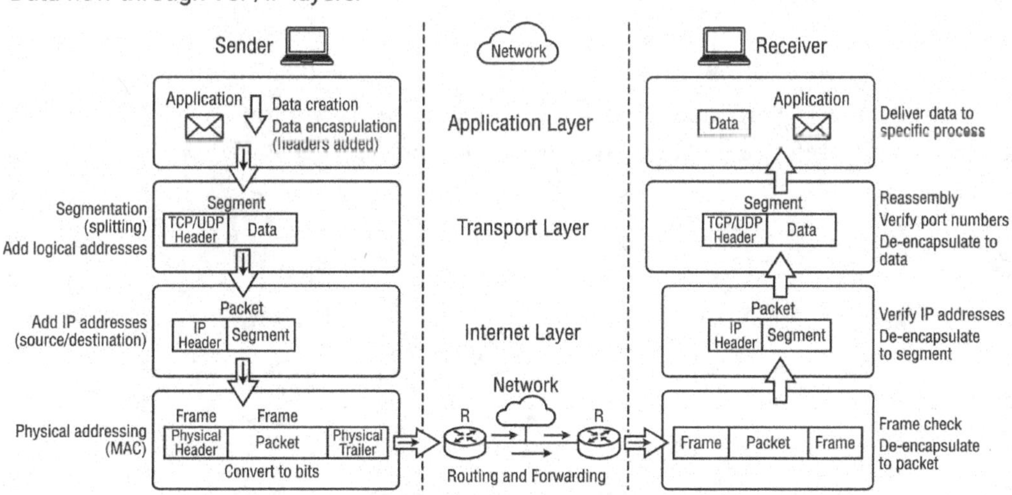

Data flow through TCP/IP layers.

Importance of the TCP/IP Model

The TCP/IP model plays a crucial role in modern networking because it forms the foundation of the Internet.

Almost every network communication today — including web browsing, email, video streaming, and cloud services — relies on the TCP/IP protocol suite.

Some key advantages of the TCP/IP model include:

It supports communication between different types of networks.

It is highly scalable and supports large networks such as the Internet.

It provides reliable and efficient data communication.

It is widely supported by networking devices and operating systems.

Because of these advantages, the TCP/IP model has become the standard architecture used in global networking.

Summary

The TCP/IP model is the practical networking architecture used on the Internet. It consists of four layers: Application Layer, Transport Layer, Internet Layer, and Network Access Layer.

Each layer performs specific tasks that help ensure reliable and efficient data communication between devices.

Protocols such as HTTP, FTP, TCP, UDP, and IP operate within this model to enable communication across the global Internet.

Understanding the TCP/IP model is essential for students studying computer networks because it explains how modern networking systems operate.

TCP/IP Layers in Detail

In the previous section, we introduced the TCP/IP Model and learned that it consists of four layers. These layers work together to ensure that data can travel from one device to another across the Internet.

The four layers of the TCP/IP model are:

Application Layer.

Transport Layer.

Internet Layer.

Network Access Layer.

Each layer performs specific communication tasks. Although these layers are fewer in number than the OSI model, they still cover all the functions required for network communication.

In this section, we will study each of these layers in detail and understand the responsibilities they perform.

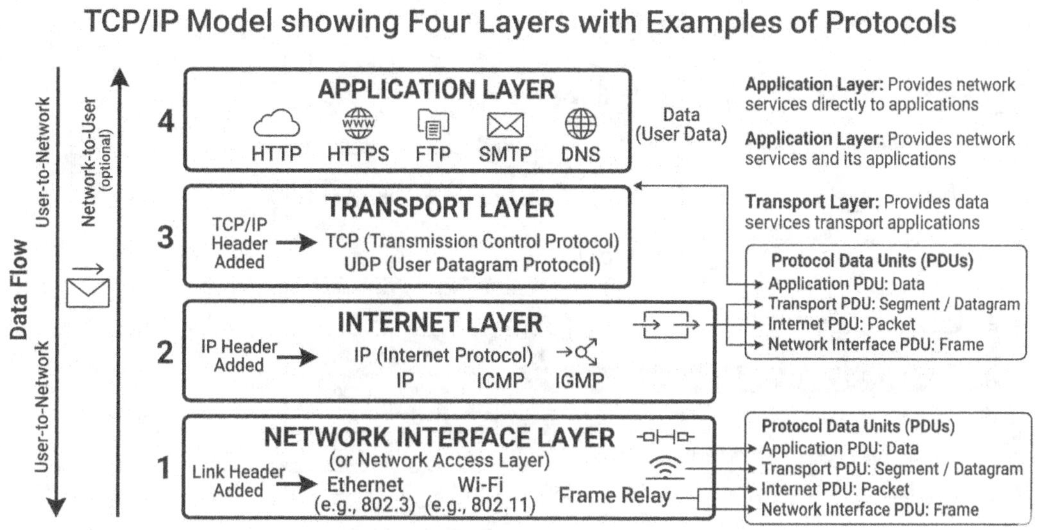

Application Layer

The Application Layer is the topmost layer of the TCP/IP model. This layer provides network services directly to the user applications.

Whenever a user interacts with the Internet through an application such as a web browser or email software, the communication starts at the application layer.

This layer allows software applications to send and receive data over the network.

Some of the important functions performed by the application layer include:

Providing network services to user applications.

Handling file transfers.

Managing email communication.

Supporting web browsing.

Resolving domain names.

Many commonly used Internet protocols operate at this layer.

Some important protocols include:

HTTP (HyperText Transfer Protocol)

HTTP is used for communication between web browsers and web servers. When you open a website, your browser sends an HTTP request to the web server, and the server responds by sending the webpage.

For example, when a user visits a website like www.example.com, the browser sends an HTTP request to the server hosting that website.

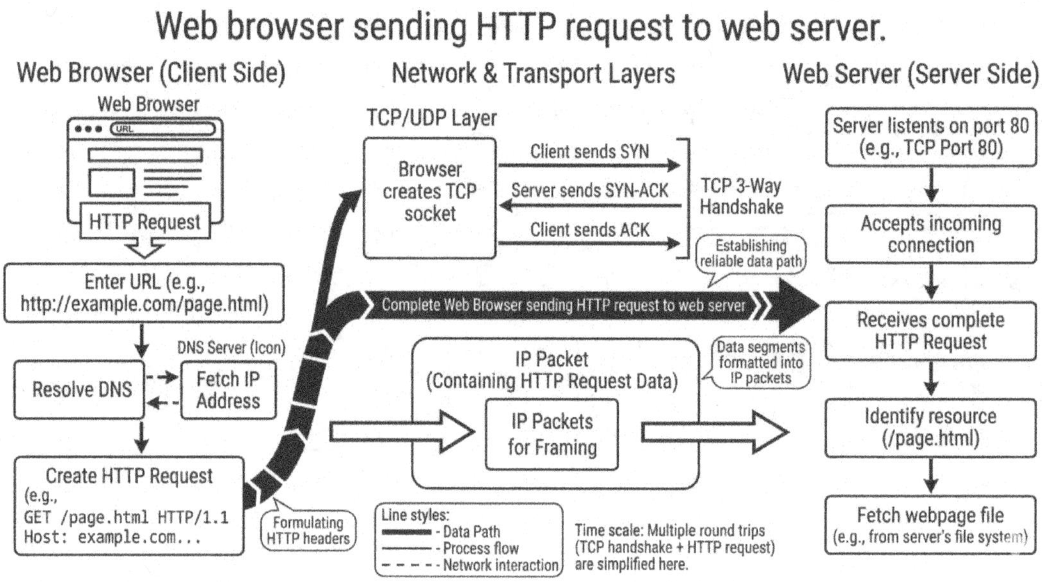

FTP (File Transfer Protocol)

FTP is used for transferring files between computers over a network.

For example, a web developer may use FTP to upload website files from their computer to a web server.
FTP allows users to:

Upload files to servers.

Download files from servers.

Manage remote file systems.

SMTP (Simple Mail Transfer Protocol)

SMTP is used for sending emails across networks.

When a user sends an email, the email client sends the message to the mail server using SMTP.

The mail server then forwards the message to the recipient's mail server.

DNS (Domain Name System)

DNS is responsible for translating domain names into IP addresses.

Humans prefer using easy-to-remember names such as www.google.com, but computers communicate using numerical IP addresses.

DNS converts the domain name into the corresponding IP address so that the device can locate the server on the Internet.

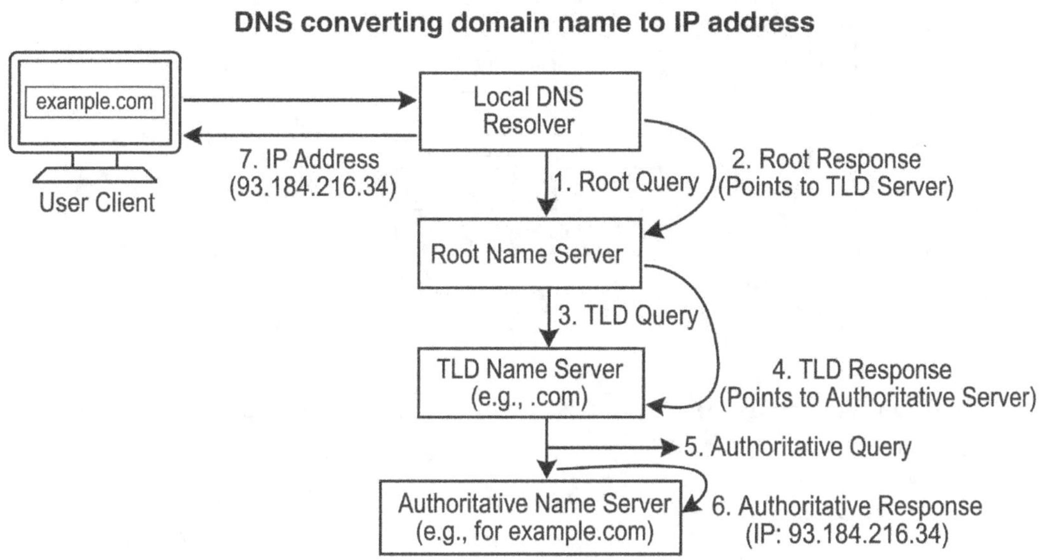

Transport Layer

The Transport Layer is responsible for ensuring reliable communication between the source and destination devices.

This layer manages end-to-end communication, meaning it ensures that data sent from one application reaches the correct application on the receiving device.

The transport layer performs several important tasks.

Segmentation

Large data messages are divided into smaller units called segments before being transmitted across the network.

Dividing the data into segments improves efficiency and allows data to travel through the network more easily.

At the receiving end, the segments are reassembled to reconstruct the original message.

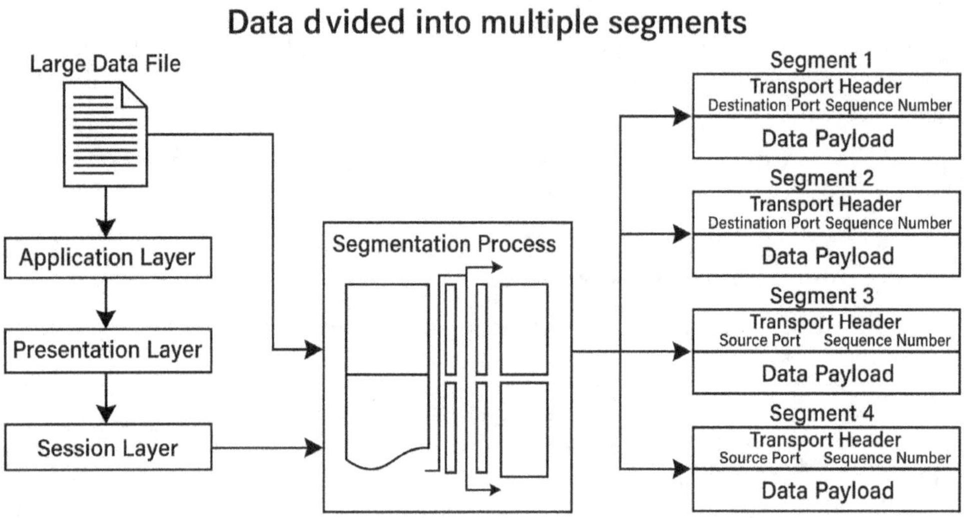

Error Control

The transport layer ensures that data is delivered correctly. If a segment is lost or corrupted during transmission, the transport layer can request retransmission.

This helps ensure reliable communication.

Flow Control

Flow control prevents the sender from transmitting data faster than the receiver can process it.

This ensures that the receiving system is not overloaded.

Important Transport Layer Protocols.

Two major protocols operate at the transport layer.

TCP (Transmission Control Protocol)

TCP provides reliable communication. It ensures that all segments are delivered successfully and in the correct order.

TCP is commonly used in applications such as:

Web browsing.

Email communication.

File transfers.

UDP (User Datagram Protocol)

UDP provides faster communication but does not guarantee reliability.

It does not check whether packets are delivered or not.

UDP is commonly used in applications such as:

Video streaming.

Online gaming.

Voice communication.

Comparison between TCP and UDP communication

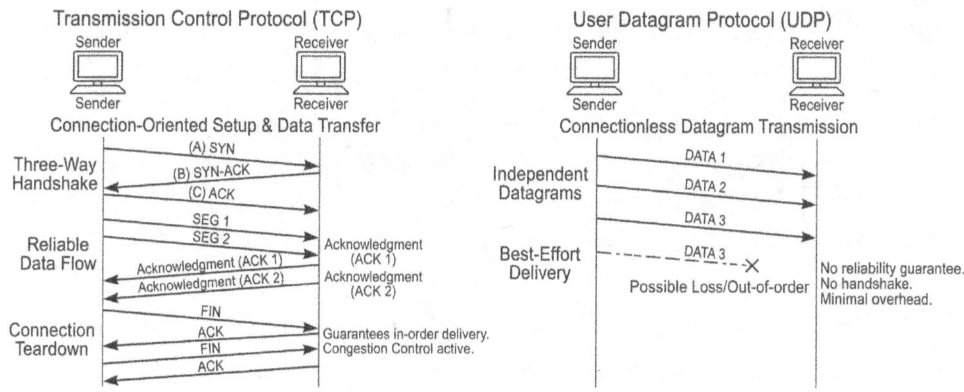

Comparison of Key Features:

Property	TCP	UDP
Connection Type	Connection-oriented	Connectionless
Reliability	Reliable (Retransmissions)	Unreliable (No retransmissions)
Sequence	Guaranteed In-order	Out-of-order possible
Handshake	3-way handshake	None
Speed	Medium (overhead slower)	Fast
Overhead	High	Low
Usage	Web browsing, file transfer, email	Streaming, voice calls, DNS

Internet Layer

The Internet Layer is responsible for addressing and routing data packets through the network.

Its main function is to ensure that packets travel from the source network to the destination network.

The Internet Layer performs several important tasks.

Logical Addressing

Every device connected to the Internet has a unique IP address.

This address helps identify the source and destination devices.

For example, an IPv4 address may look like:

192.168.1.1
These addresses allow routers to determine where the packet should be sent.

Routing

When data travels across multiple networks, routers determine the best path for the packet to reach the destination.

This process is called routing.

Routers analyze the destination IP address and forward the packet accordingly.

Router directing packets across multiple networks.

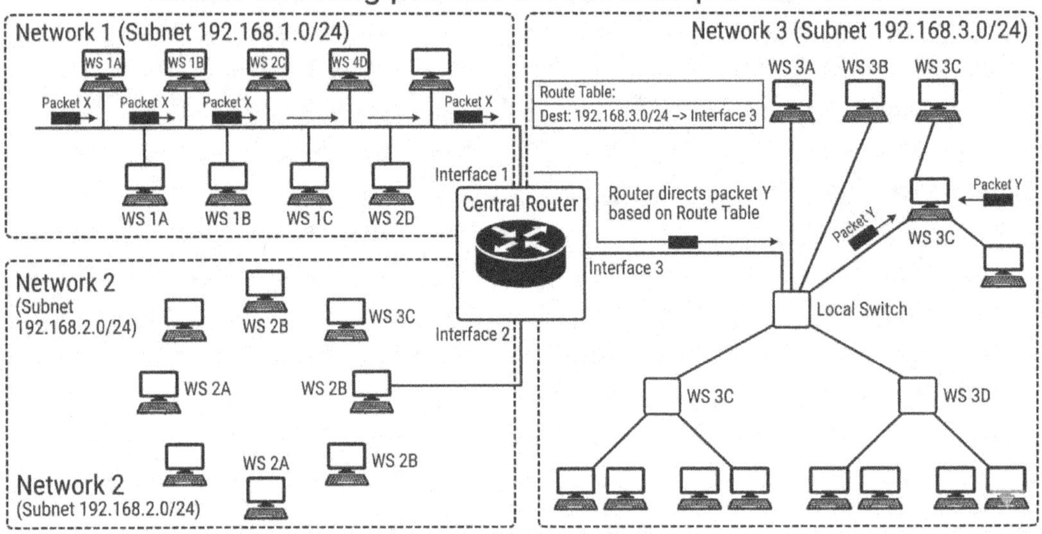

Important Protocols at Internet Layer

Several protocols operate at this layer.

Some important ones include:

IP (Internet Protocol) – responsible for addressing and packet delivery.

ICMP (Internet Control Message Protocol) – used for error reporting and diagnostics.

ARP (Address Resolution Protocol) – used to convert IP addresses into MAC addresses.

Network Access Layer

The Network Access Layer is the lowest layer of the TCP/IP model. It handles the physical transmission of data through the communication medium.

This layer combines the functions of the Physical Layer and Data Link Layer of the OSI model.

The responsibilities of this layer include:

Framing data packets.

Error detection.

Physical addressing using MAC addresses.

Transmitting bits through cables or wireless signals.

Examples of technologies used at this layer include:

Ethernet networks.

Wi-Fi networks.

Fiber optic communication systems.

Devices that operate at this layer include:

Network Interface Cards (NIC).

Switches.

Network cables.

Ethernet communication between two devices.

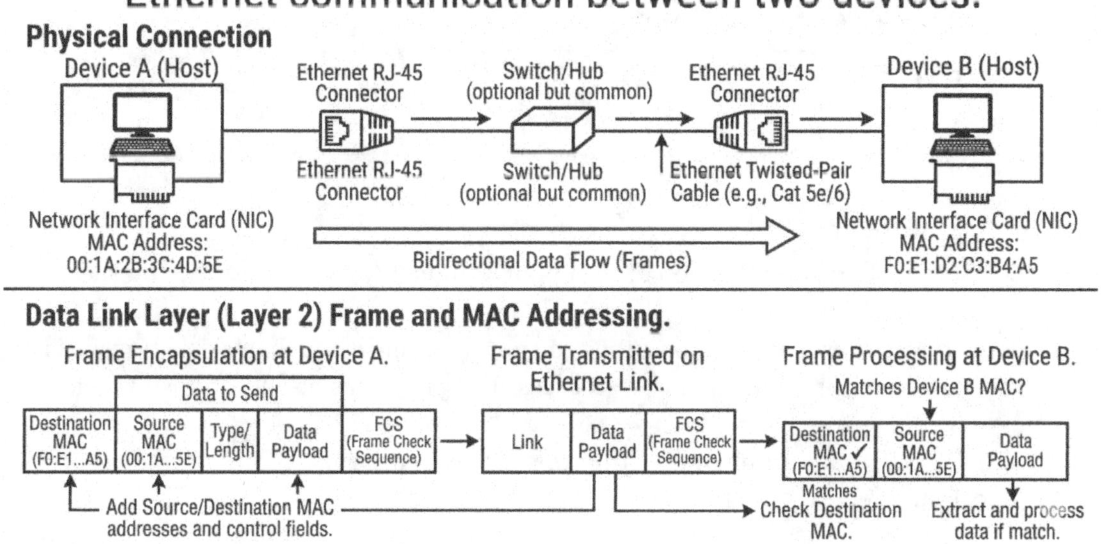

How TCP/IP Layers Work Together

The layers of the TCP/IP model work together during communication.

When a user sends data:

The Application Layer prepares the data.

The Transport Layer divides the data into segments.

The Internet Layer adds IP addressing information.

The Network Access Layer transmits the data through the communication medium.

At the receiving device, the process happens in the reverse order until the original message is delivered to the application.

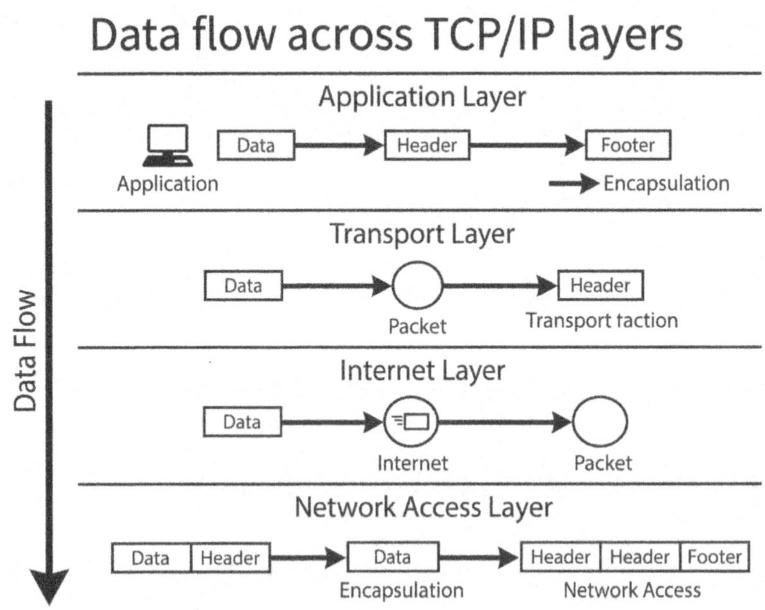

Summary

The TCP/IP model consists of four layers that work together to support communication across the Internet.

The application layer provides services to user applications, the transport layer ensures reliable data transmission, the Internet layer handles addressing and routing, and the network access layer manages physical transmission.

Protocols such as HTTP, FTP, TCP, UDP, and IP operate within this model and enable communication between millions of devices across the global Internet.

Understanding these layers is essential for students because they form the foundation of modern networking technologies.

Comparison between OSI Model and TCP/IP Model

In the previous sections, we studied two important networking models: the OSI Reference Model and the TCP/IP Model. Both models are used to describe how communication takes place between devices in a computer network.

Although both models explain the process of network communication, they are different in their structure, development, and practical usage.

The OSI model was developed by the International Organization for Standardization (ISO) as a theoretical framework for understanding network communication. On the other hand, the TCP/IP model was developed earlier by the United States Department of Defense as a practical communication model used for building large networks such as the Internet.

Today, the TCP/IP model is widely used in real-world networking systems, while the OSI model is mainly used for learning and understanding networking concepts.

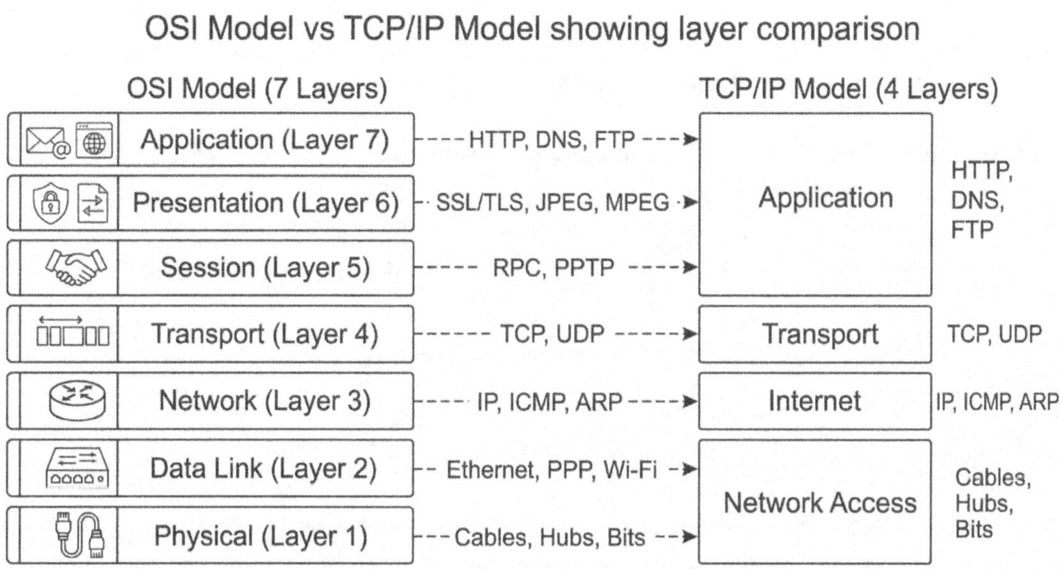

Number of Layers

One of the main differences between the two models is the number of layers.

The OSI model consists of seven layers:

Application Layer.

Presentation Layer.

Session Layer.

Transport Layer.

Network Layer.

Data Link Layer.

Physical Layer.

Each of these layers performs specific tasks during data communication.

In contrast, the TCP/IP model consists of four layers:

Application Layer.

Transport Layer.

Internet Layer.

Network Access Layer.

The TCP/IP model combines several functions of the OSI layers into fewer layers.

For example, the Application Layer of the TCP/IP model includes the functions of the Application, Presentation, and Session layers of the OSI model.

Similarly, the Network Access Layer of TCP/IP includes the functions of both the Data Link and Physical layers of the OSI model.

Development and Purpose

Another important difference lies in the way the models were developed.

The OSI model was developed as a theoretical model to help standardize networking concepts and guide the design of communication systems. It was created mainly for educational and reference purposes.

The TCP/IP model, however, was developed as a practical communication model. It was designed to support communication across interconnected networks, especially in the early Internet.

Because TCP/IP was used in real networks from the beginning, it became widely adopted and eventually formed the foundation of modern Internet communication.

Layer Design Approach

The OSI model follows a strict layered structure. Each layer performs specific functions, and communication occurs only between adjacent layers.

This strict separation makes the OSI model very clear and easy to understand.

The TCP/IP model, on the other hand, follows a more flexible approach. Its layers are not as strictly separated as in the OSI model. Some functions may overlap between layers.

Because of this flexibility, the TCP/IP model is easier to implement in real networking environments.

Protocol Implementation

The OSI model was designed before specific protocols were defined. It was developed first as a framework, and protocols were later designed based on it.

In contrast, the TCP/IP model was built around existing communication protocols, especially the Transmission Control Protocol (TCP) and the Internet Protocol (IP).

These protocols were already being used in network communication when the TCP/IP model was formally defined.

As a result, the TCP/IP model is closely connected to actual Internet technologies.

Usage in Modern Networking

Today, the TCP/IP model is used in almost every networking system around the world. The Internet, cloud services, mobile networks, and many enterprise networks operate using TCP/IP protocols.

Although the OSI model is not directly implemented in most real networks, it remains extremely important for understanding how communication works in a layered structure.

Many networking professionals use the OSI model to analyze and troubleshoot network problems, because it clearly separates communication tasks into layers.

Example of Layer Mapping

To understand the relationship between the two models, it is useful to see how their layers correspond to each other.

The Application Layer of TCP/IP performs the tasks of the Application, Presentation, and Session layers of the OSI model.

The Transport Layer of TCP/IP corresponds to the Transport Layer of the OSI model.

The Internet Layer of TCP/IP performs the same role as the Network Layer of the OSI model, handling addressing and routing.

Finally, the Network Access Layer of TCP/IP combines the responsibilities of the Data Link and Physical layers of the OSI model.

Mapping of OSI layers to TCP/IP layers

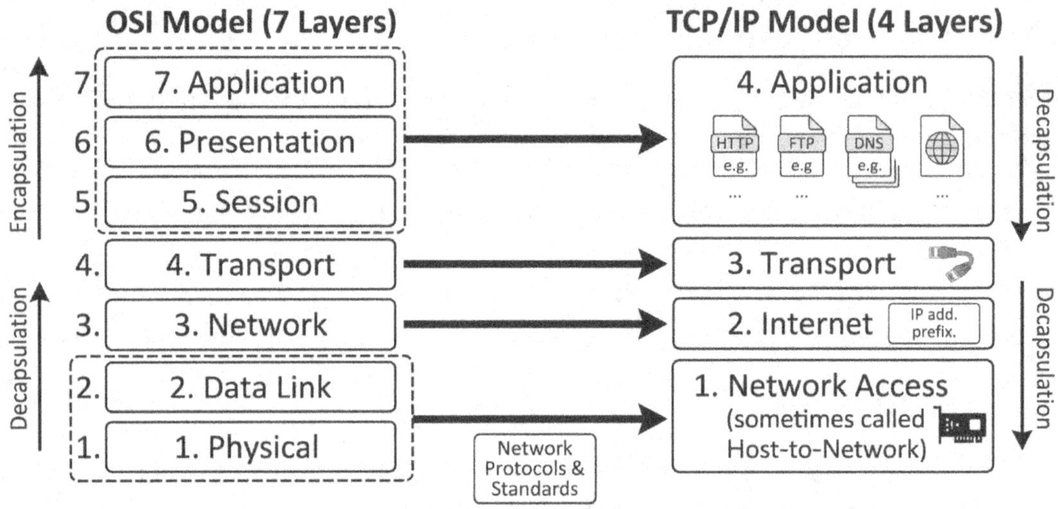

Advantages of the OSI Model

The OSI model offers several advantages.

First, it provides a very clear and structured representation of network communication.

Second, it divides complex networking tasks into smaller layers, making the system easier to understand.

Third, it is widely used as a teaching tool for networking students.

Because of these advantages, the OSI model remains an important conceptual framework.

Advantages of the TCP/IP Model

The TCP/IP model also provides several important advantages.

It is a practical model that is used in real networks around the world.

It supports communication between different types of networks, allowing the Internet to connect millions of devices.

The TCP/IP protocol suite is also highly scalable and reliable, making it suitable for large networks.

Importance of Understanding Both Models

Even though the TCP/IP model is used in real networking systems, understanding the OSI model is still very important for networking students.

The OSI model provides a detailed explanation of how communication tasks are organized, while the TCP/IP model explains how these tasks are implemented in real networks.

Together, these two models help students understand both the theoretical and practical aspects of networking.

Summary

Both the OSI model and the TCP/IP model describe how communication occurs in computer networks, but they differ in their structure and purpose.

The OSI model consists of seven layers and is mainly used as a conceptual framework for understanding networking. The TCP/IP model consists of four layers and forms the foundation of real-world Internet communication.

Understanding the relationship between these two models helps students gain a deeper understanding of how modern networking systems operate.

Internet Communication Overview

In the previous sections, we studied the TCP/IP model and its layers, as well as the comparison between the OSI model and the TCP/IP model. Now it is important to understand how communication actually takes place on the Internet.

The Internet is a massive global network that connects millions of smaller networks together. These networks may belong to organizations, universities, companies, government institutions, or individual users. All these networks communicate using the TCP/IP protocol suite.

When a user sends information over the Internet, the data does not travel directly from the sender's computer to the receiver's computer in a single step. Instead, the data passes through multiple devices and networks before reaching its final destination.

This entire process is known as Internet communication.

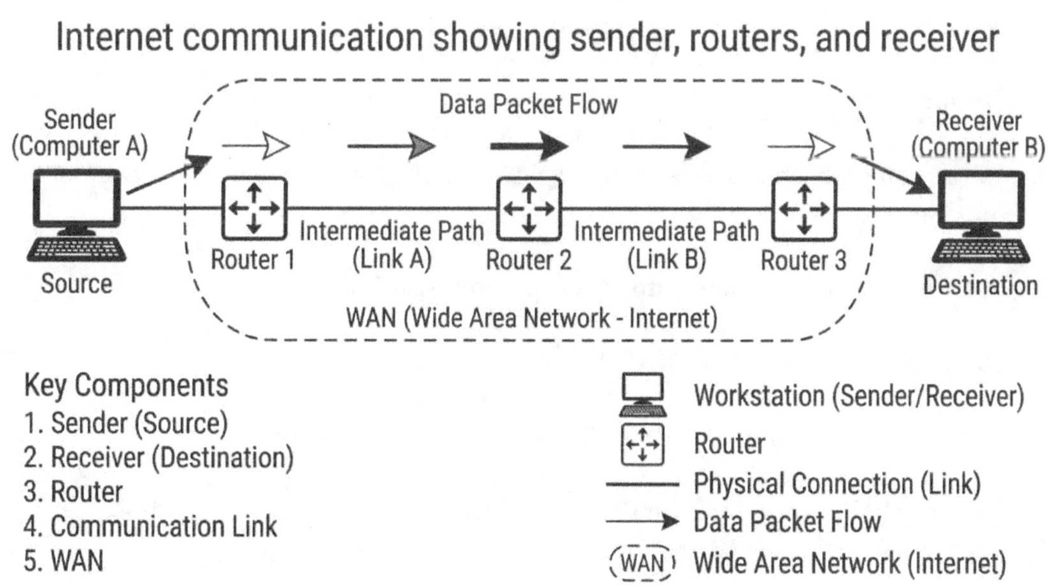

Basic Concept of Internet Communication

Internet communication works on the principle of packet switching. This means that the data being transmitted is divided into smaller units called packets.

Each packet contains not only the actual data but also important control information such as:

Source address.
Destination address.
Sequence number.
Error detection information.

These packets travel independently through different routes in the network until they reach the destination device.

Once all packets arrive at the destination, they are reassembled to reconstruct the original message.

Steps in Internet Communication

To understand the process more clearly, let us look at the step-by-step process that occurs when a user accesses a website on the Internet.

Step 1: User Sends a Request

The communication process begins when a user performs an action such as opening a website in a web browser.

For example, a user types the address: www.example.com into the browser.

At this stage, the browser prepares a request to retrieve the webpage from the web server.

This request is created using the HTTP protocol at the application layer.

Step 2: Domain Name Resolution

Humans prefer using easy-to-remember domain names such as www.example.com, but computers communicate using IP addresses.

Therefore, the system must convert the domain name into its corresponding IP address.

This process is handled by the Domain Name System (DNS).

The DNS server translates the domain name into the correct IP address of the web server.

For example, the domain name may be converted into an IP address such as:

192.168.10.15

DNS converting domain name into IP address

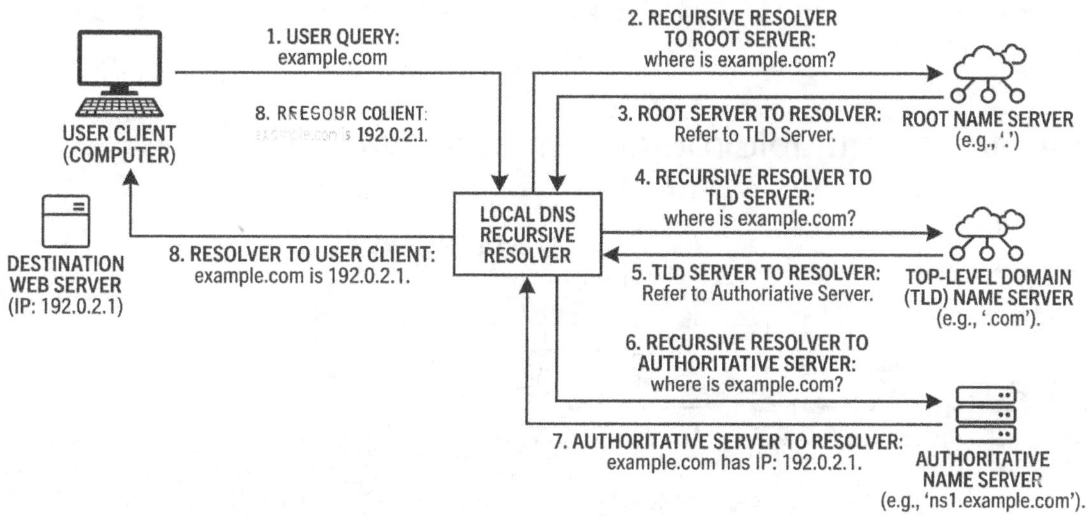

Step 3: Data Segmentation

Once the request is ready, the Transport Layer divides the data into smaller segments.

Dividing data into smaller units helps ensure efficient transmission across the network.

Each segment contains additional information such as port numbers and sequence numbers, which help the receiving system reconstruct the original data.

Step 4: Packet Creation and Addressing

Next, the segments move to the Internet Layer, where each segment is converted into a packet.

At this stage, the Internet Protocol (IP) adds the following information:

Source IP address.
Destination IP address.

This addressing information allows networking devices such as routers to determine where the packet should be sent.

Step 5: Transmission through Network Devices

The packets are then transmitted through the network using the Network Access Layer.

During transmission, the packets travel through multiple networking devices such as:

Routers.
Switches.
Network gateways.

Routers analyze the destination IP address of each packet and determine the best path for the packet to travel.

Because the Internet consists of many interconnected networks, packets may travel through several routers before reaching their destination.

Pa cket traveling throιgh multiple routers across networks.

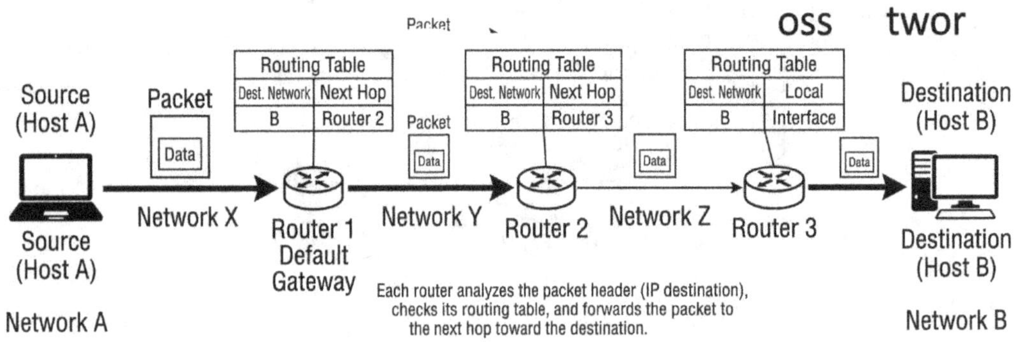

Step 6: Arrival at the Destination

When the packets reach the destination network, they are delivered to the receiving device.

At this stage, the reverse process begins.

The packets are passed upward through the TCP/IP layers.

The transport layer reassembles the segments into the original message, ensuring that all segments are received and arranged in the correct order.

Step 7: Data Delivered to the Application

Finally, the reconstructed data reaches the Application Layer, where it is delivered to the user application.

For example, the web browser receives the webpage data from the server and displays it to the user.

This entire process usually takes only a fraction of a second, even though the data may have traveled through multiple networks and routers.

Role of Routers in Internet Communication

Routers play a very important role in Internet communication.

A router is a networking device that connects different networks together and forwards data packets between them.

Each router maintains a routing table that helps determine the best path for sending packets toward their destination.

When a router receives a packet, it examines the destination IP address and decides where the packet should be forwarded next.

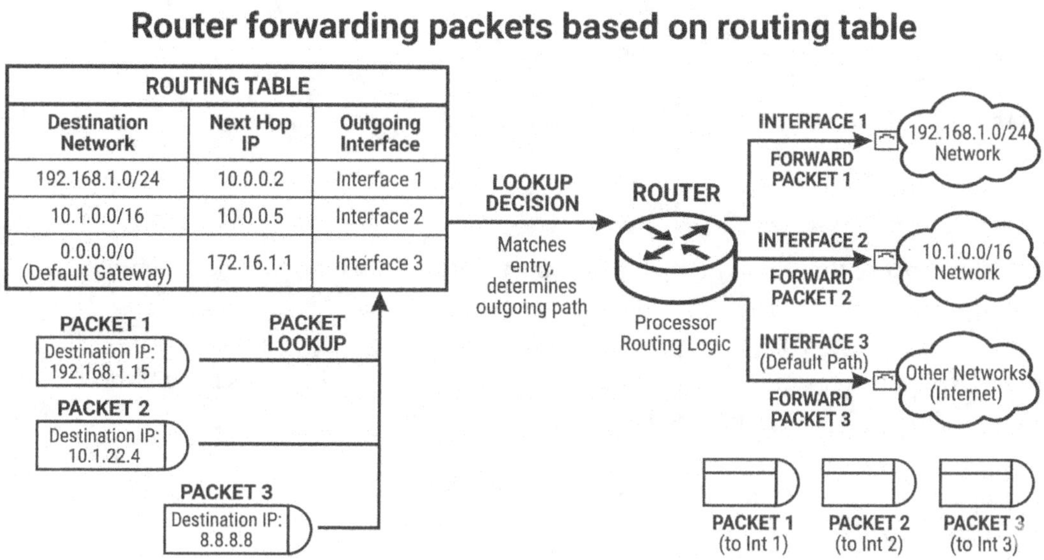

Because packets may travel through different routes, they may not always arrive in the same order in which they were sent.

The transport layer ensures that these packets are properly reassembled.

Packet Switching in the Internet

The Internet uses a communication technique known as packet switching.

In packet switching, large messages are divided into smaller packets before transmission. These packets travel independently through the network and may follow different paths.

Packet switching offers several advantages:

Efficient use of network resources.
Ability to handle large amounts of traffic.
Improved reliability because packets can be rerouted if a network path fails.

This technique allows the Internet to support millions of simultaneous users.

Importance of Internet Communication

Internet communication is essential for many modern technologies and services.

Today, almost every digital service depends on Internet communication, including:

Web browsing.
Email communication.
Video conferencing.
Online gaming.
Cloud computing.
Social media platforms.

All these services rely on the TCP/IP protocol suite to transmit data efficiently across networks.

Summary

Internet communication is the process through which data is transmitted across interconnected networks using the TCP/IP protocol suite.

The process begins when a user sends a request, followed by domain name resolution, segmentation of data, packet creation, and transmission through routers and networks.

Finally, the packets reach the destination device, where they are reassembled and delivered to the application.

This structured communication process allows the Internet to connect millions of devices around the world and support a wide range of digital services.

CHAPTER FIVE

Signals and Data Representation

Analog Signals

In computer networks, data must travel from one device to another through some type of communication medium such as cables, optical fiber, or wireless signals. However, computers cannot send raw data directly through these media. Instead, the data must first be converted into signals that can travel through the transmission medium.

A signal is a form of energy that carries information from one device to another. Signals can travel through various media such as electrical wires, fiber optic cables, or wireless airwaves.

In communication systems, signals are mainly classified into two types:

Analog Signals.
Digital Signals.

In this section, we will focus on analog signals, which are one of the fundamental concepts in data communication.

What is an Analog Signal?

An analog signal is a continuous signal that changes smoothly over time. The value of an analog signal can take any value within a given range.

Unlike digital signals that use only two levels (0 and 1), analog signals vary continuously and can represent many different values.

For example, the sound of a human voice is an analog signal. When we speak, the sound waves travel through the air as continuous vibrations. These vibrations can vary in strength and frequency depending on the tone and loudness of the voice.

Similarly, analog signals are used in many communication systems such as:

Radio broadcasting.
Television broadcasting.
Telephone communication.
Audio recording systems.

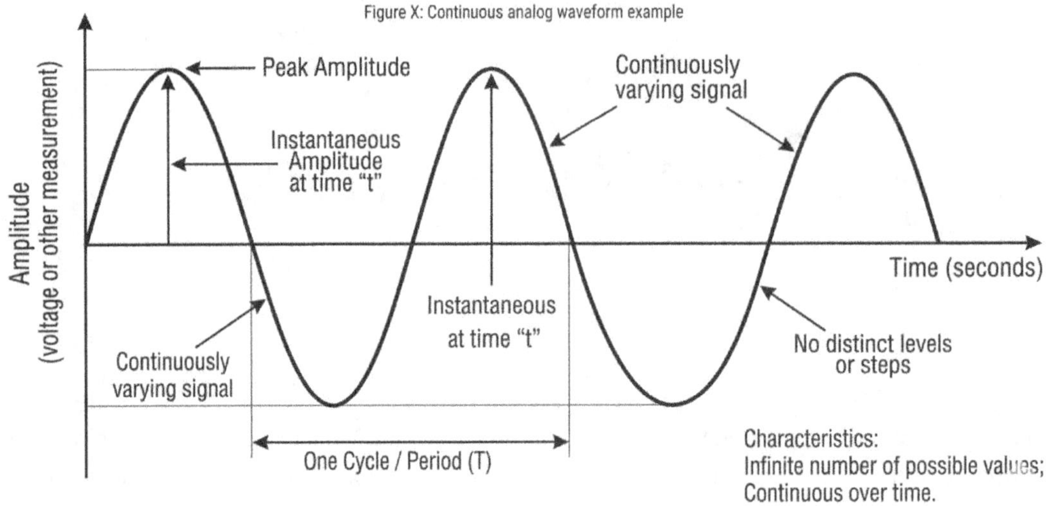

Continuous analog waveform.

Figure X: Continuous analog waveform example

Characteristics of Analog Signals

Analog signals are described using several important characteristics. These characteristics help us understand how the signal behaves and how it carries information.

The most important characteristics of analog signals include:

Amplitude.
Frequency.
Phase.

Let us understand each of these in detail.

Amplitude

Amplitude refers to the strength or height of the signal wave.

It represents the maximum value reached by the signal above or below the central reference line. In many communication systems, amplitude determines the power or intensity of the signal.

For example, when we increase the volume of a sound, the amplitude of the sound wave increases.

In electrical signals, amplitude is usually measured in volts.

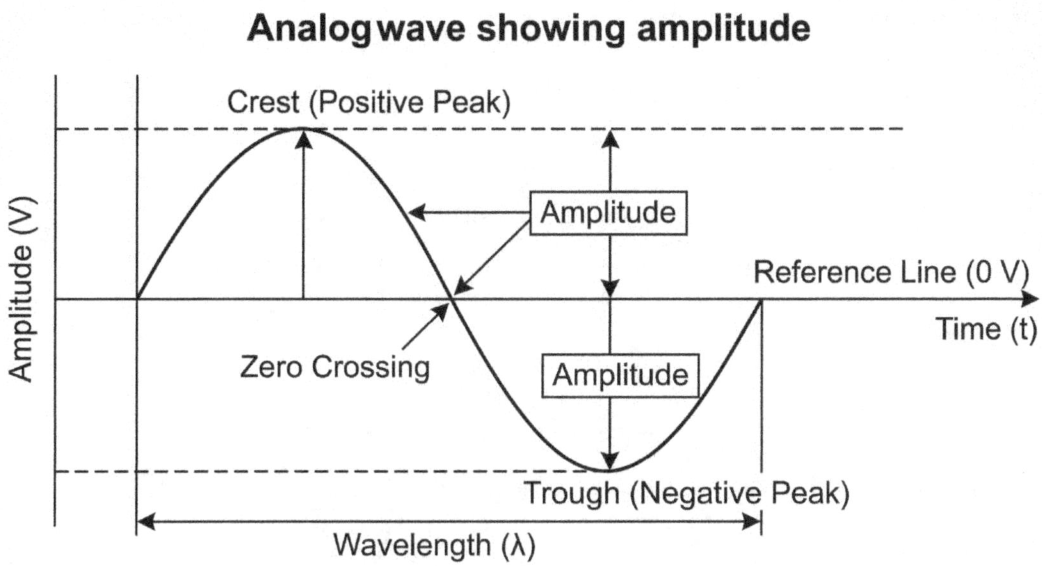

A higher amplitude generally indicates a stronger signal, while a lower amplitude indicates a weaker signal.

Frequency

Frequency refers to the number of cycles that a signal completes in one second.

It indicates how fast the signal oscillates or repeats itself.

Frequency is measured in Hertz (Hz).

For example:

If a signal completes one cycle per second, its frequency is 1 Hz.

If it completes one thousand cycles per second, its frequency is 1000 Hz or 1 kHz.

In communication systems, frequency is very important because different communication channels operate at different frequency ranges.

For example:

Radio broadcasting uses specific frequency bands.

Wi-Fi communication also uses particular frequency ranges.

Analog wave showing frequency cycles.

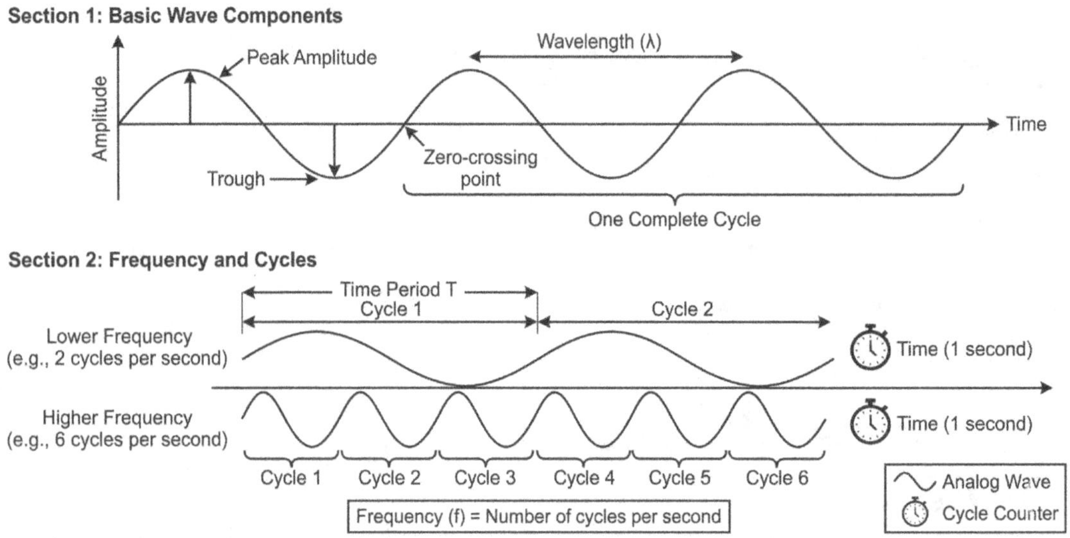

Phase

Phase refers to the position of the waveform relative to time.

It indicates how the signal wave is shifted compared to another signal.

Phase differences can occur when two signals start at different points in time.

For example, two signals may have the same frequency and amplitude but may start at slightly different points along the time axis.

Phase Difference

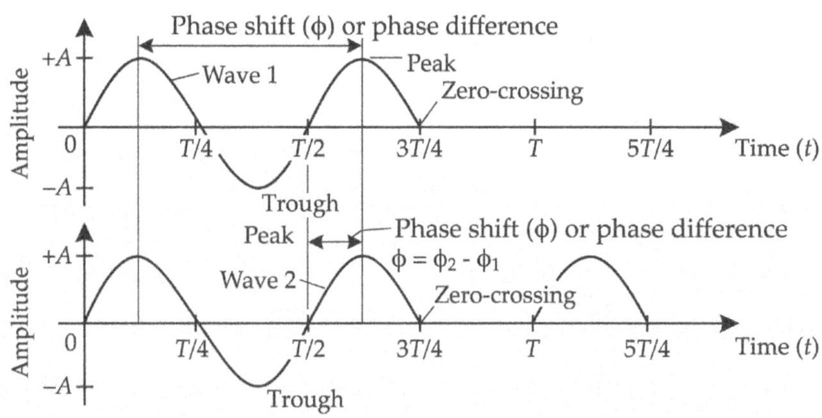

Two sinusoidal waves with identical frequency and amplitude, demonstrating a phase difference.

Phase is an important factor in many communication techniques such as signal synchronization and modulation.

Analog Signals in Real Life

Analog signals are commonly used in everyday technologies.

For example, traditional telephone systems use analog signals to transmit voice communication. When a person speaks into a telephone, the microphone converts the sound waves into electrical analog signals. These signals travel through the telephone network and are converted back into sound at the receiver's end.

Another example is radio broadcasting. In radio systems, audio signals are converted into analog electromagnetic waves that travel through the air and are received by radio receivers.

Similarly, television broadcasting originally used analog signals to transmit audio and video information.

Advantages of Analog Signals

Analog signals offer several advantages in communication systems.

First, they can represent continuous real-world phenomena such as sound, temperature, and light.

Second, analog systems are relatively simple in terms of signal generation and transmission.

Third, analog signals can represent very fine variations in information because they are continuous.

Because of these characteristics, analog signals are widely used in audio systems and broadcasting technologies.

Limitations of Analog Signals

Despite their advantages, analog signals also have certain limitations.

One major disadvantage is that analog signals are more sensitive to noise and interference. During transmission, external disturbances such as electromagnetic interference may distort the signal.

Once distortion occurs, it is difficult to recover the original signal accurately.

Another limitation is that analog signals are not easily processed or stored by modern digital systems. Because computers work with digital data, analog signals must often be converted into digital form before processing.

Due to these limitations, many modern communication systems use digital signals instead of analog signals.

Analog vs Real World Information

Many real-world signals are naturally analog in nature.

Examples include:

Human speech.
Music.
Temperature readings.
Light intensity.

Pressure changes.

Communication systems often convert these real-world analog signals into electrical signals so that they can be transmitted through networks.

In many modern technologies, analog signals are later converted into digital signals so that computers can process them more efficiently.

Summary

An analog signal is a continuous signal that varies smoothly over time and can represent a wide range of values.

Analog signals are characterized by three main properties: amplitude, frequency, and phase. These characteristics determine how the signal behaves and how it carries information.

Analog signals are widely used in systems such as radio broadcasting, telephone communication, and audio transmission. However, they are more sensitive to noise and interference compared to digital signals.

Understanding analog signals is an important step in learning how information is transmitted through communication systems.

Digital Signals

In the previous section, we studied analog signals, which are continuous signals that vary smoothly over time. However, modern computer systems do not work directly with continuous signals. Computers process and store information in the form of binary digits, which are 0 and 1.

To transmit this type of information through communication systems, digital signals are used.

A digital signal is a signal that represents information using discrete values, typically two levels: 0 and 1.

These two levels correspond to the binary system used by computers.

Unlike analog signals, which vary continuously, digital signals change in distinct steps.

Digital signal waveform showing binary levels

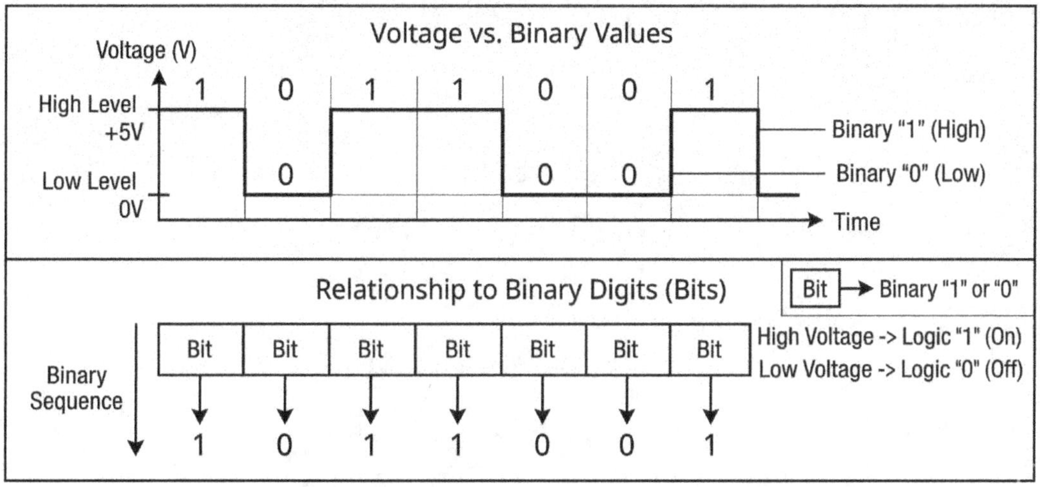

What is a Digital Signal?

A digital signal is a signal that represents data using binary values.

In most digital communication systems, two voltage levels are used:

A high voltage level represents binary 1

A low voltage level represents binary 0

These voltage levels are transmitted through communication channels such as network cables or wireless networks.

For example, when a computer sends data over a network, it converts the information into a sequence of binary digits (bits). These bits are then transmitted as digital signals.

Binary Representation of Data

Computers use the binary number system to represent all types of data.

Binary numbers consist of only two digits:

0 and 1
These digits are called bits.

Groups of bits are used to represent characters, numbers, and other types of information.

For example, the letter A may be represented using binary code such as:

01000001
This binary representation allows computers to store and transmit information efficiently.

Binary data representation using bits

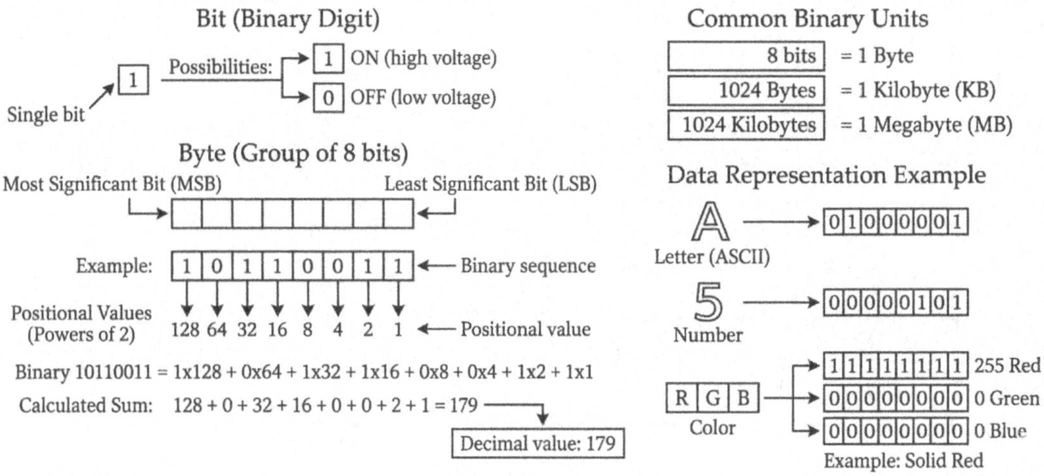

Digital Signal Characteristics

Digital signals also have certain characteristics that define how the signal behaves during transmission.

Some important characteristics include:

Bit interval.
Bit rate.
Signal levels.
Bit Interval.

The bit interval refers to the time required to transmit one bit.

For example, if a system transmits one bit every millisecond, the bit interval is 1 millisecond.

The bit interval determines how long each binary value remains on the communication medium before the next bit is transmitted.

Bit Rate

The bit rate refers to the number of bits transmitted per second.

It is usually measured in bits per second (bps).

For example:

1 kbps = 1000 bits per second.
1 Mbps = 1 million bits per second.
1 Gbps = 1 billion bits per second.

Higher bit rates allow faster data transmission across networks.

For instance, modern high-speed networks may support speeds such as 1 Gbps or even higher.

Digital signal showing bit intervals

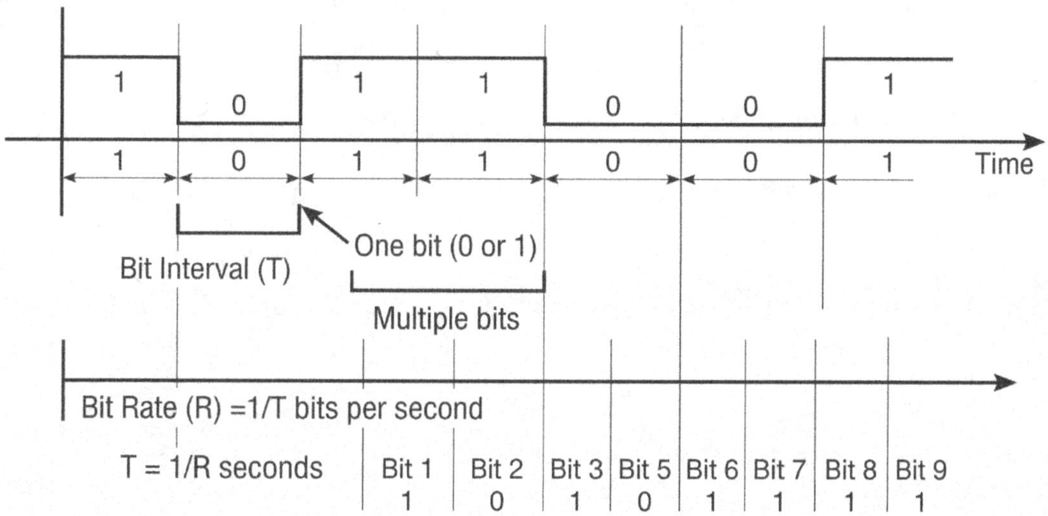

Signal Levels

Digital signals typically use two signal levels representing binary values.

However, some communication systems use multiple signal levels to transmit more bits in a single signal.

For example:

Two-level signals represent one bit at a time.

Four-level signals can represent two bits at once.

This technique helps increase data transmission speed.

Advantages of Digital Signals

Digital signals offer several advantages compared to analog signals.

One major advantage is that digital signals are less affected by noise and interference. Even if the signal becomes slightly distorted during transmission, it can often be reconstructed accurately.

Another advantage is that digital signals are easier to store and process using computers.

Digital systems also allow the use of error detection and correction techniques, which improve reliability during data transmission.

Additionally, digital signals can be easily encrypted, which helps protect data during communication.

Digital Signals in Computer Networks

Digital signals are widely used in modern computer networks.

For example, when a computer sends data through an Ethernet cable, the information is transmitted as digital signals.

Similarly, wireless networks such as Wi-Fi convert digital data into radio signals that can travel through the air.

Many digital communication systems use advanced encoding techniques to ensure efficient and reliable transmission.

These systems allow high-speed communication between devices across local networks and the global Internet.

Conversion between Analog and Digital Signals

In many situations, real-world signals such as sound or video are originally analog in nature. However, modern computer systems process data in digital form.

Therefore, these analog signals must be converted into digital signals before processing.

This process is known as analog-to-digital conversion.

For example, when a person speaks into a microphone during a video call, the sound waves are converted into digital signals so that the computer can transmit them through the network.

Similarly, digital signals may sometimes be converted back into analog form for playback through speakers or display devices.

Analog signal converted to digital signal.

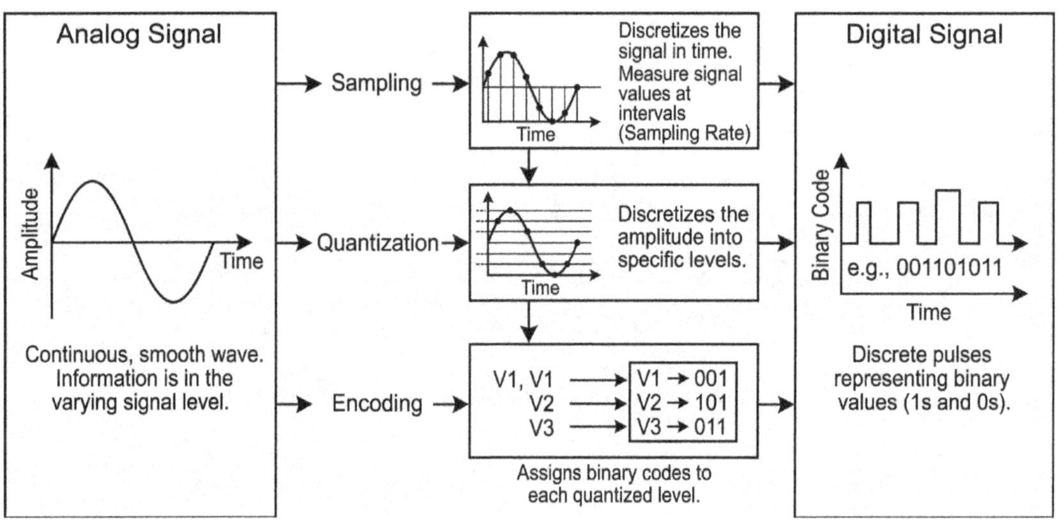

Applications of Digital Signals

Digital signals are used in many modern technologies.

Some examples include:

Computer networks.

Internet communication.

Mobile communication systems.

Digital television broadcasting.

Online video streaming.

Digital audio systems.

These technologies rely on digital signals to transmit large amounts of data efficiently and reliably.

Summary

A digital signal represents information using discrete values, usually in the form of binary digits 0 and 1.

Digital signals are widely used in modern communication systems because they are more reliable, easier to process, and less affected by noise compared to analog signals.

Important characteristics of digital signals include bit interval, bit rate, and signal levels. Digital signals form the foundation of modern networking technologies and enable efficient data communication across networks.

Signal Characteristics

In the previous sections, we studied analog signals and digital signals. Both of these signals are used to carry information from one device to another in communication systems. However, to understand how signals behave during transmission, it is important to study their characteristics.

Signal characteristics describe the properties of a signal that determine how the signal carries information and how it travels through the communication medium.

Some important signal characteristics include:

Amplitude.

Frequency.

Period.

Phase.

Bandwidth.

Understanding these characteristics helps engineers design efficient communication systems and also helps students understand how signals behave in networking environments.

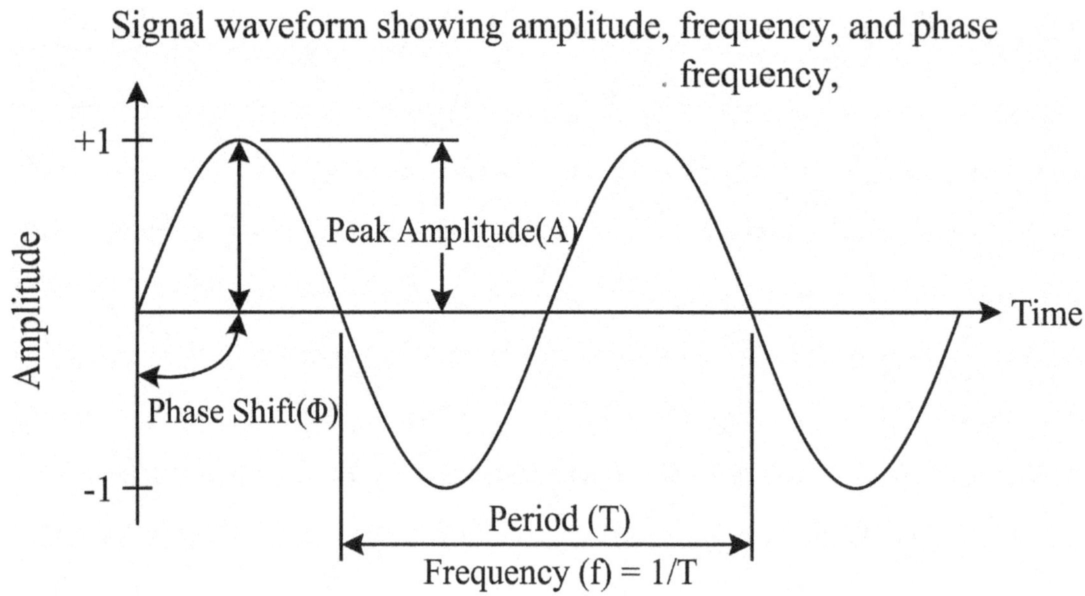

Amplitude

Amplitude refers to the maximum height or strength of a signal wave measured from the central reference line.

In simple terms, amplitude indicates the power or intensity of the signal.

For example, in an electrical signal, amplitude may represent the voltage level of the signal. In sound signals, amplitude determines the loudness of the sound.

If the amplitude of a signal increases, the signal becomes stronger. If the amplitude decreases, the signal becomes weaker.

Amplitude is usually measured in units such as volts, watts, or decibels, depending on the type of signal being used.

Signal wave showing amplitude measurement

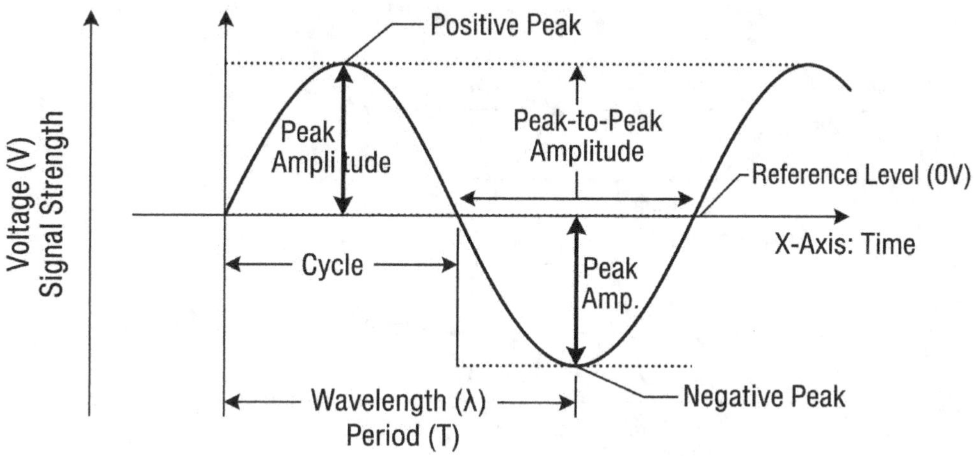

Higher amplitude signals generally carry stronger energy, but extremely high amplitudes may also cause distortion in some communication systems.

Frequency

Frequency refers to the number of cycles that a signal completes in one second.

Frequency tells us how quickly the signal wave oscillates or repeats itself.

Frequency is measured in Hertz (Hz).

For example:

If a signal completes one cycle per second, its frequency is 1 Hz.
If a signal completes 1000 cycles per second, its frequency is 1000 Hz or 1 kHz.

Frequency is very important in communication systems because different communication technologies operate within specific frequency ranges.

For example:

Radio broadcasting operates in specific frequency bands.

Wi-Fi networks operate in frequency bands such as 2.4 GHz and 5 GHz.

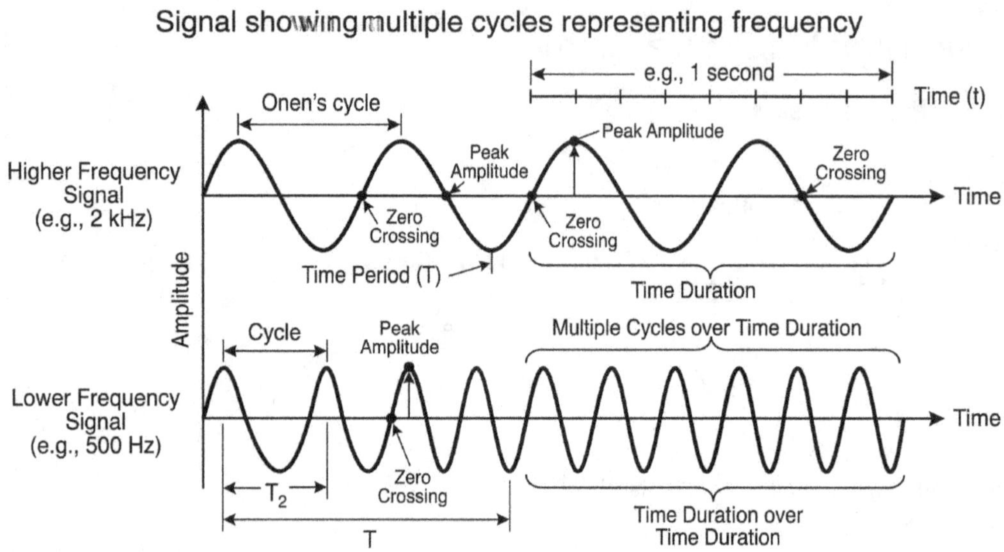

Higher frequency signals usually allow faster transmission of information.

Period

The period of a signal is the time required to complete one full cycle of the signal.

In other words, the period represents the duration of one wave cycle.

The period is usually measured in seconds.

The relationship between frequency and period is very important.

If the frequency of a signal is high, the period becomes smaller. If the frequency is low, the period becomes larger.

The mathematical relationship between frequency and period is:

Period = 1 / Frequency

For example:

If the frequency of a signal is 10 Hz, then the period is 1/10 seconds, which equals 0.1 seconds.

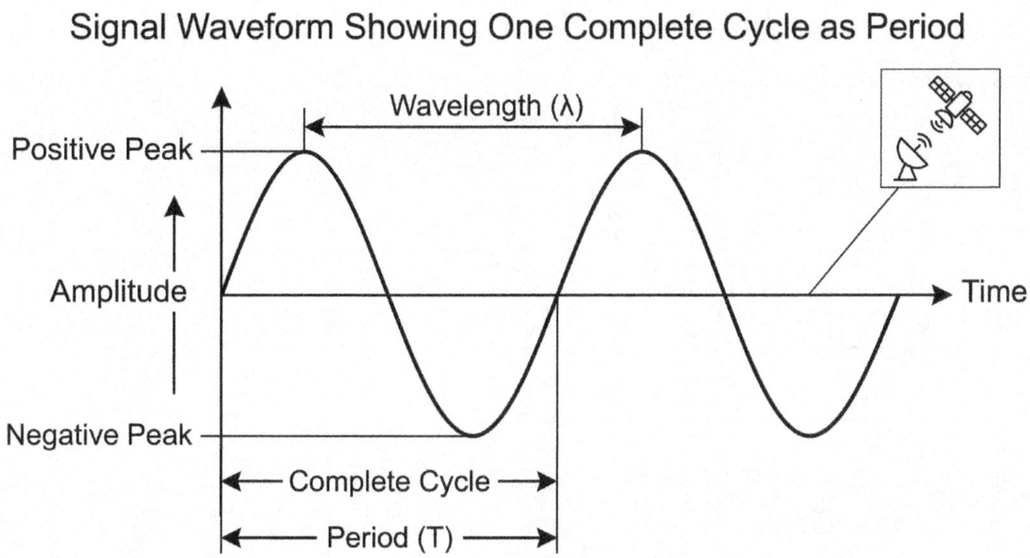

This relationship helps engineers analyze signal behavior in communication systems.

Phase

Phase refers to the position of a signal wave relative to time.

It describes how far a signal wave has progressed within its cycle.

Phase is usually measured in degrees or radians.

For example, a complete signal cycle corresponds to 360 degrees.

Two signals may have the same frequency and amplitude but may start at different positions in time. In such cases, they are said to have a phase difference.

Phase differences are important in many communication techniques such as modulation, signal synchronization, and wireless communication systems.

Two waves showing phase difference

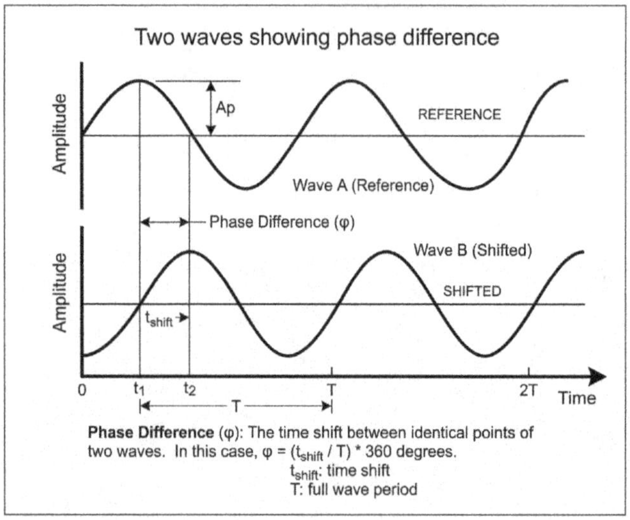

Understanding phase is particularly important in modern digital communication systems.

Bandwidth

Another important signal characteristic is bandwidth.

Bandwidth refers to the range of frequencies that a signal occupies.

In communication systems, signals are transmitted within a certain frequency range. This frequency range is known as the bandwidth.

Bandwidth is usually measured in Hertz (Hz).

For example:

If a communication channel can transmit frequencies between 1000 Hz and 5000 Hz, then the bandwidth is:

5000 Hz – 1000 Hz = 4000 Hz

This means the channel has a bandwidth of 4000 Hz.

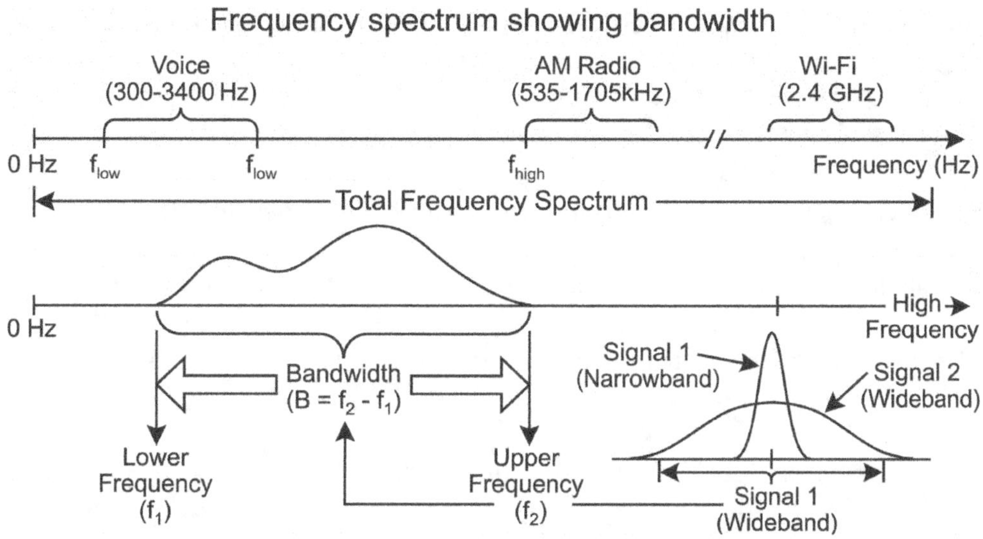

Bandwidth is very important because it determines how much data can be transmitted through a communication channel.

Generally, higher bandwidth allows faster data transmission.

For example:

Telephone lines have relatively low bandwidth.

Optical fiber networks provide very high bandwidth.

Because of this, fiber optic communication supports much higher Internet speeds.

Relationship between Signal Characteristics

The characteristics of signals are often related to each other.

For example:

Higher frequency signals usually have smaller periods.

Higher bandwidth allows higher data transmission rates.

Signal amplitude determines signal strength.

Understanding these relationships helps engineers design communication systems that are both efficient and reliable.

Importance of Signal Characteristics in Networking

Signal characteristics play an important role in computer networks because they affect how data travels through communication channels.

For example:

If the bandwidth of a communication channel is low, the data transmission speed will also be limited.

If signal amplitude becomes too weak during transmission, the signal may not reach the destination correctly.

Similarly, interference and noise may affect the signal frequency and phase, which can cause errors in communication.

Therefore, communication systems must be carefully designed to maintain proper signal characteristics during transmission.

Summary

Signal characteristics describe the properties that determine how signals behave during transmission.

Important signal characteristics include Amplitude, Frequency, Period, Phase, and Bandwidth. These properties help define the strength, speed, and behavior of signals in communication systems.

Understanding these characteristics is essential for designing reliable communication networks and ensuring efficient data transmission.

These concepts form the foundation for studying advanced topics such as signal encoding, modulation techniques, and multiplexing.

Analog vs Digital Communication

In the previous sections, we studied analog signals and digital signals, as well as the important characteristics of signals such as amplitude, frequency, and bandwidth. Now it is important to understand how these signals are used in communication systems.

Communication systems can generally be divided into two types:

Analog Communication.
Digital Communication.

Both of these methods are used to transmit information from one place to another. However, they differ in the way signals are generated, transmitted, and processed.

Understanding the difference between analog and digital communication helps students understand how modern networking systems operate.

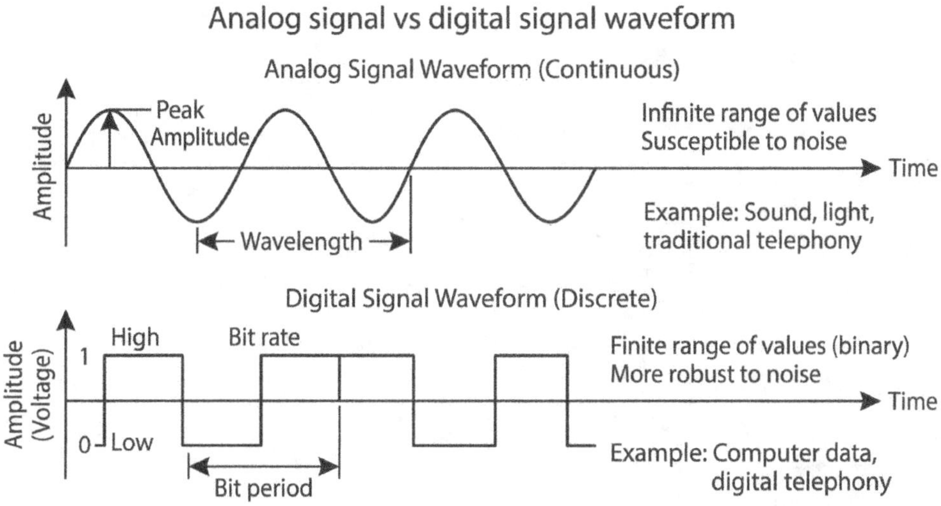

Analog Communication

Analog communication is a communication method in which information is transmitted using continuous signals.

In this type of communication, the signal varies smoothly over time and can take any value within a range.

Analog communication is commonly used in systems where real-world signals such as sound or light must be transmitted.

For example, when a person speaks into a traditional telephone, the sound waves are converted into electrical analog signals. These signals travel through communication lines and are converted back into sound at the receiver's end.

Similarly, early radio and television broadcasting systems also used analog communication techniques.

Some examples of analog communication systems include:

Traditional telephone systems.

AM and FM radio broadcasting.

Analog television transmission.

Audio recording systems.

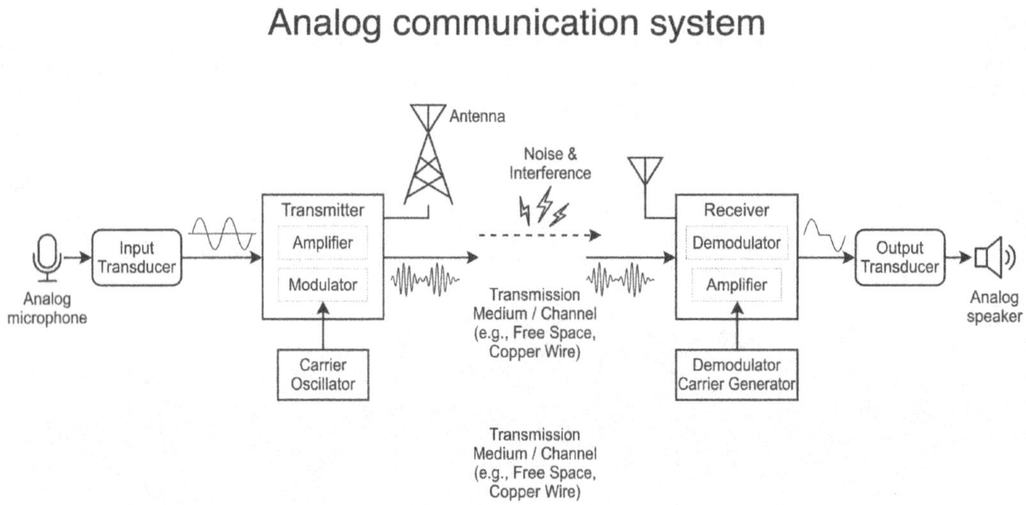

Characteristics of Analog Communication

Analog communication has several key characteristics.

First, analog signals are continuous in nature, meaning they change smoothly without sudden jumps.

Second, analog signals can represent very fine variations in information such as sound waves and light intensity.

Third, analog communication systems are relatively simple in terms of signal generation and transmission.

However, analog signals are also more sensitive to noise and interference. During transmission, external disturbances may distort the signal.

Once the signal is distorted, it becomes difficult to recover the original information accurately.

Digital Communication

Digital communication is a communication method in which information is transmitted using discrete signals, typically represented by binary digits 0 and 1.

In digital communication, data is converted into binary form before transmission.

Modern computer networks and Internet communication systems primarily use digital communication because computers operate using binary data.

For example, when a computer sends a file across a network, the information is converted into a sequence of binary bits. These bits are then transmitted through communication channels such as Ethernet cables or wireless networks.

Examples of digital communication systems include:

Computer networks.

Internet communication.

Mobile communication systems.

Digital television broadcasting.

Wi-Fi communication.

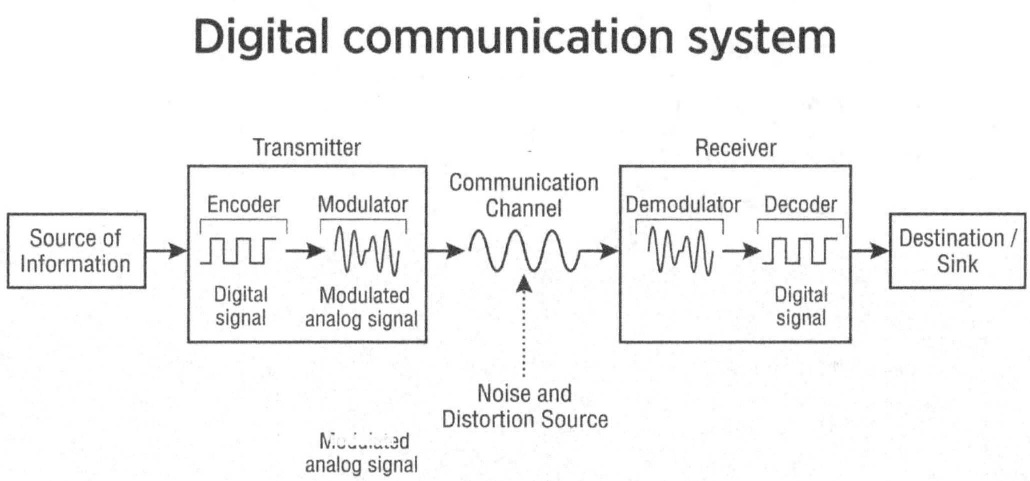

Characteristics of Digital Communication

Digital communication has several advantages over analog communication.

First, digital signals are less affected by noise and interference. Even if the signal becomes slightly distorted during transmission, the original data can often be recovered correctly.

Second, digital communication allows the use of error detection and correction techniques, which improve reliability during transmission.

Third, digital signals are easier to store, process, and encrypt, which makes them suitable for modern computer systems.

Digital communication also supports high-speed data transmission, which is essential for Internet services, video streaming, and cloud computing.

Key Differences between Analog and Digital Communication

Although both communication methods are used to transmit information, they differ in several important ways.

In analog communication, signals vary continuously and can take any value within a range. In digital communication, signals use discrete levels, usually represented by binary digits.

Analog communication systems are generally more sensitive to noise and interference. Digital communication systems are more resistant to noise because signals can be regenerated during transmission.

Another important difference is that analog systems are often simpler in design, while digital systems require additional processes such as encoding, modulation, and signal processing.

Despite the complexity, digital communication has become the preferred method in modern networking systems due to its reliability and efficiency.

Conceptual Comparison of Analog and Digital Communication

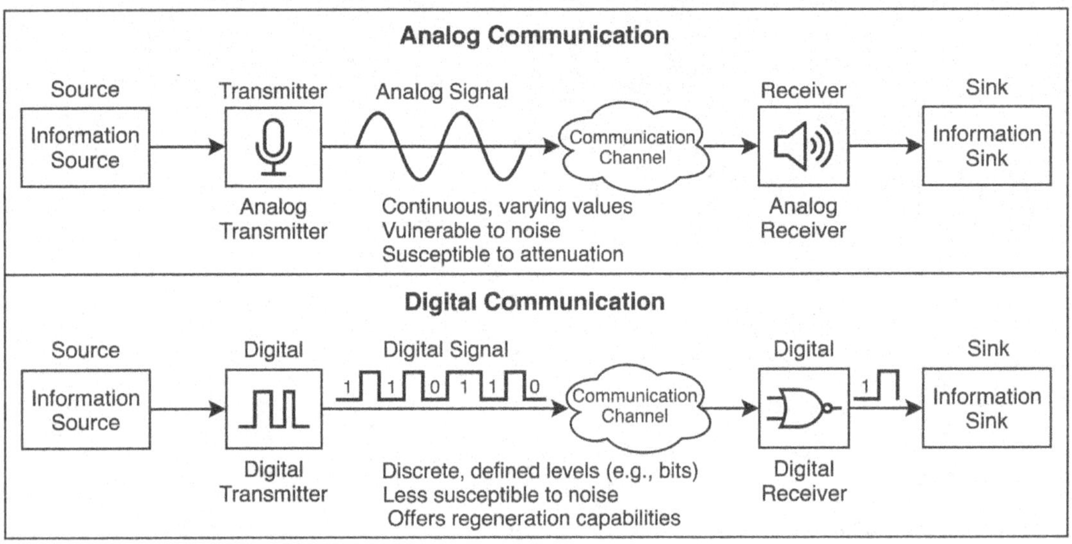

Why Modern Networks Use Digital Communication

Most modern communication systems have shifted from analog communication to digital communication.

There are several reasons for this transition.

Digital communication allows data to be transmitted at very high speeds, which is necessary for modern Internet applications such as video streaming and online gaming.

Digital signals can also be easily compressed, encrypted, and processed using computer systems.

Another advantage is that digital signals can be regenerated during transmission, which reduces the effects of noise and improves overall communication quality.

Because of these advantages, modern communication technologies such as fiber optic networks, mobile networks, and satellite communication systems rely heavily on digital communication.

Real-World Example

Consider the example of modern mobile communication systems.

When a person speaks during a phone call, the sound waves are first captured by the microphone. These sound waves are then converted into digital signals by the mobile device.

The digital signals are transmitted through the mobile network to the receiving device.

At the receiver's end, the digital signals are converted back into sound so that the other person can hear the conversation.

This process allows communication to occur clearly even across long distances.

Summary

Analog communication uses continuous signals to transmit information, while digital communication uses discrete signals represented by binary digits.

Although analog communication was widely used in earlier communication systems, digital communication has become the dominant method in modern networking technologies.

Digital communication offers several advantages, including higher reliability, better resistance to noise, and easier processing by computer systems.

Understanding the differences between analog and digital communication helps students understand how modern communication systems and computer networks operate.

CHAPTER SIX

Encoding, Modulation, and Multiplexing

Digital to Digital Encoding

In modern computer networks, data is usually generated in digital form, which means it is represented using binary digits 0 and 1. However, this binary data cannot always be transmitted directly through communication media such as cables or wireless channels.

Before digital data is transmitted, it must be converted into a form that can travel through the communication medium. This process is known as encoding.

Digital-to-digital encoding is the process of converting digital data (binary bits) into digital signals that can be transmitted through communication channels.

In this process, binary data is represented using specific signal patterns that allow the receiving device to correctly interpret the information.

Digital data converted into digital signal waveform

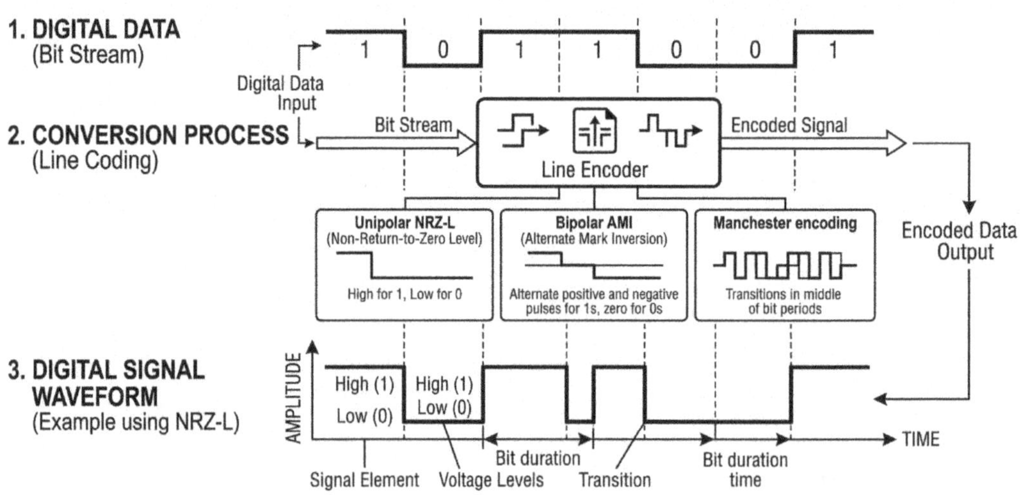

Digital-to-digital encoding is commonly used in computer networks, Ethernet communication, and other digital communication systems.

Why Digital Encoding is Required

Digital encoding plays a very important role in data communication systems.

Although computers generate data in binary form, the communication medium may require signals to follow specific patterns to ensure reliable transmission.

Encoding helps in achieving the following objectives:

First, it ensures that the receiver can correctly interpret the transmitted data.

Second, it helps maintain synchronization between the sender and receiver, meaning both systems stay aligned while transmitting and receiving bits.

Third, encoding techniques help reduce errors caused by noise or signal distortion.

Fourth, encoding improves the efficient use of the communication channel.

Because of these advantages, digital encoding is widely used in networking technologies.

Basic Concept of Line Coding

The most common form of digital-to-digital encoding is known as line coding.

Line coding refers to the method used to represent binary data using digital signal levels.

In line coding, different voltage levels or signal transitions are used to represent the binary digits 0 and 1.

For example, a high voltage level may represent binary 1, while a low voltage level may represent binary 0.

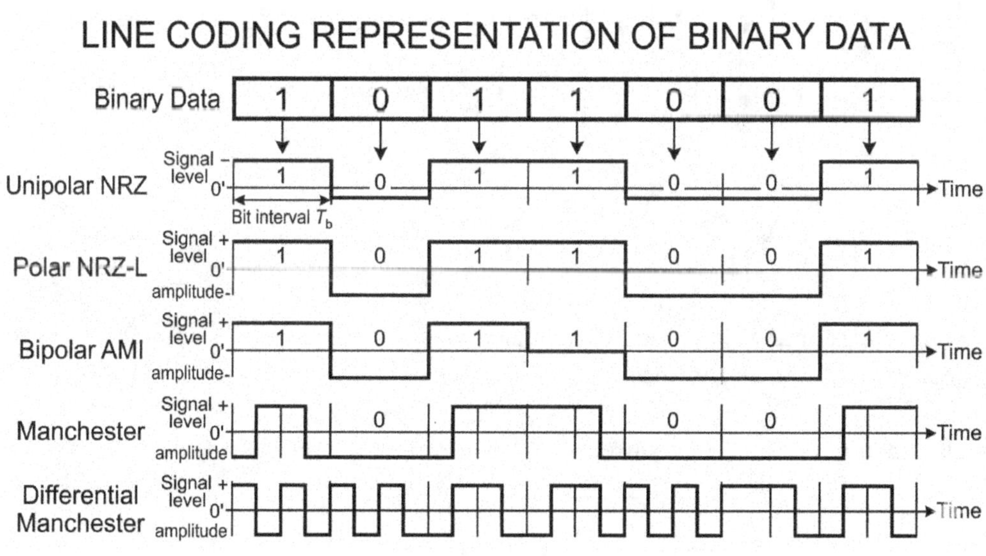

Different line coding techniques are used depending on the communication system and its requirements.

Types of Digital Encoding Techniques

Several digital encoding techniques are used in communication systems. Some commonly used methods include:

Unipolar Encoding.
Polar Encoding.
Bipolar Encoding.
Manchester Encoding.

Each of these methods represents binary data using different signal patterns.

Unipolar Encoding

In Unipolar Encoding, only one polarity of voltage is used.

Typically:

Binary 1 is represented by a positive voltage level.

Binary 0 is represented by zero voltage.

This means the signal moves between a positive voltage and zero.

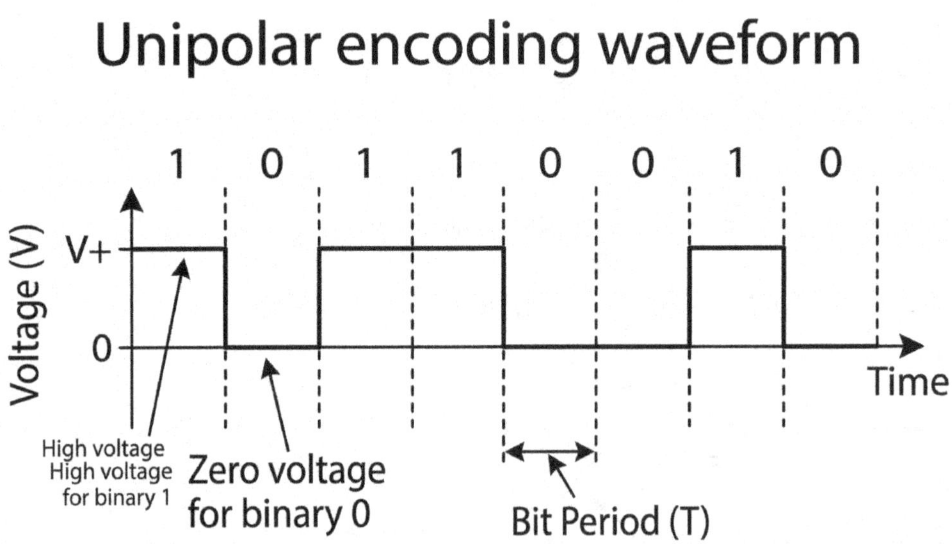

Although this method is simple, it has certain disadvantages. One major problem is that long sequences of zeros may cause synchronization issues between the sender and receiver.

Because of this limitation, unipolar encoding is not widely used in modern communication systems.

Polar Encoding

In Polar Encoding, two voltage levels are used: one positive and one negative.

Typically:

Binary 1 is represented by a positive voltage.

Binary 0 is represented by a negative voltage.

This method improves signal balance and helps maintain synchronization between the sender and receiver.

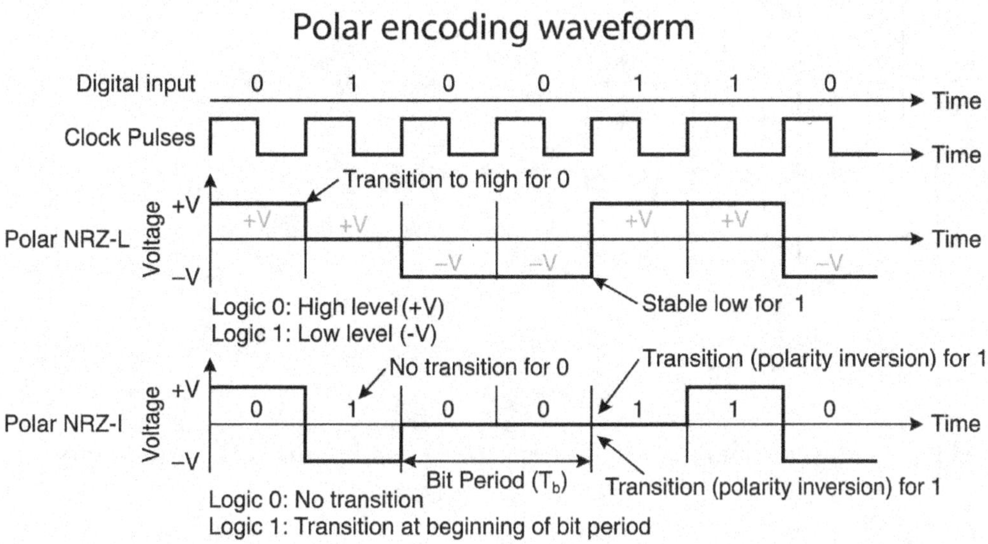

Polar encoding is more reliable than unipolar encoding and is commonly used in communication systems.

Bipolar Encoding

In Bipolar Encoding, three voltage levels are used:

Positive voltage.
Negative voltage.
Zero voltage.

In this technique:

Binary 0 is represented by zero voltage.

Binary 1 alternates between positive and negative voltage levels.

This alternating pattern helps reduce signal distortion and improves error detection.

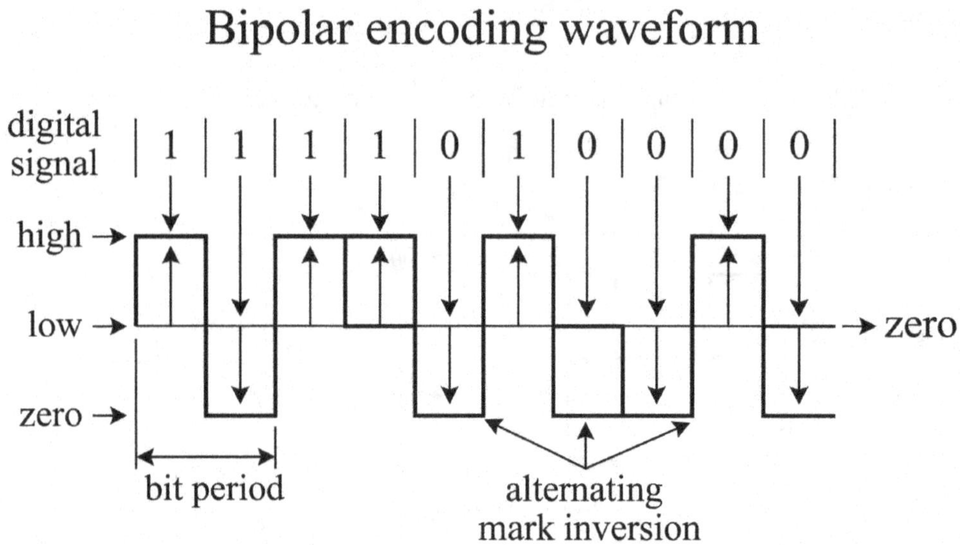

Bipolar encoding is widely used in certain telecommunication systems because it improves signal reliability.

Manchester Encoding

Manchester Encoding is another popular digital encoding technique used in communication systems such as Ethernet networks.

In Manchester encoding, each bit period is divided into two halves.

A transition from high to low represents binary 1.

A transition from low to high represents binary 0.

This method ensures that a signal transition always occurs in the middle of each bit, which helps maintain synchronization between the sender and receiver.

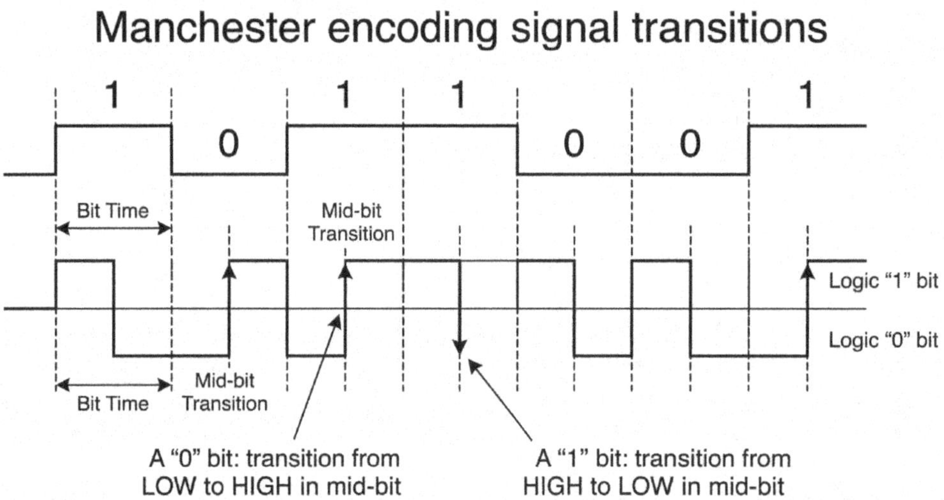

Because of its reliability and synchronization advantages, Manchester encoding is used in many networking standards.

Importance of Digital Encoding in Networks

Digital encoding techniques are essential in computer networks because they allow digital data to be transmitted reliably across communication channels.

Encoding ensures that signals remain synchronized, reduces transmission errors, and allows efficient use of network bandwidth.

Without proper encoding techniques, digital communication systems would struggle to maintain reliable communication over long distances.

Real-World Applications

Digital encoding techniques are used in many real-world technologies.

For example:

Ethernet networks use Manchester encoding to transmit data between computers.

Telecommunication systems use various encoding techniques to ensure reliable voice and data communication.

Optical fiber networks also use advanced encoding schemes to transmit high-speed digital signals.

These technologies allow modern networks to support high-speed Internet communication and large-scale data transmission.

Summary

Digital-to-digital encoding is the process of converting binary data into digital signals that can be transmitted through communication channels.

Line coding techniques such as Unipolar, Polar, Bipolar, and Manchester encoding are used to represent binary digits using specific signal patterns.

These encoding techniques help maintain synchronization between sender and receiver, reduce transmission errors, and improve the efficiency of communication systems.

Understanding digital encoding is important because it forms the foundation of many modern networking technologies.

Analog to Digital Conversion (PCM)

In many communication systems, the information that we want to transmit is analog in nature. For example, human voice, music, and video signals are naturally analog signals because they vary continuously over time.

However, modern computer networks and digital systems process information in digital form, using binary digits (0 and 1).

Therefore, before analog signals can be transmitted through digital communication systems, they must first be converted into digital signals. This process is known as analog-to-digital conversion.

One of the most widely used techniques for analog-to-digital conversion is Pulse Code Modulation (PCM).

Pulse Code Modulation (PCM) is a method used to convert analog signals into digital signals so that they can be transmitted through digital communication systems.

PCM is widely used in technologies such as:

Digital telephony.
Audio recording systems.
Voice over IP (VoIP) communication.
Digital television broadcasting.

Analog signal being converted into digital signal using PCM

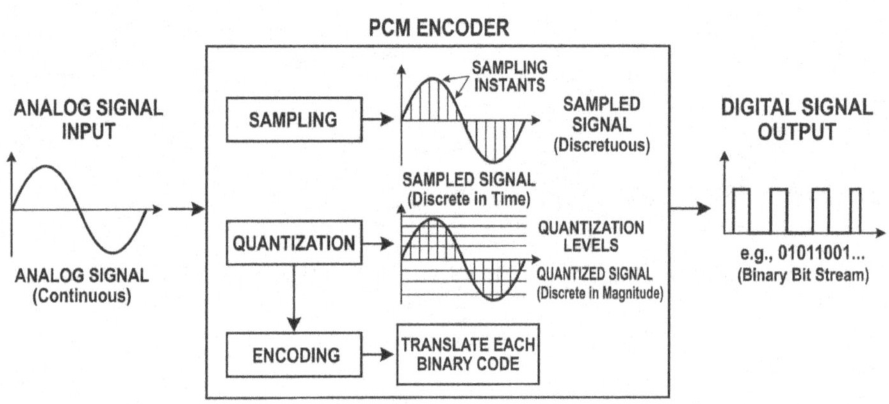

Basic Idea of Pulse Code Modulation

The main idea behind PCM is to represent an analog signal using a series of digital values.

In this technique, the continuous analog signal is measured at regular time intervals. These measured values are then converted into binary numbers that represent the signal digitally.

Once the analog signal is converted into digital form, it can be transmitted through computer networks and digital communication systems.

At the receiver's side, the digital signal can be converted back into the original analog signal.

Steps Involved in PCM

The Pulse Code Modulation process involves three main steps:

Sampling.
Quantization.
Encoding.

Each step plays an important role in converting analog signals into digital form.

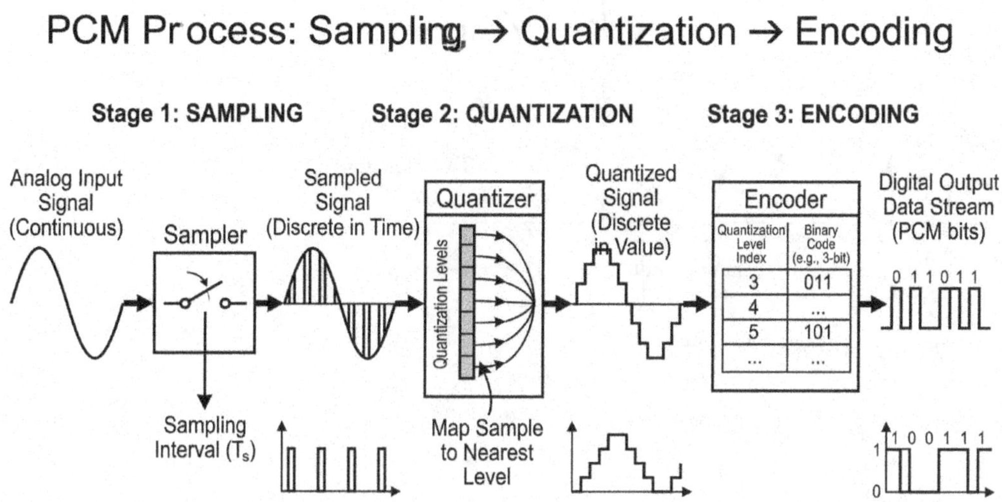

Sampling

The first step in PCM is sampling.

Sampling is the process of measuring the amplitude of an analog signal at regular intervals of time.

Instead of transmitting the entire continuous waveform, the system records the value of the signal at specific time points.

For example, when recording audio, the system may measure the signal thousands of times per second.

These measured values are called samples.

The more samples taken per second, the more accurately the digital signal represents the original analog signal.

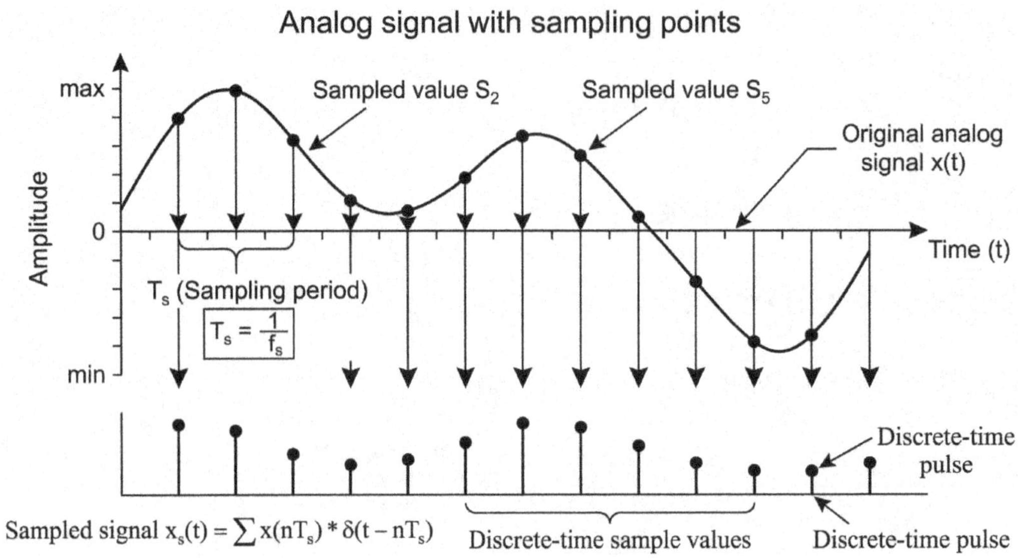

In digital audio systems, common sampling rates include:

8000 samples per second (telephone communication)
44100 samples per second (CD quality audio)

Higher sampling rates result in better sound quality because the digital signal becomes a more accurate representation of the original analog signal.

Quantization

The second step in PCM is quantization.

After sampling the analog signal, the next step is to assign each sample a numerical value.

However, digital systems cannot represent an infinite range of values. Therefore, the continuous range of signal amplitudes is divided into a finite number of levels.

Each sample is then approximated to the nearest available level.

This process of mapping sampled values to predefined levels is called quantization.

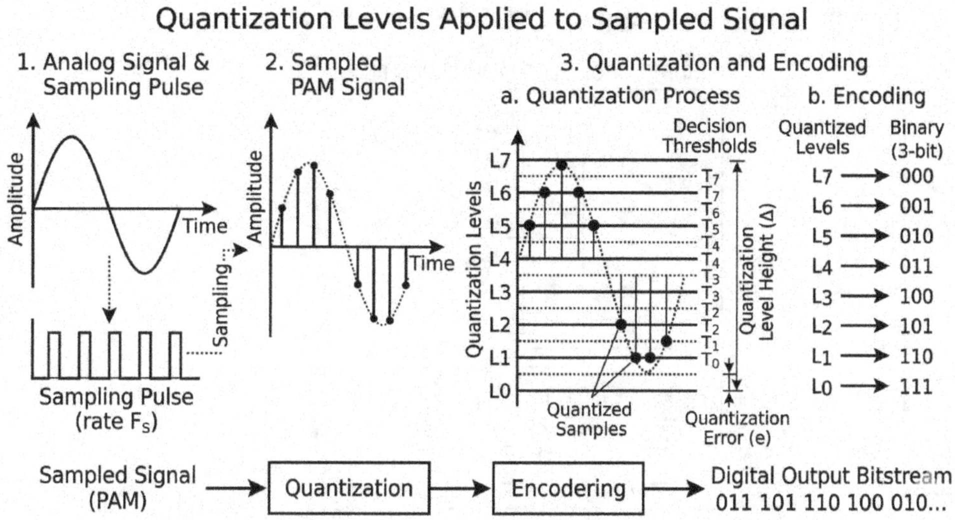

Because quantization approximates the actual signal values, a small error known as quantization error may occur.

However, by increasing the number of quantization levels, the accuracy of the digital signal can be improved.

Encoding

The final step in PCM is encoding.

During this step, the quantized values are converted into binary numbers.

Each quantized level is assigned a unique binary code.

These binary codes are then transmitted through the communication channel as digital signals.

For example, a sample value may be represented by a binary number such as:

101101

This binary representation allows the signal to be transmitted through digital communication systems.

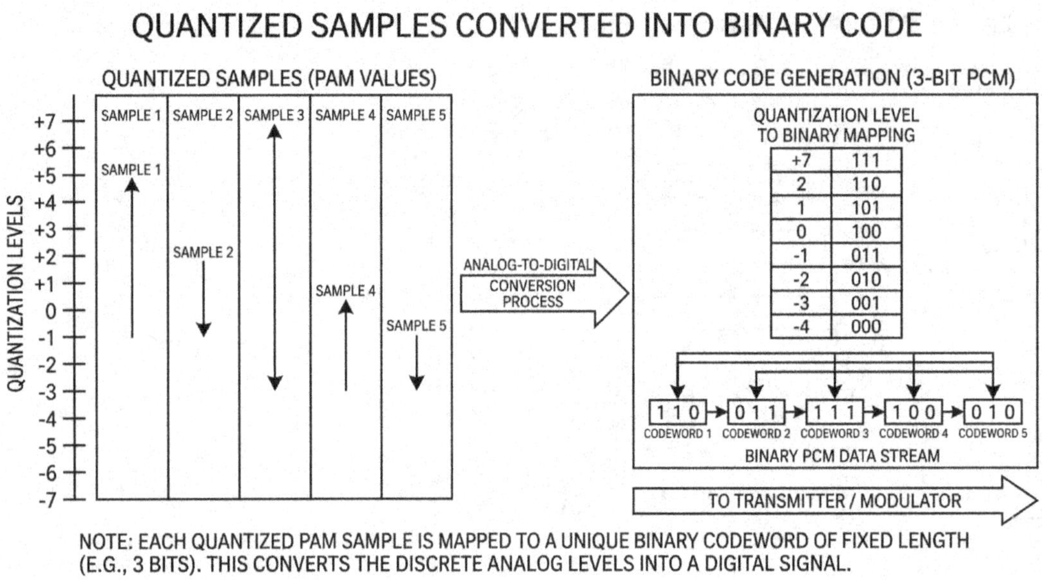

PCM in Real-World Communication Systems

PCM is widely used in modern digital communication systems.

One common example is digital telephone networks.

When a person speaks into a telephone, the microphone converts the sound waves into analog electrical signals. These signals are then converted into digital form using PCM.

The digital signals are transmitted through the communication network and converted back into analog signals at the receiver's end so that the listener can hear the voice.

Another example is digital audio recording, where sound signals are converted into digital data and stored on devices such as computers and music players.

Advantages of PCM

Pulse Code Modulation offers several advantages in digital communication systems.

First, it allows analog signals to be transmitted using digital communication techniques.

Second, digital signals generated by PCM are less affected by noise and interference compared to analog signals.

Third, digital signals can be easily stored, processed, and transmitted by computer systems.

Finally, PCM allows the use of error detection and correction techniques, which improve communication reliability.

Limitations of PCM

Although PCM is widely used, it also has some limitations.

One limitation is that PCM requires high bandwidth because the analog signal is converted into a large number of digital bits.

Another limitation is that the PCM process requires additional hardware components such as analog-to-digital converters and digital-to-analog converters.

Despite these limitations, PCM remains one of the most important techniques used in modern communication systems.

Summary

Pulse Code Modulation (PCM) is a widely used technique for converting analog signals into digital signals.

The PCM process involves three main steps: sampling, quantization, and encoding. Through these steps, continuous analog signals are converted into binary data that can be transmitted through digital communication systems.

PCM is widely used in technologies such as digital telephony, audio recording, and Internet communication.

Understanding PCM helps students understand how real-world analog signals such as voice and music are transmitted through modern digital networks.

Digital to Analog Modulation

In the previous section, we studied Pulse Code Modulation (PCM), which converts analog signals into digital signals. However, in many communication systems the opposite situation also occurs. Sometimes we have digital data, but the communication channel requires analog signals for transmission.

For example, traditional telephone networks were designed to carry analog signals. When computers needed to communicate through telephone lines, digital data had to be converted into analog signals before transmission.

This conversion process is known as digital-to-analog modulation.

Digital-to-analog modulation is the process of converting digital data into analog signals so that the data can be transmitted through analog communication channels.

This technique is widely used in:

Modems.
Wireless communication systems.
Radio communication.
Satellite communication.
Broadband communication systems.

Digital data converted into analog modulated signal.

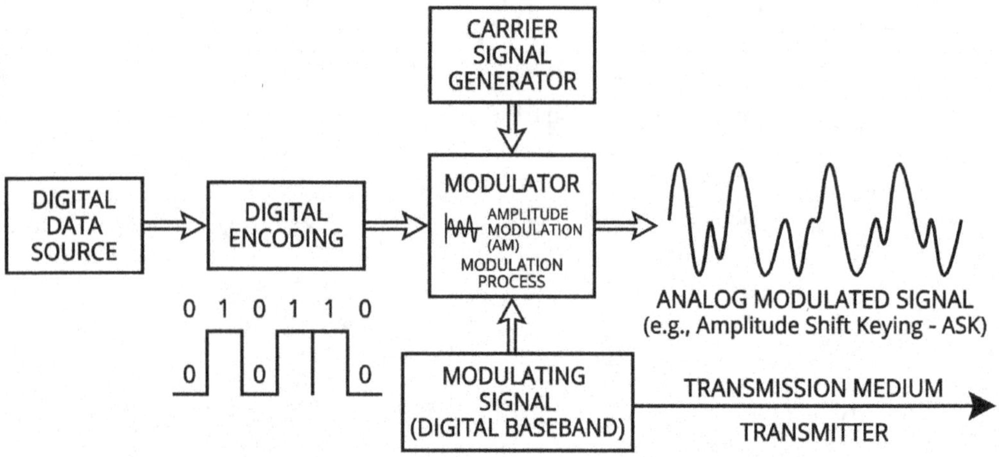

Digital data converted into analog modulated signal.

Basic Concept of Modulation

To understand digital-to-analog modulation, we must first understand the concept of modulation.

Modulation is the process of modifying a property of a signal called a carrier signal in order to transmit information.

A carrier signal is a high-frequency analog signal that carries information from the sender to the receiver.

The digital data is embedded into this carrier signal by modifying certain characteristics of the signal.

These characteristics include:

Amplitude.
Frequency.
Phase.

Depending on which characteristic is modified, different modulation techniques are used.

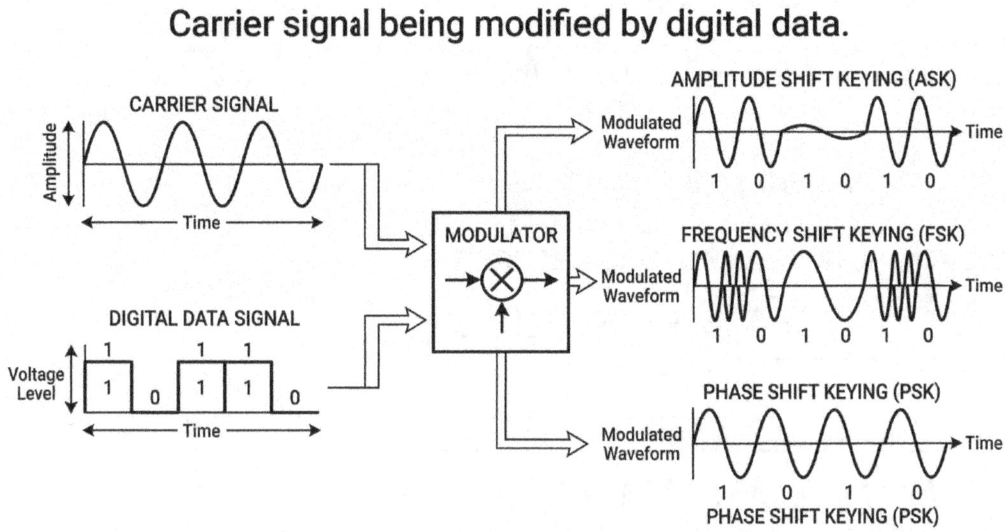

Why Modulation is Necessary

Modulation is necessary for several reasons.

First, it allows digital data to be transmitted through analog communication channels, such as telephone lines or wireless systems.

Second, modulation allows signals to travel over long distances without significant loss of information.

Third, modulation helps multiple signals share the same communication medium without interfering with each other.

Because of these advantages, modulation is widely used in communication systems.

Types of Digital to Analog Modulation

There are three main types of digital-to-analog modulation techniques used in communication systems:

Amplitude Shift Keying (ASK).
Frequency Shift Keying (FSK).
Phase Shift Keying (PSK).

Each technique represents digital data by modifying a specific property of the carrier signal.

Amplitude Shift Keying (ASK)

In Amplitude Shift Keying (ASK), the amplitude of the carrier signal is changed according to the digital data being transmitted.

In this technique:

Binary 1 is represented by a carrier signal with a higher amplitude.

Binary 0 is represented by a carrier signal with a lower amplitude or no signal.

This means the strength of the signal changes depending on whether the transmitted bit is 0 or 1.

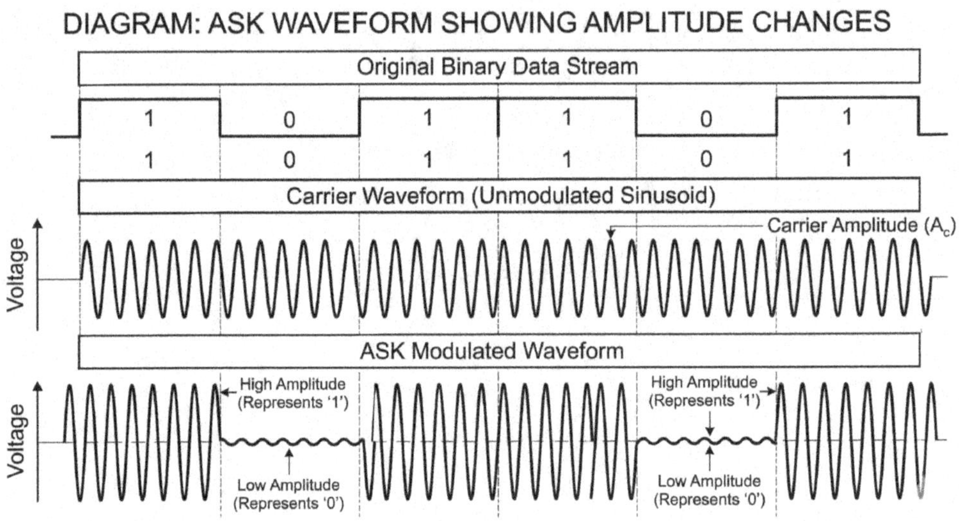

ASK is one of the simplest modulation techniques, but it is also more sensitive to noise because any interference that affects signal amplitude may cause errors.

ASK is sometimes used in optical communication systems and radio communication systems.

Frequency Shift Keying (FSK)

In Frequency Shift Keying (FSK), the frequency of the carrier signal is changed according to the digital data.

In this technique:

Binary 1 is represented by a carrier signal with one frequency.

Binary 0 is represented by a carrier signal with another frequency.

The amplitude of the signal remains constant, but the frequency changes depending on the bit being transmitted.

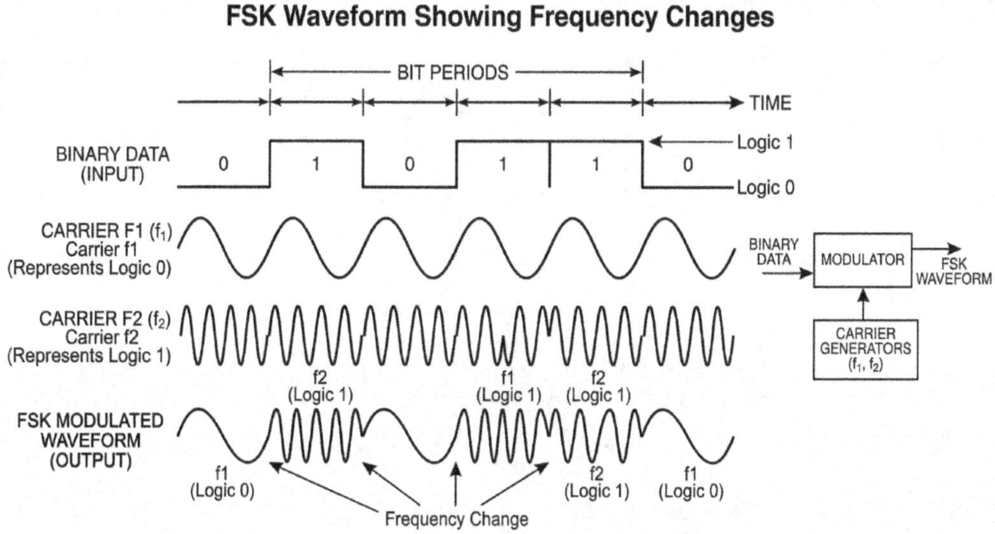

FSK is more resistant to noise compared to ASK because noise usually affects amplitude rather than frequency.

FSK is widely used in:

Radio communication.
Caller ID systems.
Low-speed data communication.

Phase Shift Keying (PSK)

In Phase Shift Keying (PSK), the phase of the carrier signal is changed according to the digital data.

The phase refers to the position of the signal waveform relative to time.

In a simple form of PSK:
Binary 1 may be represented by a signal with a certain phase.

Binary 0 may be represented by a signal with a different phase.

One common form of PSK is Binary Phase Shift Keying (BPSK), where the phase of the signal changes by 180 degrees depending on the transmitted bit.

PSK waveform showing phase shifts.

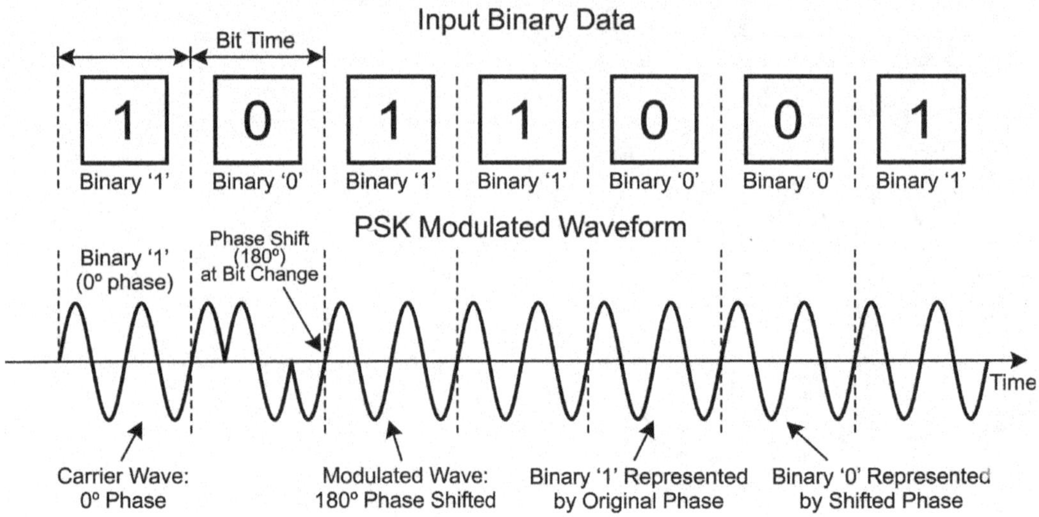

PSK is widely used in modern communication systems because it provides better noise resistance and efficient data transmission.

Advanced forms of PSK are used in technologies such as:

Wi-Fi networks.
Satellite communication.
Mobile communication systems.

Role of Modems in Digital to Analog Modulation

A device called a modem performs digital-to-analog modulation in many communication systems.

The word modem comes from Modulator–Demodulator.

The modem performs two main functions:

Modulation – converting digital data into analog signals for transmission.
Demodulation – converting received analog signals back into digital data.

Modems were widely used in traditional Internet connections over telephone lines.

Diagram Title: Modem performing modulation and demodulation.

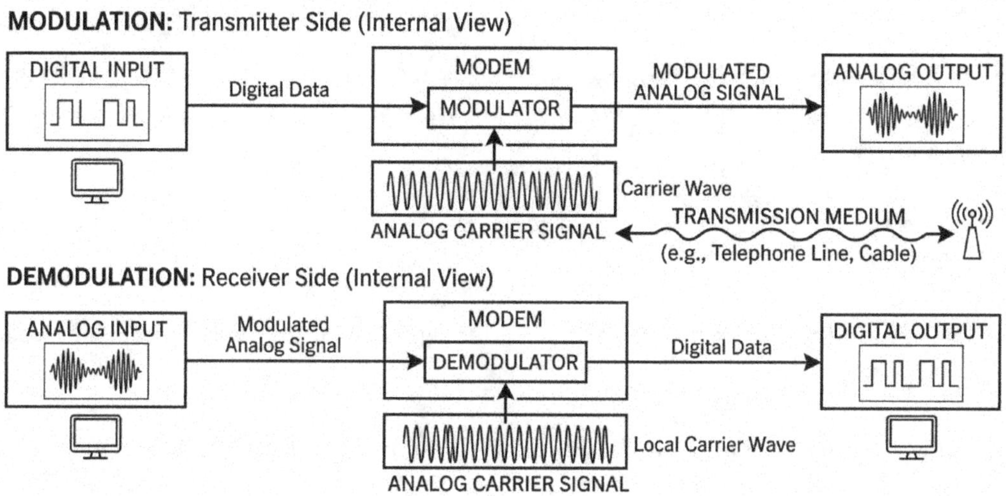

Even though modern broadband technologies use more advanced methods, the basic concept of modulation remains very important.

Importance of Digital to Analog Modulation

Digital-to-analog modulation plays an important role in communication systems.

It allows digital devices such as computers to communicate through analog communication channels.

It also makes wireless communication possible by allowing digital information to be transmitted using radio waves.

Modern communication technologies such as Wi-Fi, mobile networks, and satellite communication systems rely heavily on advanced modulation techniques.

Summary

Digital-to-analog modulation is the process of converting digital data into analog signals for transmission through analog communication channels.

This process is achieved by modifying certain characteristics of a carrier signal such as amplitude, frequency, or phase.

Three common modulation techniques are Amplitude Shift Keying (ASK), Frequency Shift Keying (FSK), and Phase Shift Keying (PSK).

These techniques allow digital information to be transmitted through various communication systems, including telephone networks, wireless networks, and satellite communication systems.

Understanding modulation techniques is essential for learning how modern communication systems transmit digital data across long distances.

Analog Modulation Techniques (AM, FM, PM)

In the previous section, we studied digital-to-analog modulation, where digital data is converted into analog signals for transmission. However, in many communication systems, the original information itself is analog in nature, such as human voice, music, and video signals.

In such cases, instead of converting the information into digital form, the analog signal is transmitted directly using a technique called analog modulation.

Analog modulation is the process of modifying the properties of a carrier signal according to the analog message signal.

The carrier signal is usually a high-frequency signal, while the message signal is typically a low-frequency signal containing the actual information.

By combining the message signal with the carrier signal, the information can be transmitted efficiently over long distances.

Message signal combined with carrier signal to produce modulated signal

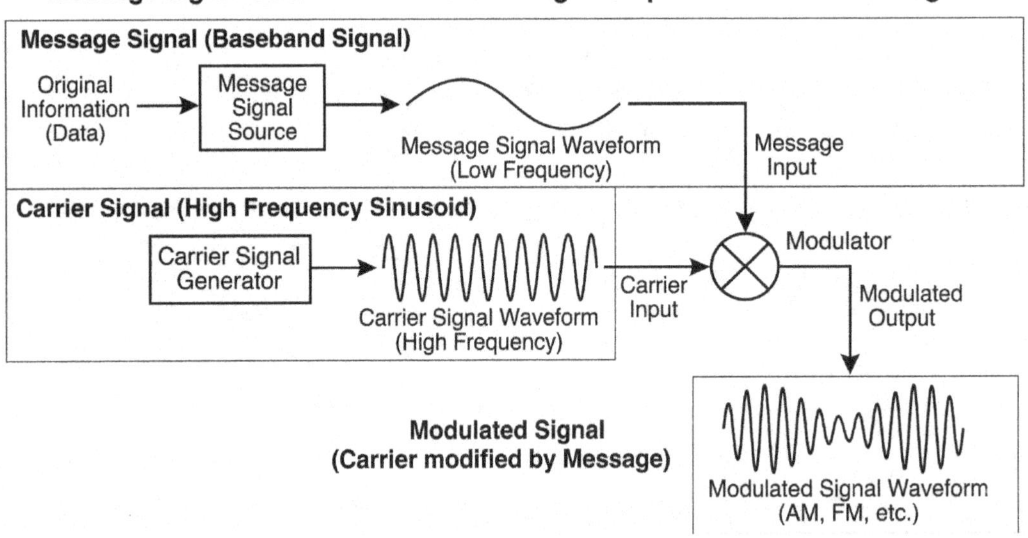

Why Analog Modulation is Required

Analog signals such as sound waves usually have low frequencies. If these signals were transmitted directly, they would not travel long distances effectively and could easily suffer from interference.

Therefore, communication systems use a high-frequency carrier signal to carry the information.

The process of combining the message signal with the carrier signal is known as modulation.

Analog modulation provides several advantages:

First, it allows signals to travel longer distances.

Second, it allows multiple signals to be transmitted without interfering with each other.

Third, it improves the efficiency of communication systems.

Because of these advantages, analog modulation has been widely used in radio and television broadcasting systems.

Basic Components of Analog Modulation

An analog modulation system usually consists of three main components.

First is the message signal, which contains the actual information such as sound or voice.

Second is the carrier signal, which is a high-frequency signal used to carry the information.

Third is the modulator, which combines the message signal with the carrier signal to create the modulated signal.

At the receiver side, a device called a demodulator extracts the original message signal from the modulated signal.

Basic analog modulation system showing modulator and demodulator.

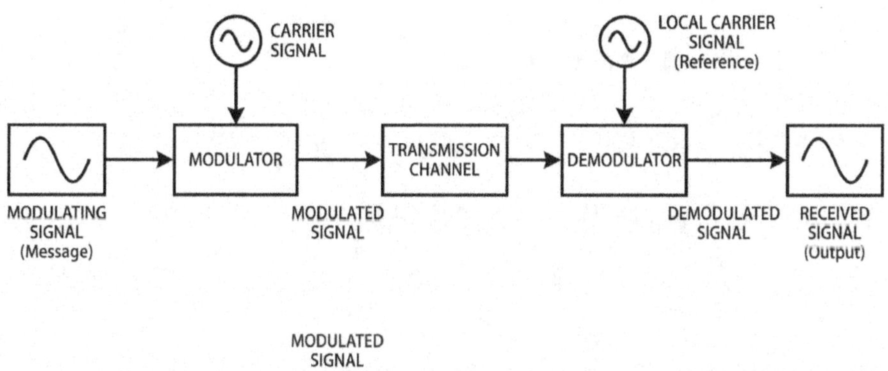

Types of Analog Modulation

Analog modulation techniques are classified based on which property of the carrier signal is modified.

There are three main types of analog modulation:

Amplitude Modulation (AM)
Frequency Modulation (FM)
Phase Modulation (PM)

Each of these techniques modifies a different characteristic of the carrier signal.

Amplitude Modulation (AM)

In Amplitude Modulation (AM), the amplitude of the carrier signal is varied according to the message signal.

The frequency and phase of the carrier signal remain constant, while its amplitude changes depending on the strength of the message signal.

For example, when the message signal increases, the amplitude of the carrier signal also increases. When the message signal decreases, the amplitude of the carrier signal decreases.

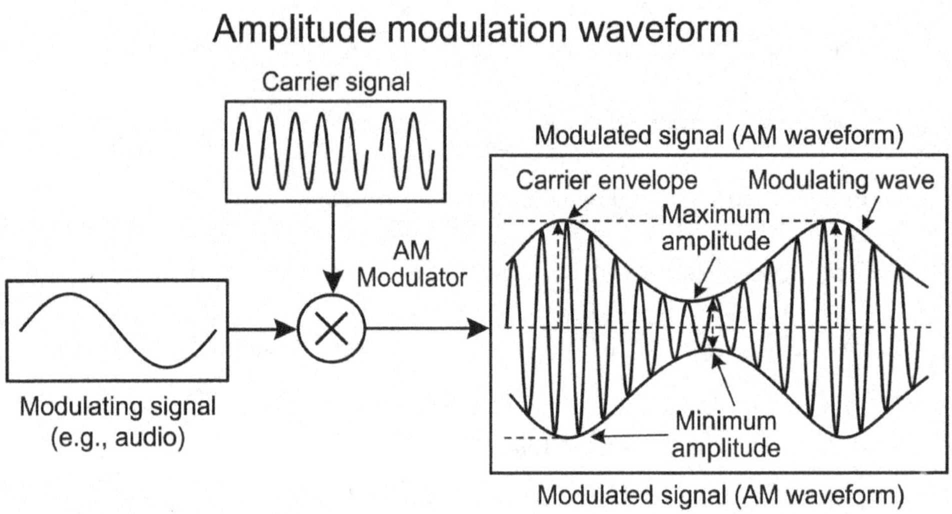

Amplitude modulation was widely used in early radio broadcasting systems.

One advantage of AM is that the equipment required for transmission and reception is relatively simple.

However, AM signals are more sensitive to noise and interference, especially because noise often affects signal amplitude.

Frequency Modulation (FM)

In Frequency Modulation (FM), the frequency of the carrier signal is varied according to the message signal, while the amplitude remains constant.

When the message signal changes, the frequency of the carrier signal increases or decreases accordingly.

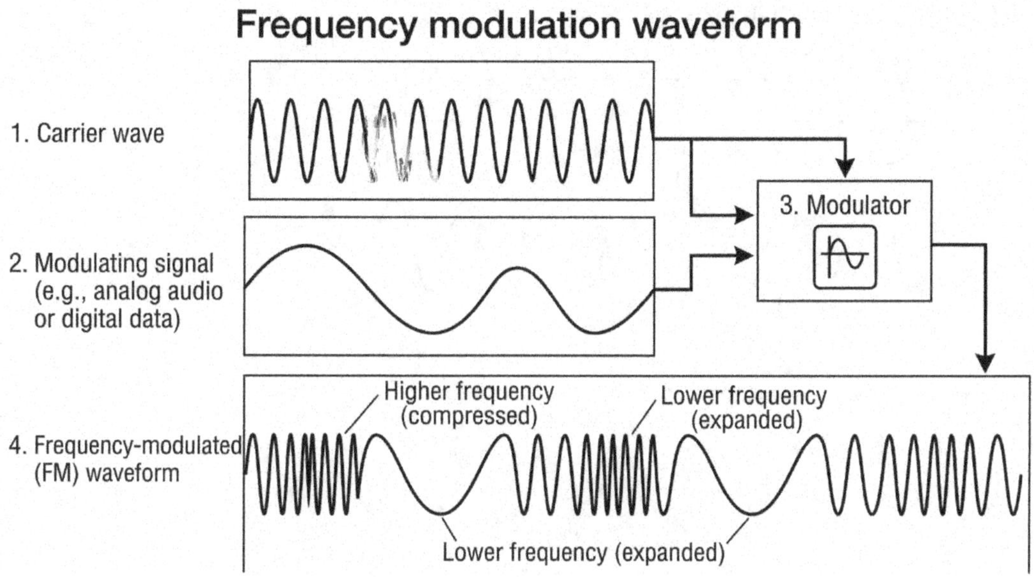

FM provides several advantages over AM.

Because the amplitude remains constant, FM signals are less affected by noise and interference.

This results in better sound quality, which is why FM is commonly used in radio broadcasting and music transmission.

FM radio stations usually operate in the 88 MHz to 108 MHz frequency band.

Phase Modulation (PM)

In Phase Modulation (PM), the phase of the carrier signal is varied according to the message signal.

The phase of the signal represents the position of the waveform relative to time.

When the message signal changes, the phase of the carrier signal shifts accordingly.

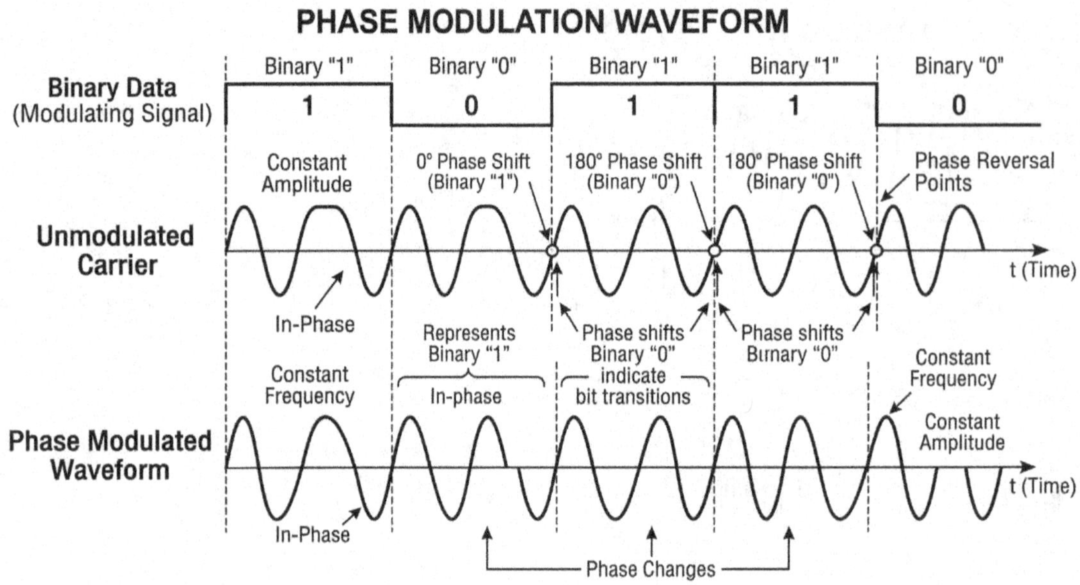

Phase modulation is commonly used in certain digital communication systems and advanced wireless communication technologies.

Although PM is not as commonly used in broadcasting as AM or FM, it plays an important role in modern communication systems.

Comparison of AM, FM, and PM

All three modulation techniques are used to transmit analog signals, but they differ in the way the carrier signal is modified.

In Amplitude Modulation, the amplitude of the carrier signal changes.

In Frequency Modulation, the frequency of the carrier signal changes.

In Phase Modulation, the phase of the carrier signal changes.

Each technique has its own advantages and applications depending on the communication system.

Comparison of AM, FM, and PM waveforms

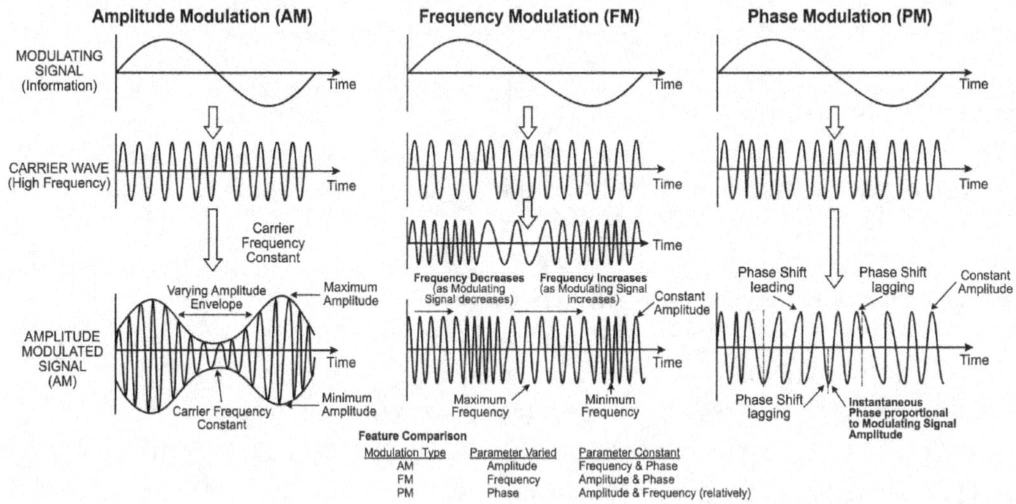

Real-World Applications of Analog Modulation

Analog modulation techniques are used in many real-world communication systems.

For example, AM radio broadcasting uses amplitude modulation to transmit voice and music signals.

FM radio broadcasting uses frequency modulation to provide high-quality audio transmission.

Analog modulation is also used in television broadcasting, aviation communication systems, and radio communication networks.

Although many modern communication systems use digital modulation techniques, analog modulation still plays an important role in broadcasting and certain wireless communication systems.

Summary

Analog modulation is the process of modifying a high-frequency carrier signal according to an analog message signal.

This technique allows information such as voice and music to be transmitted efficiently over long distances.

The three main types of analog modulation are Amplitude Modulation (AM), Frequency Modulation (FM), and Phase Modulation (PM).

Each technique modifies a different property of the carrier signal, such as amplitude, frequency, or phase.

Understanding analog modulation helps students understand how traditional communication systems such as radio broadcasting work.

Multiplexing

In modern communication systems, many users need to transmit data at the same time. If every user required a separate communication channel, the number of channels needed would be extremely large and very expensive to maintain.

To solve this problem, communication systems use a technique called multiplexing.

Multiplexing is the process of combining multiple signals and transmitting them through a single communication channel.

This technique allows several users or devices to share the same transmission medium efficiently.

At the sender's side, multiple signals are combined using a device called a multiplexer (MUX). At the receiver's side, another device called a demultiplexer (DEMUX) separates the signals back into their original form.

Multiplexing system showing multiple signals combined into one channel and separated at receiver

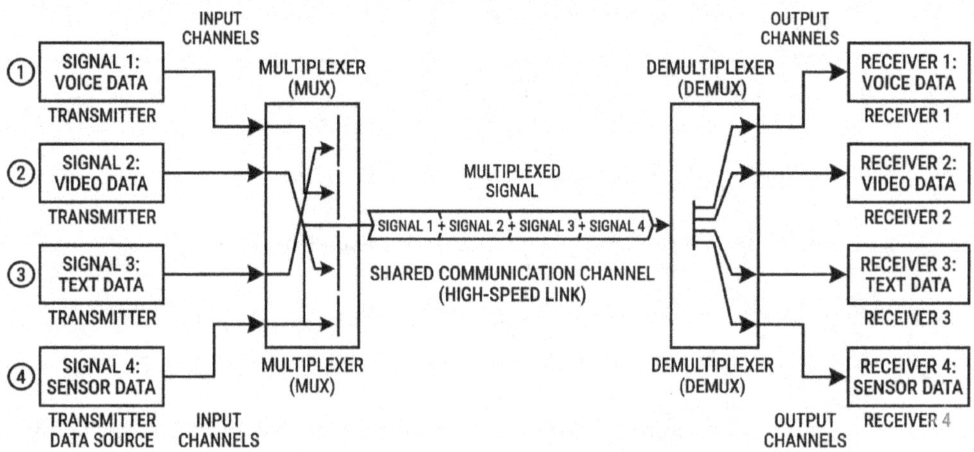

Multiplexing is widely used in communication systems such as telephone networks, television broadcasting, and computer networks.

Why Multiplexing is Needed

Multiplexing is important because communication resources such as cables, fiber optics, and wireless channels are limited.

Without multiplexing, each communication connection would require its own dedicated transmission channel. This would be inefficient and very costly.

Multiplexing helps in the following ways:

First, it allows efficient use of communication channels.
Second, it reduces the cost of communication infrastructure.
Third, it allows multiple users to share the same medium simultaneously.
Because of these advantages, multiplexing is widely used in modern networking systems.

Basic Working of Multiplexing

The working of multiplexing can be understood with a simple example.

Imagine several computers in an organization sending data to a central server through a network cable. Instead of using separate cables for each computer, multiplexing allows all data signals to be combined and transmitted through a single cable.

At the receiving end, the signals are separated and delivered to their correct destinations.

The main components involved in multiplexing are:

Multiplexer (MUX).
Communication channel.
Demultiplexer (DEMUX).

The multiplexer combines multiple input signals into a single output signal. The communication channel carries the combined signal. Finally, the demultiplexer separates the signals back into individual signals.

Block diagram showing multiplexer, channel, and demultiplexer

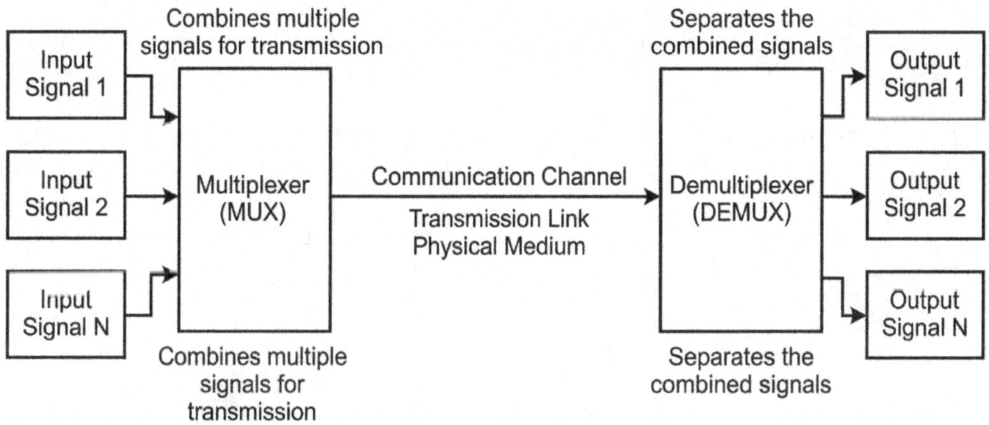

Types of Multiplexing

There are several types of multiplexing techniques used in communication systems. The most common ones include:

Frequency Division Multiplexing (FDM)
Time Division Multiplexing (TDM)
Wavelength Division Multiplexing (WDM)

Each technique combines signals in a different way.

Frequency Division Multiplexing (FDM)

In Frequency Division Multiplexing, the total available bandwidth of the communication channel is divided into several smaller frequency bands.

Each signal is transmitted using a different frequency range, so multiple signals can travel simultaneously without interfering with each other.

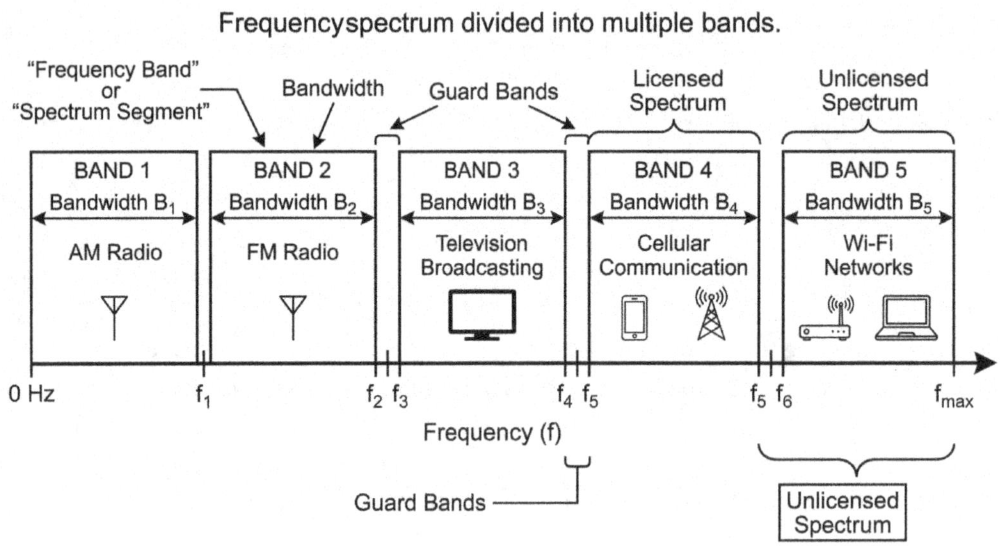

A simple example of FDM is radio broadcasting.

Different radio stations transmit signals using different frequencies. A radio receiver can tune to a specific frequency to receive a particular station.

For example:

One station may broadcast at 91.1 MHz
Another station may broadcast at 98.3 MHz

Because each station uses a different frequency band, multiple broadcasts can occur at the same time.

FDM is widely used in:

Radio broadcasting.
Television broadcasting.
Cable television networks.

Time Division Multiplexing (TDM)

In Time Division Multiplexing, multiple signals share the same communication channel but are transmitted at different time intervals.

Instead of dividing frequency, TDM divides the time of transmission into small slots.

Each signal is assigned a specific time slot during which it can transmit its data.

Time slots assigned to different signals.

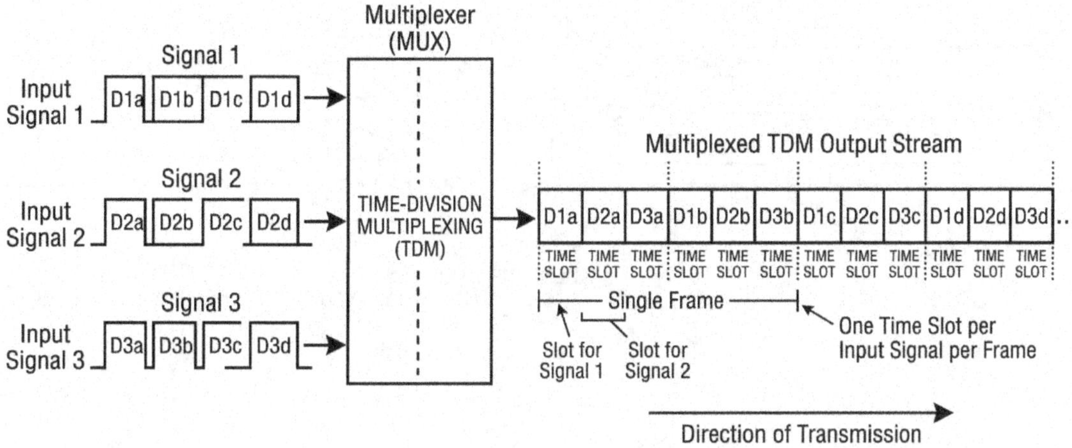

For example, if four devices are sharing the same channel, the system may allocate time slots like this:

Device 1 sends data during time slot 1.
Device 2 sends data during time slot 2.
Device 3 sends data during time slot 3.
Device 4 sends data during time slot 4.

This process repeats continuously, giving the appearance that all devices are transmitting data simultaneously.

TDM is widely used in:

Digital telephone systems.
Computer networks.
Satellite communication systems.

Wavelength Division Multiplexing (WDM)

Wavelength Division Multiplexing is mainly used in fiber optic communication systems.

In fiber optic cables, data is transmitted using light signals. WDM allows multiple signals to be transmitted simultaneously using different wavelengths of light.

Each wavelength acts as a separate communication channel within the same fiber optic cable.

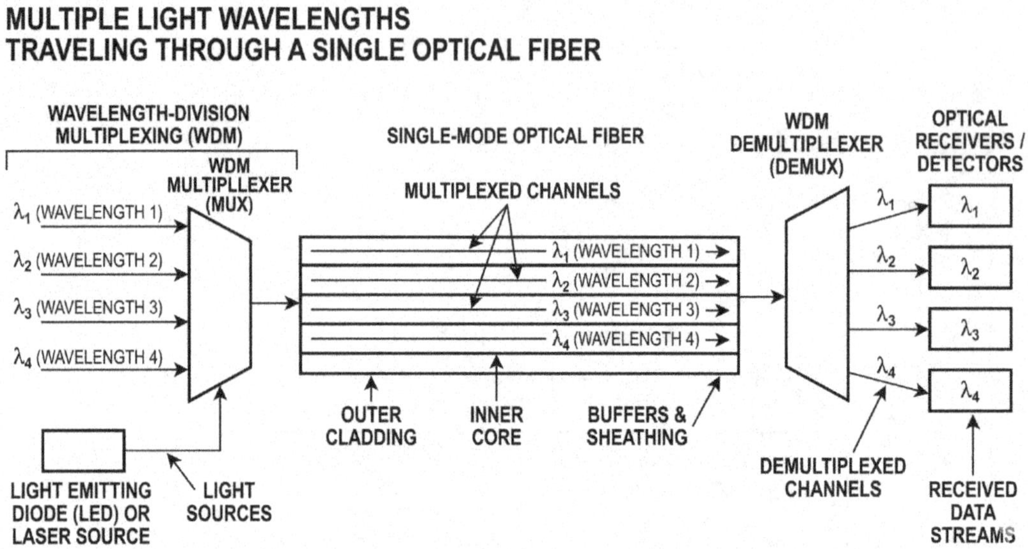

This technique greatly increases the capacity of fiber optic networks.

WDM is widely used in:

High-speed Internet networks.
Long-distance fiber optic communication.
Data center communication systems.

Advantages of Multiplexing

Multiplexing offers several advantages in communication systems.

First, it allows efficient utilization of communication channels.

Second, it reduces the cost of communication infrastructure because fewer cables and transmission media are required.

Third, multiplexing allows multiple users to communicate simultaneously without interfering with each other.

Finally, multiplexing increases the overall capacity of communication networks.

Real-World Example

Consider the example of a fiber optic Internet connection used by an Internet Service Provider.

Thousands of users may access the Internet through the same fiber optic cable. Multiplexing techniques allow the ISP to combine data from multiple users and transmit it through the same cable.

At the receiving end, the signals are separated and delivered to the correct users.

Without multiplexing, providing Internet access to millions of users would require an enormous number of cables and communication channels.

Summary

Multiplexing is a technique used to combine multiple signals and transmit them through a single communication channel.

This process improves the efficiency of communication systems and allows multiple users to share the same transmission medium.

The main types of multiplexing include Frequency Division Multiplexing (FDM), Time Division Multiplexing (TDM), and Wavelength Division Multiplexing (WDM).

Multiplexing plays a crucial role in modern communication technologies such as radio broadcasting, digital telephone networks, and fiber optic communication systems.

Understanding multiplexing helps students understand how large communication networks manage data transmission efficiently.

CHAPTER SEVEN

Switching Techniques

Circuit Switching

In communication networks, data often needs to travel from one device to another across multiple intermediate devices. When many users are communicating at the same time, the network must decide how the data will move through the network.

This process of selecting a path for data transmission is known as switching.

Switching techniques determine how data travels from the source device to the destination device through the network.

One of the earliest and most widely used switching methods in communication systems is circuit switching.

Circuit switching is a communication technique in which a dedicated communication path is established between the sender and the receiver before data transmission begins.

Once the connection is established, the entire path remains reserved for that communication session until the transmission is completed.

DIAGRAM: Circuit switching path established between two devices through multiple switches.

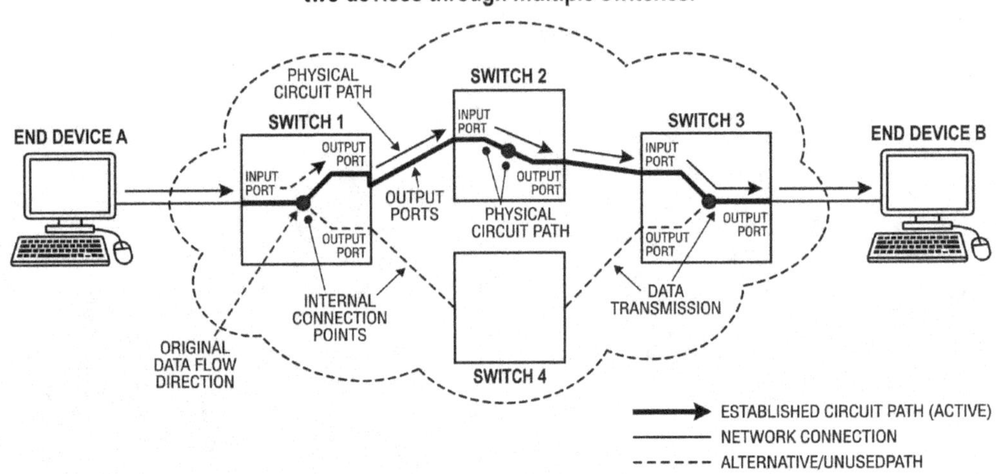

Circuit switching was widely used in traditional telephone networks, where a physical path was created between the caller and the receiver during a phone call.

Basic Idea of Circuit Switching

In circuit switching, a dedicated communication channel is created between two devices before the actual data transmission begins.

This means that the entire communication path is reserved exclusively for those two devices.

During the communication session, no other user can use that path.

Once the communication is finished, the connection is terminated and the resources become available for other users.

For example, when you make a traditional telephone call, the network establishes a connection between your phone and the receiver's phone. This connection remains active for the entire duration of the call.

Telephone network showing dedicated circuit path.

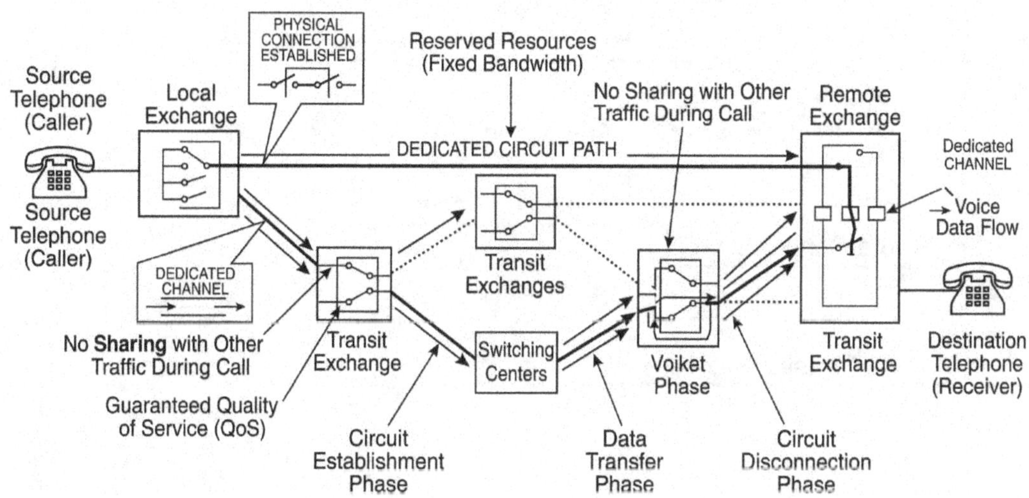

Because of this dedicated path, the communication occurs continuously without interruptions.

Phases of Circuit Switching

Circuit switching communication typically occurs in three main phases.

These phases ensure that the communication path is properly established, used, and then released.

The three phases are:

Circuit Establishment Phase.
Data Transfer Phase.
Circuit Termination Phase.
Circuit Establishment Phase.

Circuit Establishment Phase

The first phase is the circuit establishment phase.

During this phase, the network searches for an available communication path between the sender and the receiver.

Once a suitable path is found, the network reserves that path exclusively for the communication session.

This process may involve several switching devices that work together to create the connection.

For example, when you dial a phone number, the telephone network establishes a connection between your phone and the destination phone.

Circuit establishment process through multiple switches.

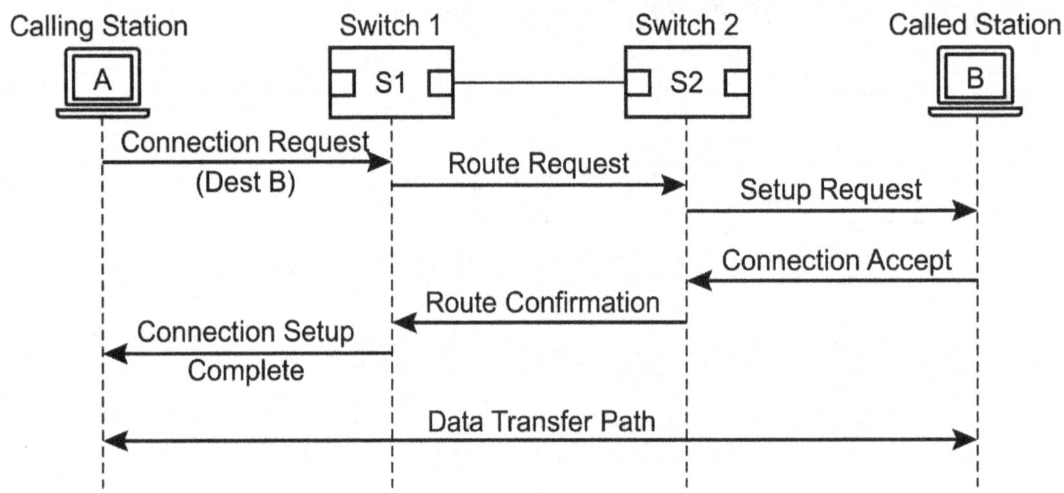

This phase may take a short amount of time before communication actually begins.

Data Transfer Phase

Once the communication path is established, the system enters the data transfer phase.

During this phase, the actual communication takes place.

Data flows continuously from the sender to the receiver through the dedicated communication path.

Because the entire path is reserved, the data transmission is usually smooth and consistent.

There is no need to repeatedly check the route for each piece of data.

This is why circuit switching is very suitable for real-time communication, such as voice calls.

Continuous data fow through dedicated circuit

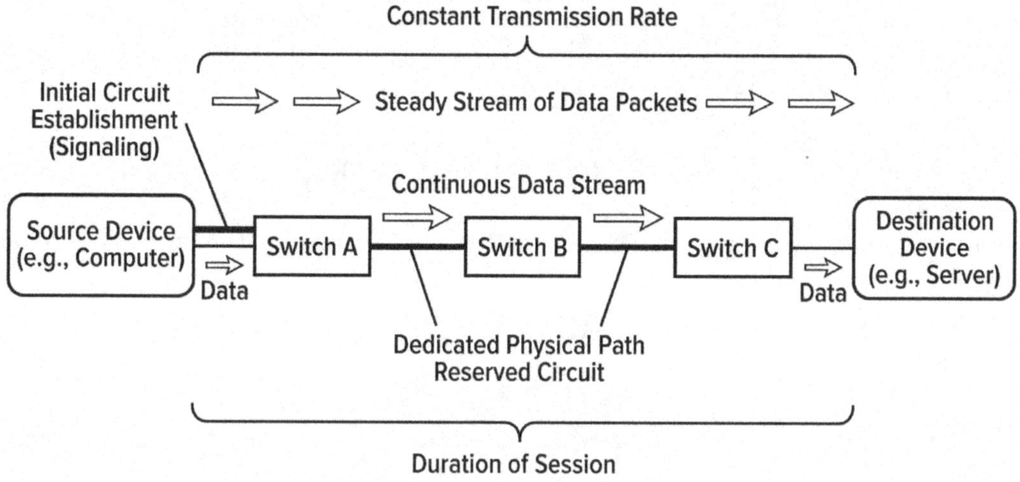

Circuit Termination Phase

The final phase is the circuit termination phase.

Once the communication session ends, the dedicated path is released.

This allows the network to free the resources so that they can be used by other users.

For example, when a phone call ends, the telephone network disconnects the circuit between the two phones.

After termination, the switches become available for establishing new connections.

Circuit disconnection after communication ends

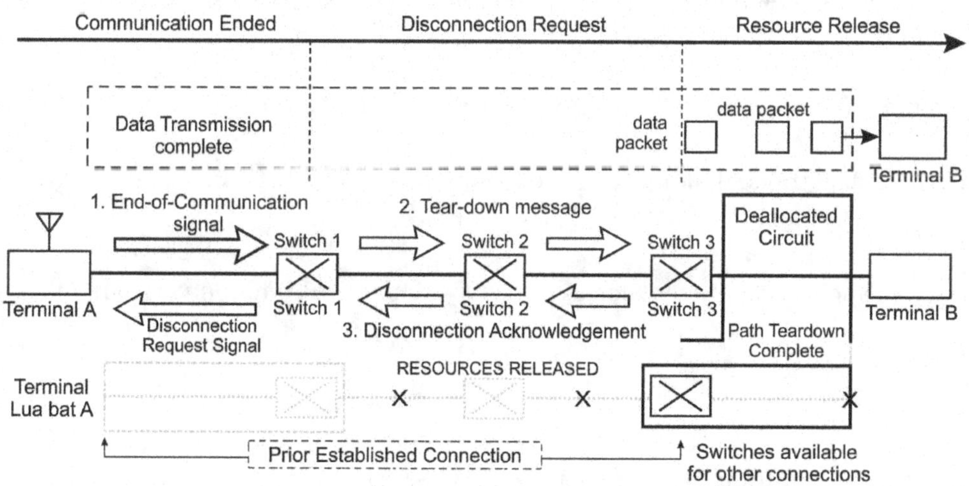

Characteristics of Circuit Switching

Circuit switching has several important characteristics.

First, a dedicated communication path is established before data transmission begins.

Second, once the connection is established, the communication occurs continuously without interruptions.

Third, the communication path remains reserved for the entire duration of the session.

Fourth, the transmission delay remains relatively constant because the path is fixed.

Because of these characteristics, circuit switching is well suited for applications that require continuous communication.

Advantages of Circuit Switching

Circuit switching offers several advantages.

One major advantage is that the communication path is dedicated, which ensures reliable and consistent communication.

Another advantage is that data transmission occurs continuously without delays caused by route selection.

Circuit switching is also very suitable for real-time voice communication, where consistent data flow is important.

Traditional telephone systems used circuit switching because voice communication requires stable and uninterrupted transmission.

Limitations of Circuit Switching

Although circuit switching provides reliable communication, it also has several limitations.

One major limitation is that the communication channel remains reserved even when no data is being transmitted. This can lead to inefficient use of network resources.

Another limitation is the time required to establish the connection before communication begins.

In modern computer networks, where data transmission is often intermittent, circuit switching is not always the most efficient method.

Because of these limitations, newer switching techniques such as packet switching are commonly used in modern networks.

Real-World Example

A good example of circuit switching is the traditional telephone network (PSTN).

When a person makes a phone call, the telephone network establishes a dedicated circuit between the caller and the receiver.

The communication continues through this circuit until the call ends.

During the call, the entire path remains reserved exclusively for those two users.

Even if there is a brief pause in the conversation, the circuit remains active until the call is disconnected.

Summary

Circuit switching is a communication technique in which a dedicated path is established between the sender and receiver before data transmission begins.

The communication process involves three phases: circuit establishment, data transfer, and circuit termination.

Although circuit switching provides reliable and continuous communication, it may lead to inefficient use of network resources because the communication channel remains reserved for the entire duration of the session.

Despite its limitations, circuit switching played an important role in traditional telephone networks and laid the foundation for modern communication technologies.

Packet Switching

In the previous section, we studied circuit switching, where a dedicated path is established between the sender and the receiver before communication begins. Although circuit switching provides continuous communication, it is not always efficient because the communication path remains reserved even when no data is being transmitted.

Modern computer networks use a different switching technique called packet switching.

Packet switching is a communication method in which data is divided into small units called packets, and each packet is transmitted independently through the network.

Unlike circuit switching, packet switching does not require a dedicated path between the sender and the receiver. Instead, packets travel through the network using the most available routes.

Data divided into packets traveling through different network paths

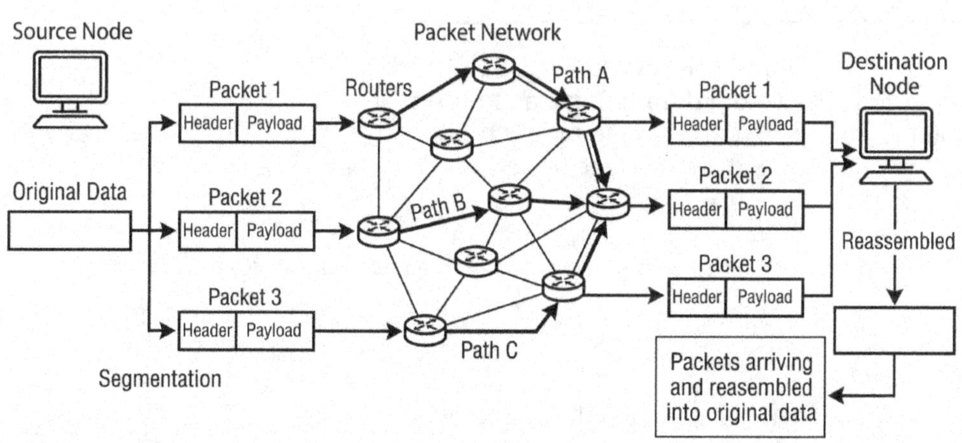

Packet switching is the foundation of modern networks such as the Internet, Wi-Fi networks, and mobile data networks.

Basic Idea of Packet Switching

In packet switching, the message or data to be transmitted is first divided into small pieces called packets.

Each packet contains two important parts:

Header.
Payload.

The header contains control information such as:

Source address.
Destination address.
Packet number.
Error detection information.

The payload contains the actual data being transmitted.

After the message is divided into packets, each packet is transmitted independently through the network.

These packets may travel through different routes to reach the destination.

Structure of a packet showing header and payload

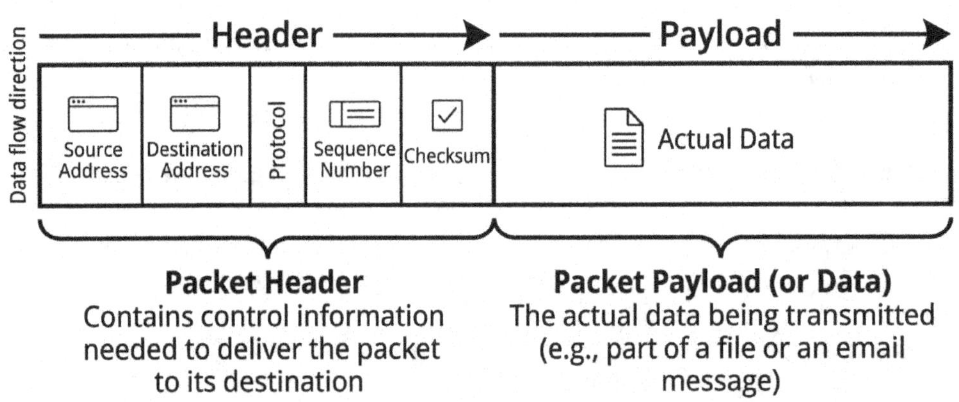

At the destination, the packets are reassembled in the correct order to reconstruct the original message.

How Packet Switching Works

The packet switching process can be explained through the following steps.

First, the sender divides the message into smaller packets.

Second, each packet is assigned a header containing important routing information.

Third, the packets are transmitted through the network using available routes.

Fourth, routers and switches in the network decide the best path for each packet.

Finally, the packets arrive at the destination and are reassembled to recreate the original message.

PACKETS TRAVELING THROUGH ROUTERS AND REACHING DESTINATION

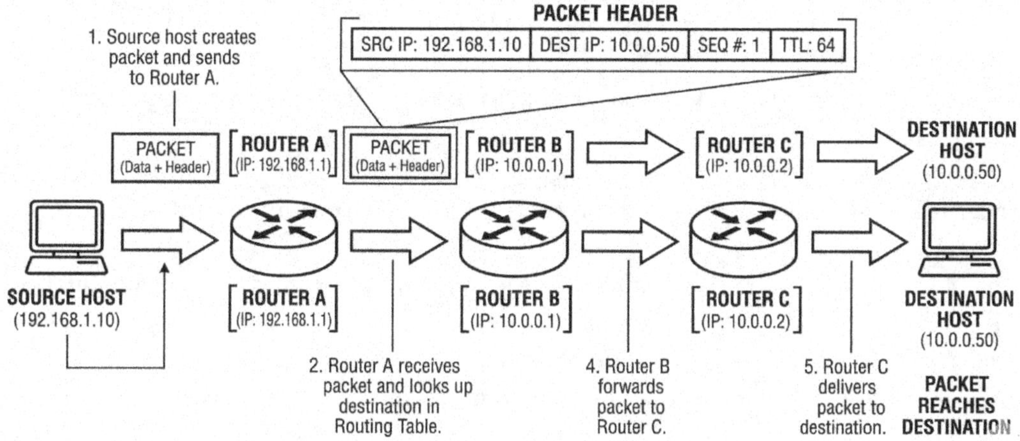

Because packets may travel through different paths, they may arrive at the destination in different orders. The receiving system rearranges them correctly using the packet sequence numbers.

Characteristics of Packet Switching

Packet switching has several important characteristics.

First, data is transmitted in the form of packets instead of continuous signals.

Second, the communication channel is not reserved for a single user.

Third, packets may take different paths through the network.

Fourth, network resources are shared among multiple users.

Because of these characteristics, packet switching allows more efficient use of network resources compared to circuit switching.

Advantages of Packet Switching

Packet switching offers several advantages in modern communication networks.

One major advantage is efficient use of network resources. Since the communication channel is shared among multiple users, the network can support many simultaneous connections.

Another advantage is greater flexibility. If one path becomes congested or unavailable, packets can be routed through alternative paths.

Packet switching also supports error detection and retransmission, which improves communication reliability.

Because of these advantages, packet switching is widely used in modern networking systems such as the Internet.

Limitations of Packet Switching

Although packet switching offers many benefits, it also has some limitations.

Since packets may travel through different routes, they may arrive at the destination at different times. This can cause delay variations, also known as jitter.

Another limitation is that network congestion may occur if too many packets are transmitted at the same time.

In some applications such as real-time voice communication, delays and jitter may affect the quality of communication.

However, modern technologies such as Quality of Service (QoS) help manage these issues in modern networks.

Real-World Example

The best example of packet switching is the Internet.

When you send an email, download a file, or watch a video online, the data is divided into small packets.

These packets travel through multiple routers across the network until they reach the destination.

For example, when you open a website, your request is divided into packets and transmitted through the Internet. The server responds by sending the webpage data in packets, which are then reassembled by your computer.

Without packet switching, the Internet would not be able to support millions of users communicating simultaneously.

Circuit Switching vs Packet Switching

Circuit switching and packet switching are two important switching techniques used in communication networks.

In circuit switching, a dedicated communication path is established before data transmission begins. In packet switching, data is divided into packets that travel independently through the network.

Circuit switching is suitable for continuous communication such as traditional telephone calls, while packet switching is better suited for modern data communication systems.

Conceptual comparison of circuit switching and packet switching

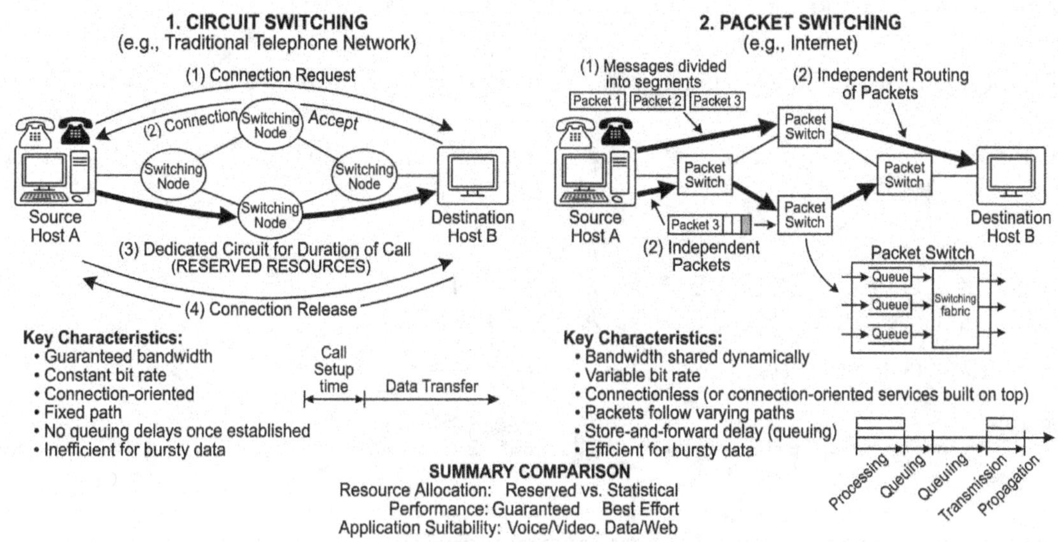

Importance of Packet Switching in Modern Networks

Packet switching is the backbone of modern computer networks.

Technologies such as Ethernet, Internet Protocol (IP), and wireless networks rely heavily on packet switching.

Because packet switching allows efficient sharing of network resources, it enables millions of devices around the world to communicate through the Internet.

Understanding packet switching helps students understand how modern communication systems handle large volumes of data efficiently.

Summary

Packet switching is a communication technique in which data is divided into small units called packets and transmitted independently through the network.

Each packet contains header information that helps it reach the correct destination.

Unlike circuit switching, packet switching does not require a dedicated communication path, making it more efficient for modern communication networks.

Packet switching is widely used in technologies such as the Internet, wireless networks, and mobile communication systems.

Message Switching

In the previous sections, we studied circuit switching and packet switching, which are two important switching techniques used in communication networks. Before packet switching became widely used, another switching technique called message switching was used in early communication systems.

Message switching is a communication method in which the entire message is sent from the source to the destination through intermediate nodes without establishing a dedicated communication path.

In this technique, the message is transmitted as a single unit, rather than dividing it into smaller packets.

Each intermediate node temporarily stores the entire message before forwarding it to the next node. This process is known as the store-and-forward technique.

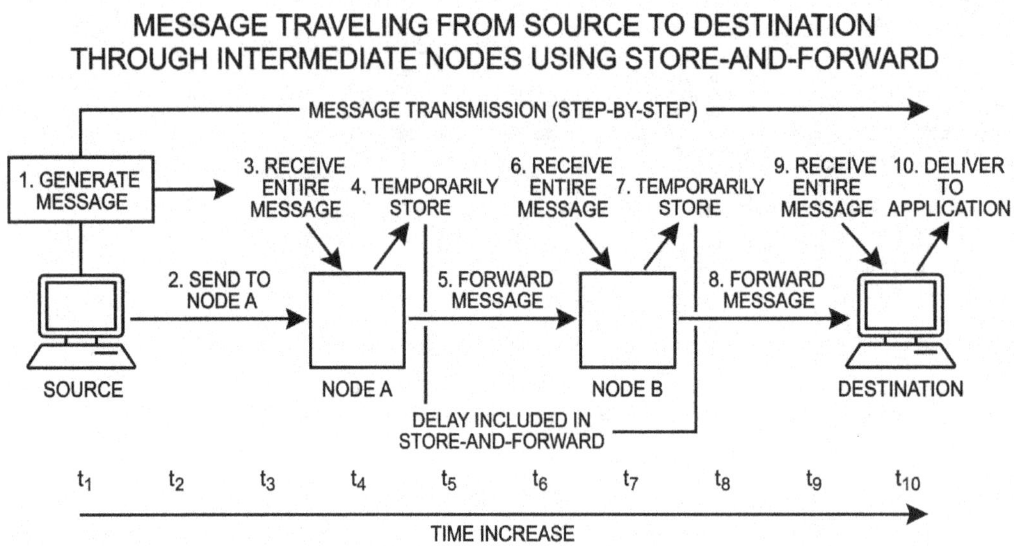

Although message switching is not commonly used in modern networks, it played an important role in the development of data communication systems.

Basic Idea of Message Switching

In message switching, the sender transmits the entire message to the first intermediate node in the network.

This node receives the message and temporarily stores it in its memory. After storing the message, the node checks the destination address and determines the next node to which the message should be forwarded.

The message is then transmitted to the next node, where the same process occurs again.

This process continues until the message finally reaches the destination.

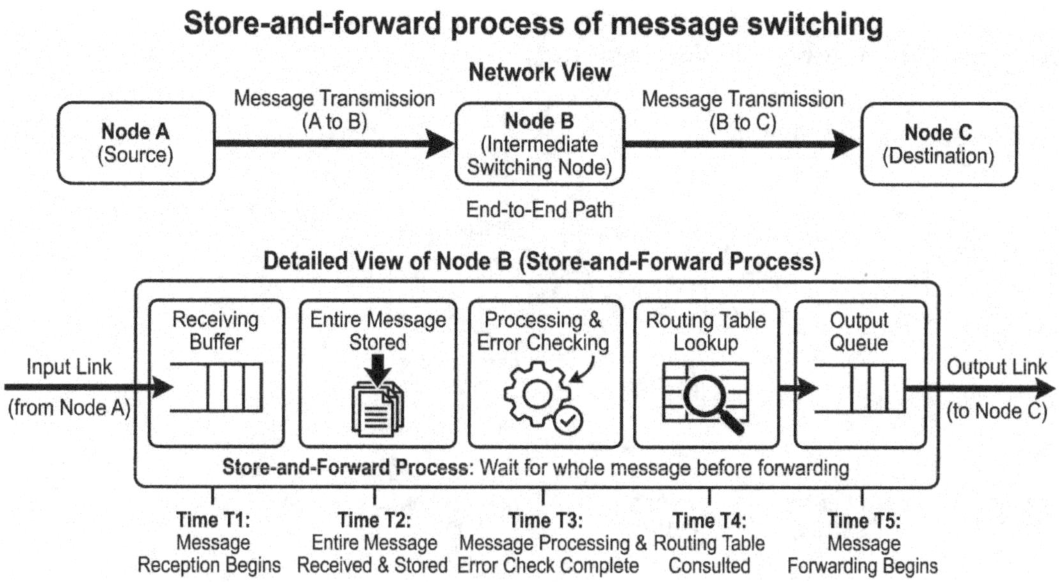

Because the entire message is stored at each intermediate node before being forwarded, this technique is called the store-and-forward switching technique.

How Message Switching Works

The message switching process can be explained in the following steps.

First, the sender creates the complete message and attaches the destination address.

Second, the message is transmitted to the nearest switching node.

Third, the switching node stores the message in its memory.

Fourth, the node determines the best path for forwarding the message to the next node.

Finally, the message continues traveling through multiple nodes until it reaches the destination.

Message moving through multiple nodes in a network.

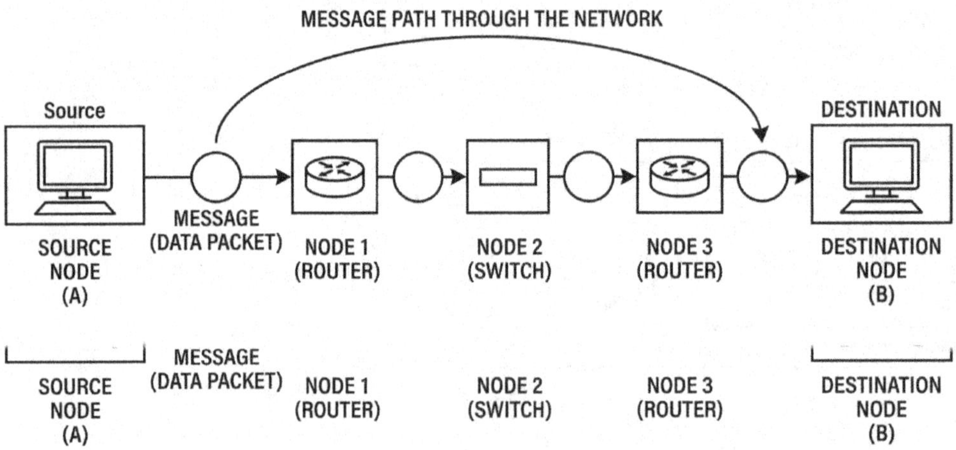

Unlike circuit switching, no dedicated communication path is established before transmission begins.

Characteristics of Message Switching

Message switching has several important characteristics.

First, the entire message is transmitted as a single unit rather than being divided into smaller parts.

Second, intermediate nodes store the complete message before forwarding it.

Third, no dedicated communication path is required between the sender and receiver.

Fourth, the communication channel is used only when the message is actually being transmitted.

Because of these characteristics, message switching allows flexible communication between network devices.

Advantages of Message Switching

Message switching offers several advantages compared to earlier communication methods.

One advantage is that it does not require a dedicated communication path. This allows the communication channel to be shared by multiple users.

Another advantage is that messages can be routed through different paths depending on network conditions.

Message switching also allows the system to store messages temporarily if the destination node is busy or unavailable.

Because of these features, message switching was considered more efficient than circuit switching in certain situations.

Limitations of Message Switching

Although message switching provided several improvements over circuit switching, it also had some important limitations.

One major limitation is that intermediate nodes must store the entire message, which requires large amounts of memory.

Another limitation is that storing and forwarding large messages can cause significant delays in communication.

If the message is very large, the node must wait until the entire message is received before forwarding it to the next node.

This delay makes message switching unsuitable for real-time communication such as voice calls.

Because of these limitations, message switching was eventually replaced by packet switching, which divides messages into smaller packets.

Message Switching vs Packet Switching

Message switching and packet switching are similar in some ways, but they also have important differences.

In message switching, the entire message is transmitted as one unit. In packet switching, the message is divided into smaller packets before transmission.

In message switching, intermediate nodes must store the complete message before forwarding it. In packet switching, nodes only store and forward smaller packets.

Because packets are smaller, packet switching allows faster and more efficient data transmission.

COMPARISON OF MESSAGE SWITCHING AND PACKET SWITCHING

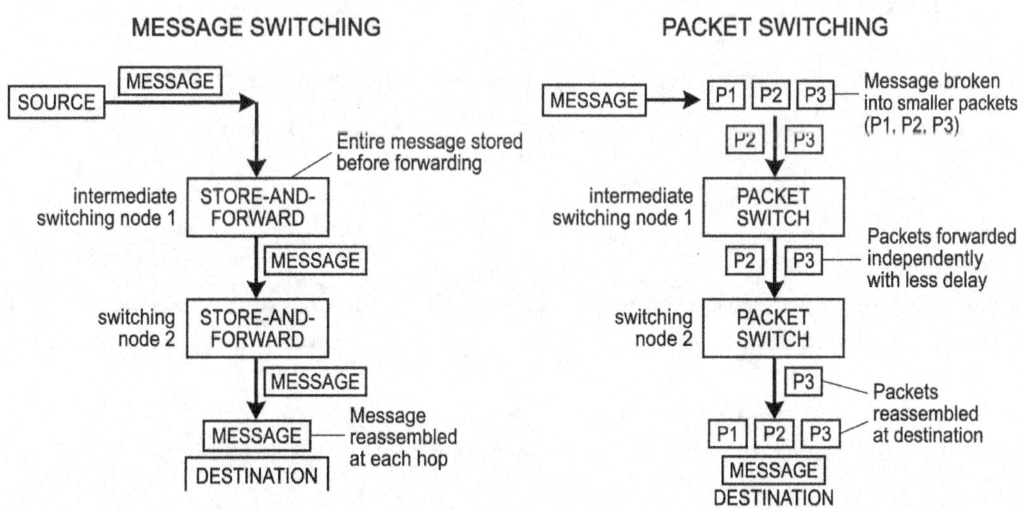

For these reasons, packet switching became the preferred method in modern computer networks.

Historical Importance of Message Switching

Message switching played an important role in early communication systems.

One well-known example of message switching was the telegraph network, where messages were transmitted through multiple relay stations before reaching their final destination.

Message switching also influenced the development of modern packet-switched networks.

Many concepts used in packet switching, such as store-and-forward transmission, originated from message switching techniques.

Understanding message switching helps students understand how communication technologies evolved over time.

Summary

Message switching is a communication technique in which the entire message is transmitted from the sender to the receiver through intermediate nodes using the store-and-forward method.

Unlike circuit switching, message switching does not require a dedicated communication path.

However, because intermediate nodes must store the complete message before forwarding it, message switching can cause significant delays.

Due to these limitations, message switching has largely been replaced by packet switching in modern communication systems.

Despite this, message switching remains an important concept for understanding the history and evolution of computer networks.

Comparison of Switching Techniques

In the previous sections, we studied three important switching techniques used in communication networks:

Circuit Switching.
Packet Switching.
Message Switching.

Each of these techniques was developed to solve communication problems in different types of networks. Although all three methods are used to transmit data from a source to a destination, the way they operate is different.

Understanding the differences between these switching techniques helps students understand how communication networks have evolved over time and why modern networks prefer packet switching.

Conceptual overviiewof circuit switching, packet switching, and message switching.

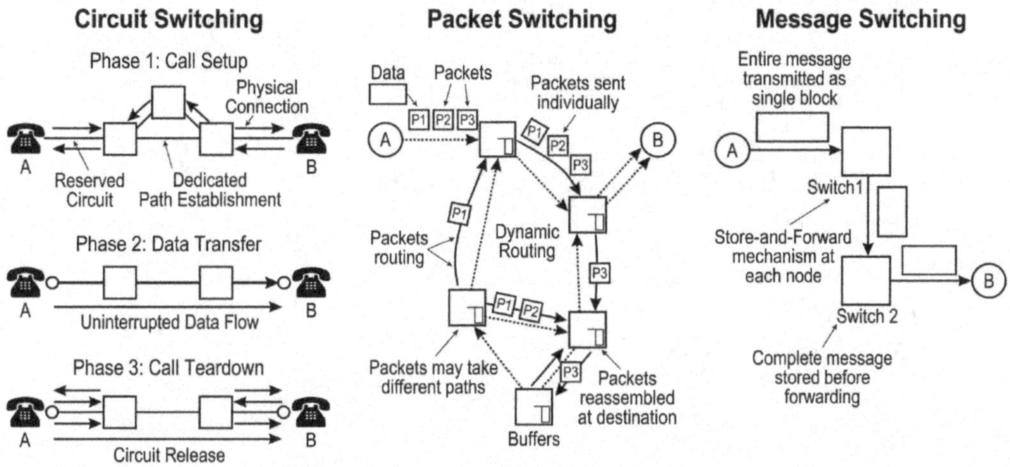

Comparison Based on Connection Establishment

One major difference between switching techniques is how the connection between devices is established.

In circuit switching, a dedicated communication path is established between the sender and the receiver before any data transmission begins. This connection remains active for the entire duration of the communication session.

In packet switching, no dedicated path is created. Instead, data is divided into packets, and each packet is transmitted independently through the network using available routes.

In message switching, a dedicated path is also not required. The entire message is transmitted from one node to another using the store-and-forward technique.

This difference makes packet switching and message switching more flexible compared to circuit switching.

Comparison Based on Data Transmission Method

Another important difference lies in how data is transmitted.

In circuit switching, data is transmitted continuously once the communication path is established. The sender and receiver communicate through the reserved circuit without interruptions.

In packet switching, data is divided into smaller units called packets. These packets are transmitted independently through the network and may travel through different paths.

In message switching, the entire message is transmitted as a single unit without dividing it into smaller packets.

Because packet switching divides data into smaller pieces, it allows more efficient transmission of information.

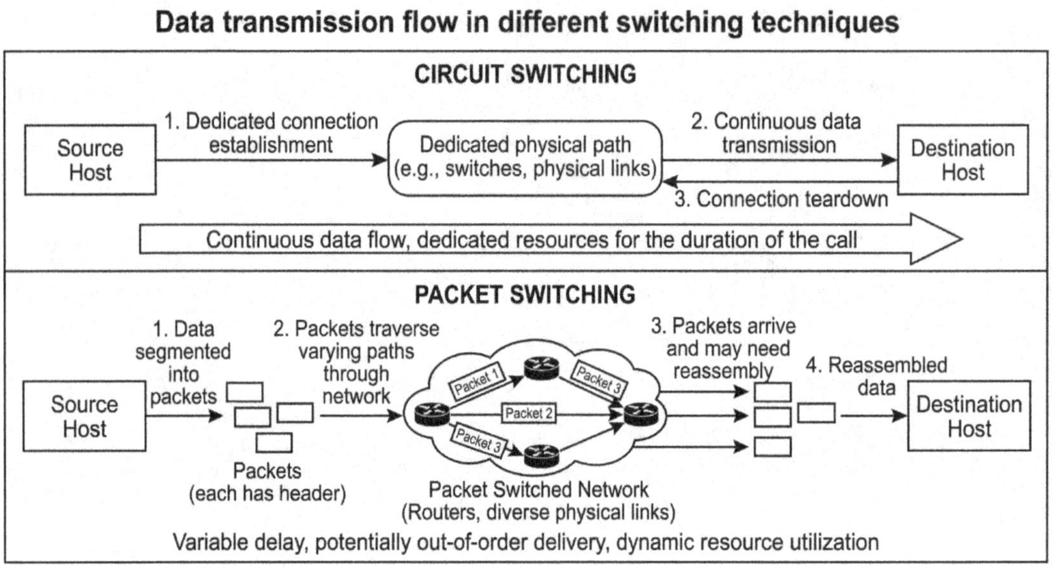

Comparison Based on Network Resource Usage

Network resource usage is another important factor when comparing switching techniques.

In circuit switching, the communication channel remains reserved for the entire duration of the communication session, even if no data is being transmitted. This leads to inefficient use of network resources.

In packet switching, the communication channel is shared by multiple users. Packets are transmitted only when data needs to be sent, which improves network efficiency.

In message switching, the communication channel is also shared among users. However, the entire message must be stored at each intermediate node before being forwarded.

Because packet switching uses network resources more efficiently, it is preferred in modern communication networks.

Comparison Based on Transmission Delay

Transmission delay is another important factor in communication systems.

In circuit switching, there is an initial delay during the connection establishment phase. However, once the connection is established, data transmission occurs continuously with minimal delay.

In message switching, delays can be significant because each intermediate node must store the entire message before forwarding it.

In packet switching, some delay may occur due to packet routing and network congestion. However, since packets are smaller, the delay is generally lower compared to message switching.

Because of this, packet switching provides a good balance between efficiency and speed.

Comparison Based on Reliability

Reliability refers to how well the communication system delivers data correctly.

In circuit switching, the communication path is fixed once established. This provides stable communication but does not easily adapt if the path becomes unavailable.

In packet switching, packets can be routed through alternative paths if one path becomes congested or unavailable. This increases reliability in large networks such as the Internet.

In message switching, reliability depends on the storage and forwarding capabilities of intermediate nodes.

Modern communication systems prefer packet switching because it offers better adaptability and reliability.

Comparison Based on Applications

Each switching technique is suitable for different types of communication systems.

Circuit switching was widely used in traditional telephone networks, where continuous communication was required.

Message switching was used in early telegraph networks and early computer communication systems.

Packet switching is widely used in modern computer networks, Internet communication, wireless networks, and mobile data communication.

Because of its flexibility and efficiency, packet switching has become the foundation of modern networking systems.

Applications of different switching techniques.

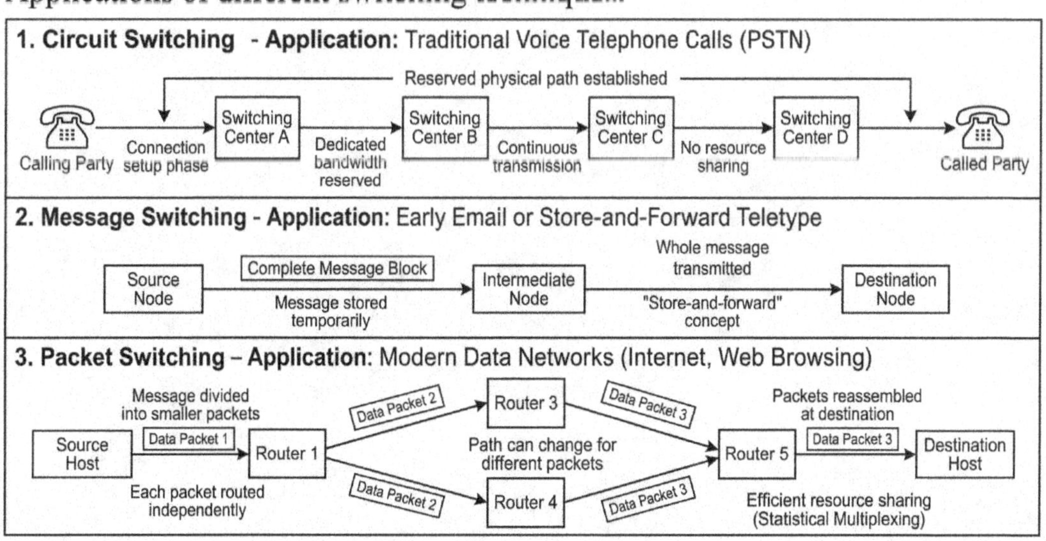

Evolution of Switching Techniques

Communication technologies have evolved significantly over time.

Initially, circuit switching was widely used for voice communication because it provided stable and uninterrupted communication.

Later, message switching introduced the concept of store-and-forward communication, which improved resource utilization.

Finally, packet switching emerged as the most efficient method for modern data communication systems.

Packet switching combines the advantages of flexible routing and efficient resource utilization, making it ideal for modern large-scale networks.

Summary

Circuit switching, message switching, and packet switching are three important switching techniques used in communication networks.

Circuit switching establishes a dedicated communication path before transmission begins. Message switching transmits the entire message using the store-and-forward technique. Packet switching divides data into smaller packets and transmits them independently through the network.

Among these techniques, packet switching is the most widely used in modern computer networks because it provides efficient resource utilization, flexibility, and improved reliability.

Understanding the differences between these switching techniques helps students understand how communication networks function and how they have evolved over time.

CHAPTER EIGHT

Data Link Layer Protocols

ALOHA Protocol

In computer networks, many devices often share the same communication channel to transmit data. When multiple devices try to send data at the same time, there is a possibility that their signals may interfere with each other. This situation is known as a collision.

To manage how devices access a shared communication channel, special communication methods called multiple access protocols are used. One of the earliest and simplest multiple access protocols developed for computer networks is the ALOHA Protocol.

The ALOHA protocol is a random access protocol that allows multiple devices to transmit data over a shared communication channel.

It was originally developed in the University of Hawaii in the early 1970s for wireless communication between computers located on different islands.

The main goal of the ALOHA protocol was to allow multiple users to send data through a common communication channel without requiring complex coordination.

MULTIPLE DEVICES TRANSMITTING DATA TO A SHARED COMMUNICATION CHANNEL USING ALOHA.

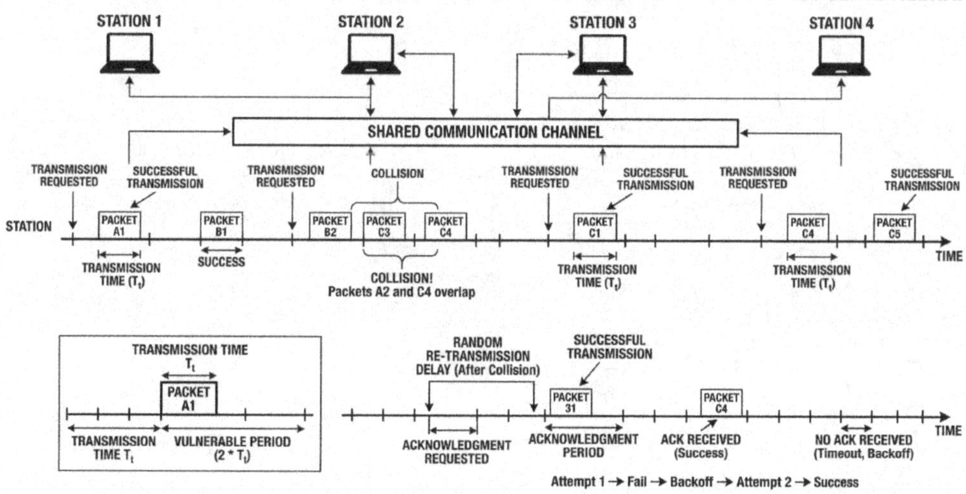

Concept of Random Access Protocols

Before understanding how ALOHA works, it is important to understand the idea of random access protocols.

In a shared communication medium, multiple devices compete for access to the same channel. Random access protocols allow devices to transmit data whenever they have data to send, without waiting for a strict schedule.

However, because many devices may attempt to transmit data at the same time, collisions can occur.

Random access protocols provide mechanisms to detect collisions and retransmit the data when necessary.

ALOHA is considered the simplest form of random access protocol.

Basic Working of the ALOHA Protocol

The operation of the ALOHA protocol is very simple.

When a device has data to send, it immediately transmits the data frame onto the communication channel without checking whether the channel is currently in use.

If the frame reaches the destination successfully, the receiver sends an acknowledgment message (ACK) back to the sender.

However, if two devices transmit data at the same time, their signals overlap and cause a collision. In such cases, the data frame becomes corrupted and cannot be correctly received.

If the sender does not receive the acknowledgment within a certain time, it assumes that a collision has occurred. The sender then waits for a random amount of time before attempting to retransmit the data.

This random waiting period reduces the probability of repeated collisions.

Collision occurring when two devices transmit data simultaneously.

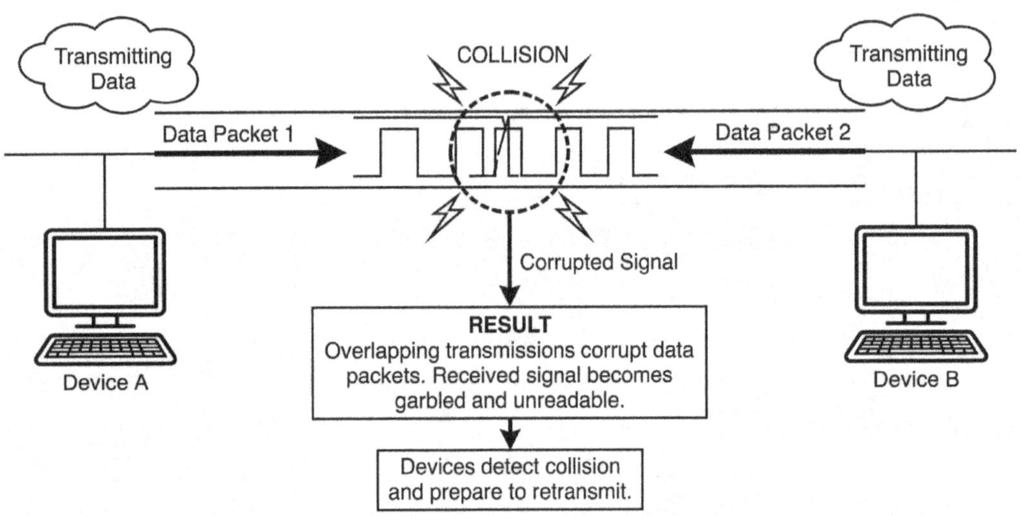

Steps in ALOHA Communication

The working of the ALOHA protocol can be explained through the following steps:

A device prepares a data frame that needs to be transmitted.

The device sends the frame immediately onto the communication channel.
The receiver checks the frame and sends an acknowledgment if it is received correctly.
If the sender receives the acknowledgment, the transmission is considered successful.
If no acknowledgment is received within a specific time, the sender assumes that a collision occurred.
The sender waits for a random time and retransmits the frame.

This process continues until the frame is successfully transmitted.

Flow of data transmission and acknowlegment in ALOHA.

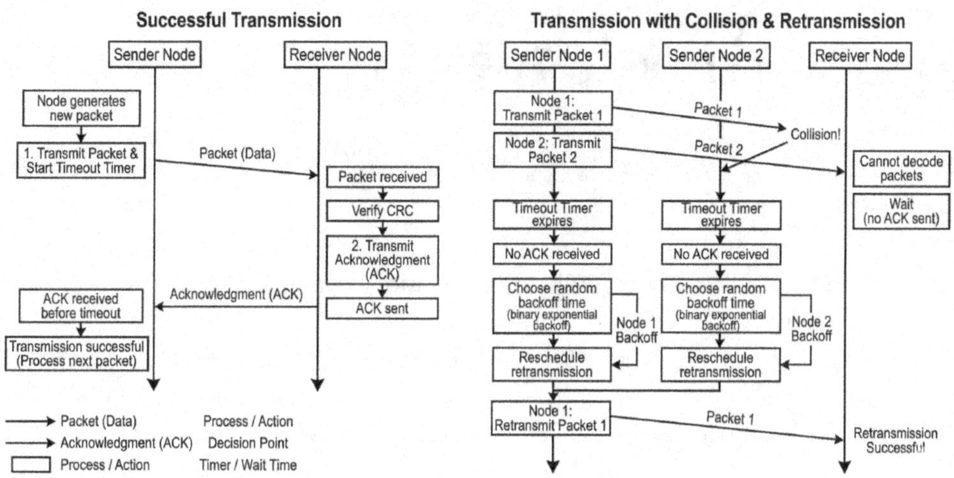

Collision in ALOHA

One of the major challenges in shared communication systems is data collision.

A collision occurs when two or more devices transmit data at the same time on the same communication channel.

When a collision happens, the signals overlap and the receiver cannot correctly interpret the transmitted data.

As a result, the data frame must be retransmitted.

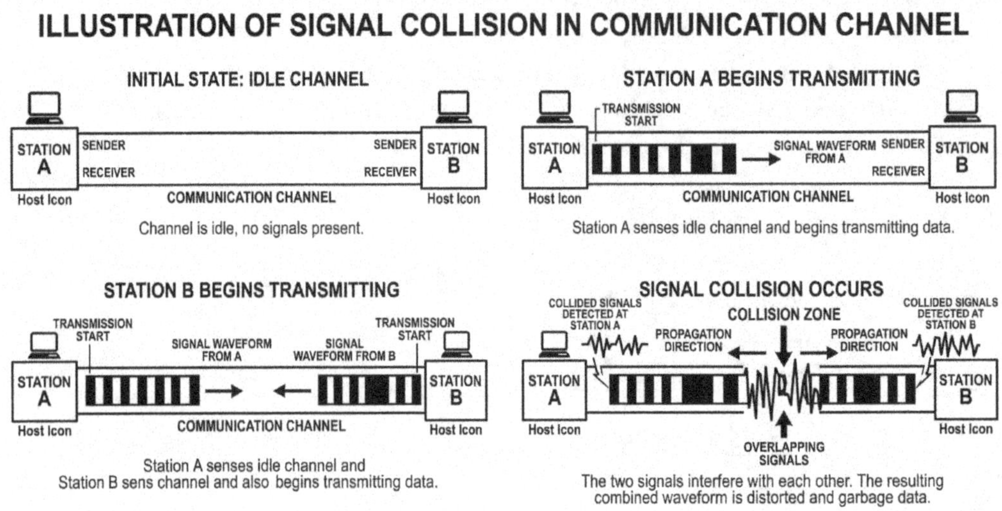

Because ALOHA allows devices to transmit data at any time, collisions are quite common in this protocol.

Vulnerable Period in ALOHA

The vulnerable period is the time during which a transmitted frame is susceptible to collisions.

In the ALOHA protocol, the vulnerable period is equal to twice the frame transmission time.

This means that if another device begins transmitting within this time interval, a collision will occur.

For example, if a frame takes T seconds to transmit, the vulnerable period will be 2T seconds.

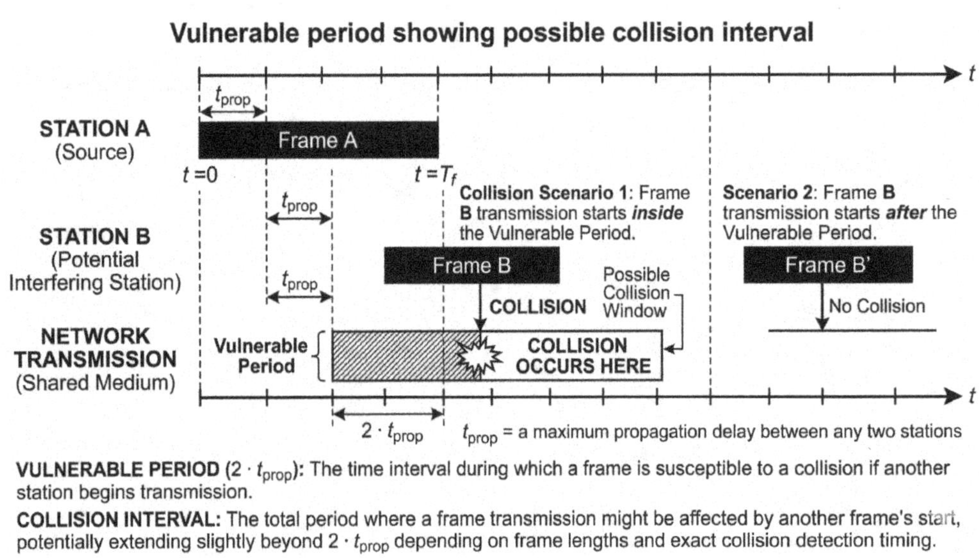

Because of this long vulnerable period, the probability of collisions in ALOHA is relatively high.

Efficiency of the ALOHA Protocol

Efficiency refers to how effectively the communication channel is utilized.

In the pure ALOHA protocol, the maximum theoretical efficiency is about 18.4%.

This means that only about 18% of the channel capacity can be used successfully for data transmission.

The remaining capacity is lost due to collisions and retransmissions.

Although this efficiency may seem low, ALOHA was an important milestone in the development of multiple access communication systems.

Later protocols such as Slotted ALOHA and CSMA/CD were developed to improve efficiency.

Advantages of ALOHA Protocol

The ALOHA protocol offers several advantages.

First, it is very simple to implement because devices transmit data without checking the channel.

Second, it allows devices to send data whenever they need to, which makes it flexible.

Third, it is suitable for communication systems where the number of users is relatively small.

Because of its simplicity, ALOHA played an important role in the early development of wireless communication systems.

Limitations of ALOHA Protocol

Although ALOHA is simple and flexible, it has some limitations.

The most significant limitation is the high probability of collisions.

Because devices transmit data without checking the channel, many transmissions may overlap and cause collisions.

Another limitation is the low channel efficiency, which means that a large portion of the communication capacity is wasted due to collisions and retransmissions.

These limitations led researchers to develop improved versions of the protocol.

Real-World Significance of ALOHA

Even though the original ALOHA protocol is not widely used today, it played a crucial role in the development of modern networking technologies.

The concepts introduced by ALOHA helped in the design of other access protocols such as:

Slotted ALOHA

CSMA (Carrier Sense Multiple Access)
CSMA/CD used in Ethernet networks

These protocols significantly improved network efficiency and reliability.

Understanding the ALOHA protocol helps students understand the basic challenges of shared communication channels and how networking protocols evolved over time.

Summary

The ALOHA protocol is one of the earliest random access protocols designed for communication over shared channels.

It allows devices to transmit data whenever they have data to send, but collisions may occur if multiple devices transmit simultaneously.

If a collision occurs, the sender waits for a random time and retransmits the data frame.

Although the efficiency of the ALOHA protocol is relatively low, it laid the foundation for more advanced communication protocols used in modern computer networks.

Slotted ALOHA

In the previous section, we studied the ALOHA protocol, which allows devices to transmit data whenever they have data to send. Although this method is simple, it has a major drawback: collisions occur frequently because devices can transmit data at any time.

To reduce the number of collisions and improve network efficiency, an improved version of the ALOHA protocol was developed. This improved version is known as Slotted ALOHA.

The Slotted ALOHA protocol is a random access protocol in which time is divided into equal time slots, and devices are allowed to transmit data only at the beginning of a time slot.

By restricting transmissions to specific time slots, the chances of collisions are significantly reduced.

DIAGRAM TITLE: TIME DIVIDED INTO SLOTS WITH DEVICES TRANSMITTING ONLY AT SLOT BOUNDARIES

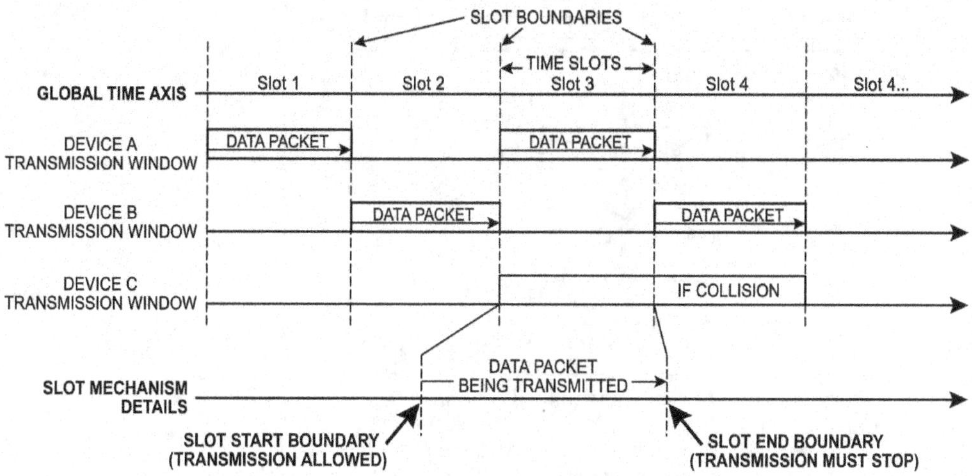

Need for Slotted ALOHA

In the original ALOHA protocol, devices transmit frames whenever they want. This means that frames can start at any moment, and overlapping transmissions are very common.

Because of this, the vulnerable period in pure ALOHA is very large, which increases the probability of collisions.

Researchers realized that if transmissions could be synchronized into fixed time intervals, the vulnerable period could be reduced.

This idea led to the development of Slotted ALOHA.

By allowing transmissions only at the beginning of specific time slots, the protocol reduces the possibility of overlapping transmissions.

Basic Concept of Time Slots

In Slotted ALOHA, time is divided into equal intervals called slots.

Each slot is designed to be exactly long enough to transmit one data frame.

This means that a device must wait until the start of the next available slot before transmitting its frame.

If two or more devices attempt to transmit during the same time slot, a collision will occur. However, if only one device transmits during a slot, the transmission will be successful.

Time slots showing successful transmission and collision.

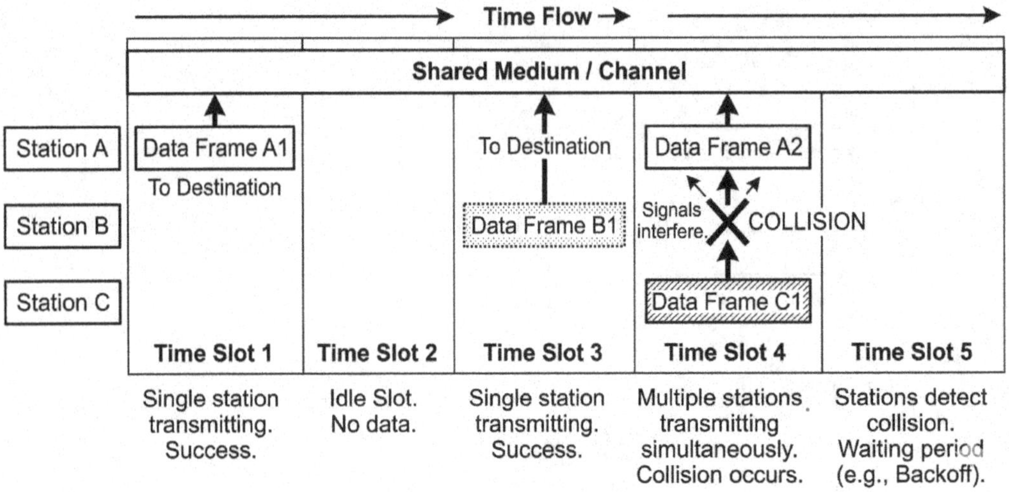

This method significantly reduces the vulnerable period compared to pure ALOHA.

Working of Slotted ALOHA

The operation of the Slotted ALOHA protocol can be explained through the following steps.

Time is divided into equal slots.
A device that wants to transmit data waits for the beginning of the next time slot.
The device transmits its frame at the start of the slot.
If only one device transmits during that slot, the transmission is successful.
If two or more devices transmit in the same slot, a collision occurs.

When a collision occurs, the devices wait for a random number of time slots before attempting to retransmit.

Two devices transmitting in the same slot causing collision

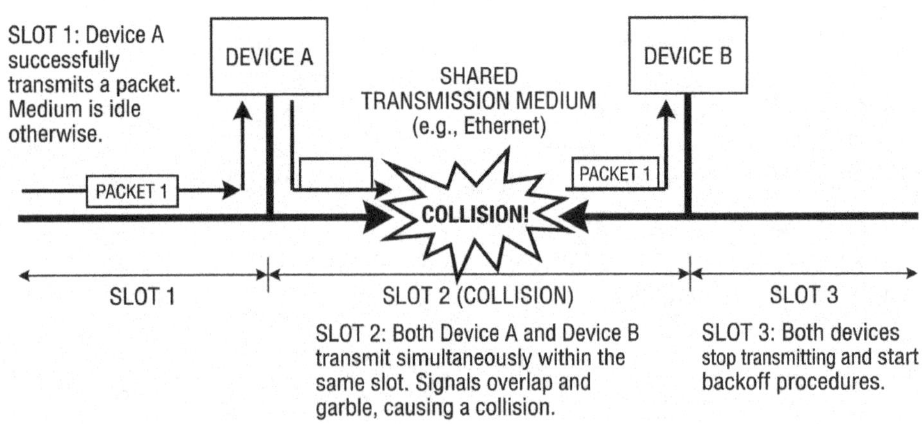

The random waiting period helps prevent repeated collisions.

Vulnerable Period in Slotted ALOHA

The vulnerable period is the time interval during which another transmission can cause a collision.

In pure ALOHA, the vulnerable period is 2T, where T is the time required to transmit a frame.

In Slotted ALOHA, the vulnerable period is reduced to T, which means the frame is vulnerable only during its own time slot.

Vulnerability period comparison between Pure ALOHA and Slotted ALOHA.

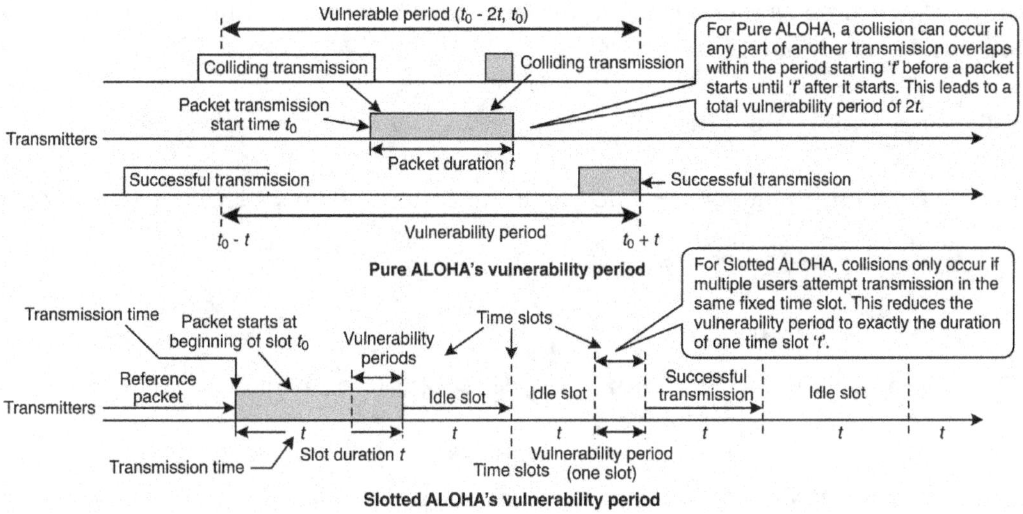

Because the vulnerable period is smaller, Slotted ALOHA experiences fewer collisions than pure ALOHA.

Efficiency of Slotted ALOHA

One of the main improvements of Slotted ALOHA over pure ALOHA is higher channel efficiency.

The maximum theoretical efficiency of pure ALOHA is approximately 18.4%.

In contrast, the maximum efficiency of Slotted ALOHA is approximately 36.8%.

This means that Slotted ALOHA can utilize the communication channel almost twice as efficiently as pure ALOHA.

Although this improvement is significant, collisions can still occur when multiple devices attempt to transmit during the same slot.

Advantages of Slotted ALOHA

Slotted ALOHA provides several advantages over the original ALOHA protocol.

First, it reduces the probability of collisions by synchronizing transmissions.

Second, it improves channel utilization and efficiency.

Third, it provides a simple method for managing communication in networks with multiple users.

Because of these advantages, Slotted ALOHA became an important step in the development of more advanced access protocols.

Limitations of Slotted ALOHA

Despite its improvements, Slotted ALOHA still has some limitations.

One limitation is that devices must synchronize their clocks so that they know when each time slot begins. This synchronization may require additional system complexity.

Another limitation is that collisions can still occur if multiple devices choose the same slot for transmission.

Because of these limitations, further improvements were developed in later protocols such as Carrier Sense Multiple Access (CSMA) and CSMA/CD.

Real-World Applications

Although Slotted ALOHA is not commonly used in modern wired networks, its principles are used in several communication systems.

For example, Slotted ALOHA is used in some satellite communication systems and wireless communication technologies where multiple users share the same communication channel.

The protocol provides a simple method for managing shared communication resources.

Summary

The Slotted ALOHA protocol is an improved version of the ALOHA protocol that divides time into equal slots. Devices are allowed to transmit data only at the beginning of these slots.

This method reduces the vulnerable period and decreases the probability of collisions, leading to higher channel efficiency.

Although collisions can still occur, Slotted ALOHA provides a significant improvement over the original ALOHA protocol and helped inspire more advanced multiple access protocols used in modern computer networks.

CSMA/CD Protocol

(Carrier Sense Multiple Access with Collision Detection)

In previous sections, we studied ALOHA and Slotted ALOHA protocols, which allow multiple devices to share a common communication channel. Although Slotted ALOHA improves efficiency compared to pure ALOHA, collisions can still occur frequently when multiple devices attempt to transmit data at the same time.

To further reduce collisions and improve communication efficiency, a more intelligent protocol called CSMA/CD (Carrier Sense Multiple Access with Collision Detection) was developed.

CSMA/CD is a protocol used mainly in Ethernet networks to control how devices transmit data over a shared communication medium.

The main idea behind CSMA/CD is simple: before sending data, a device first checks whether the communication channel is free or already being used by another device.

Diagram Title: Multiple devices checking the channel before transmitting data.

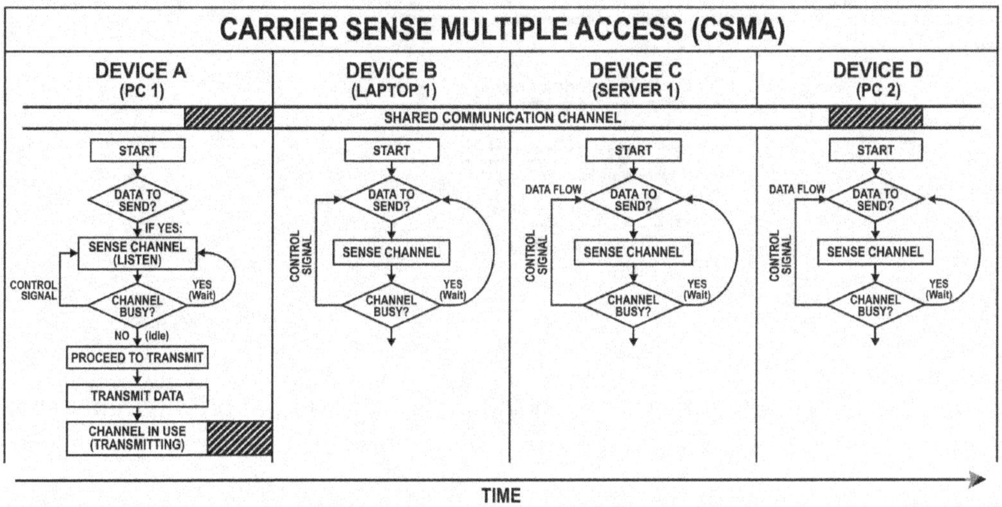

This mechanism helps reduce the number of collisions in the network.

Meaning of CSMA/CD

To understand this protocol clearly, let us break down the full form of CSMA/CD.

Carrier Sense

Carrier sense means that a device listens to the communication channel before transmitting data.

If the channel is already busy, the device waits until the channel becomes free.

Multiple Access

Multiple access means that many devices share the same communication medium.

All devices connected to the network can attempt to send data through the same channel.

Collision Detection

Collision detection means that if two devices transmit data at the same time, the system can detect the collision and stop the transmission immediately.

Once a collision is detected, the devices involved will wait for a random period of time before trying to transmit again.

Coll ision detection during simultaneous transmission.

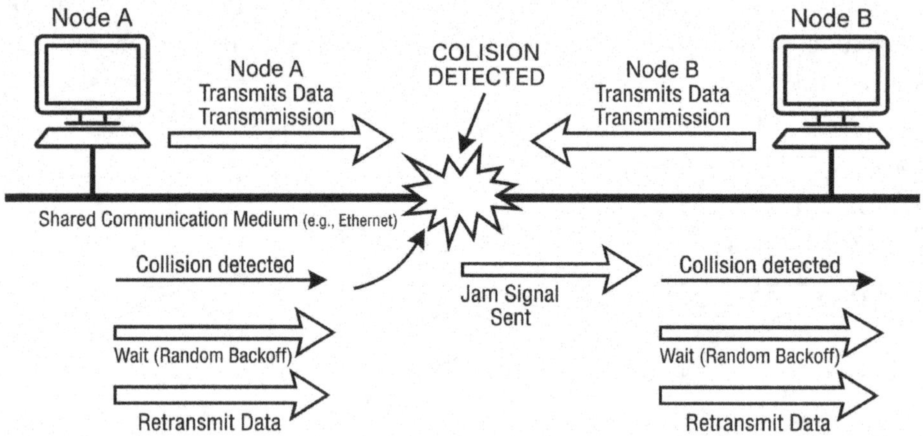

Working of CSMA/CD

The CSMA/CD protocol works through a sequence of steps that help manage communication between multiple devices.

Step 1: Listen to the Channel

Before sending data, the device checks whether the communication channel is idle or busy.
If the channel is busy, the device waits.
If the channel is free, the device begins transmitting data.

Step 2: Start Data Transmission

When the channel is free, the device starts transmitting the data frame onto the network.
During transmission, the device continues to monitor the channel to detect any possible collision.

Step 3: Collision Detection

If another device starts transmitting at the same time, a collision occurs.
The devices detect the collision by monitoring changes in the signal on the communication medium.

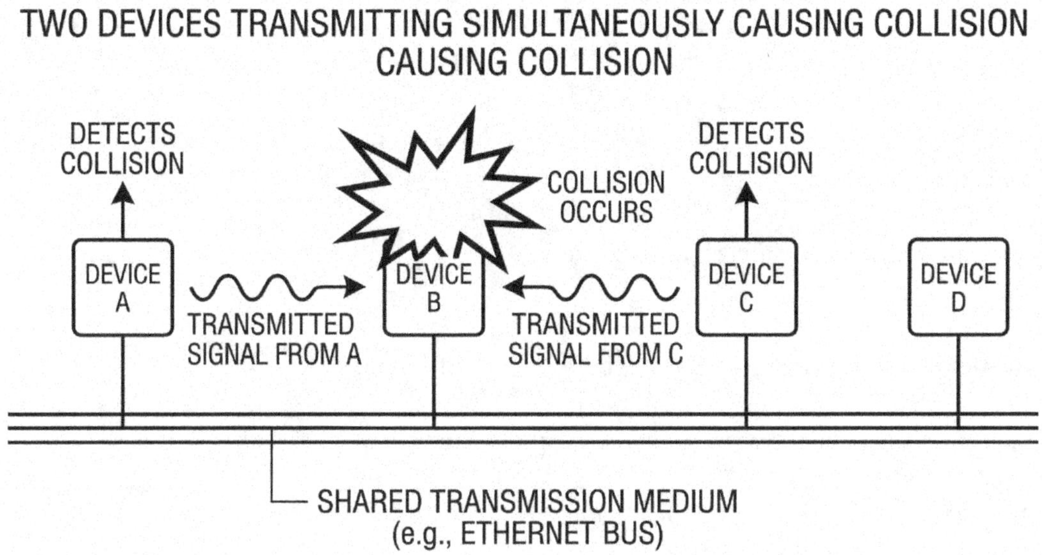

Step 4: Stop Transmission

When a collision is detected, the devices immediately stop transmitting data.
This prevents unnecessary transmission of corrupted frames.

Step 5: Send Jam Signal

After detecting a collision, the devices send a jam signal to ensure that all devices in the network become aware that a collision has occurred.
This helps maintain synchronization among devices.

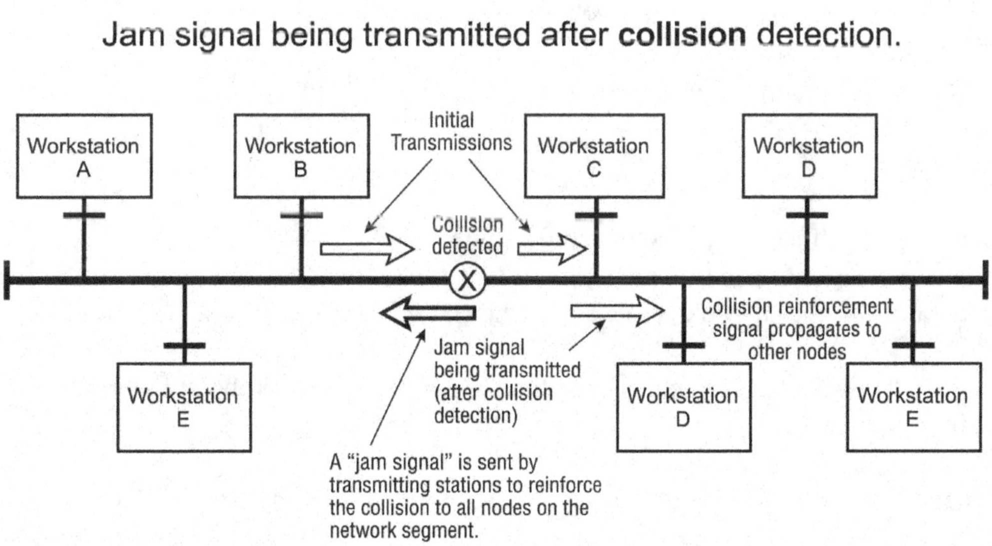

Step 6: Random Backoff Time

After the collision, each device waits for a random amount of time before attempting to retransmit the frame.
This waiting time is calculated using a method called the binary exponential backoff algorithm.

The purpose of this random delay is to reduce the chances of another collision occurring immediately.

Binary Exponential Backoff Algorithm

The binary exponential backoff algorithm is used to determine how long a device should wait before retransmitting data after a collision.

Each time a collision occurs, the waiting time increases exponentially.

For example:
After the first collision, the device waits for a random time between 0 and 1 time slot.

After the second collision, the waiting time increases between 0 and 3 time slots.

After further collisions, the waiting time range continues to increase.

This approach reduces the probability that the same devices will collide again.

Advantages of CSMA/CD

The CSMA/CD protocol provides several advantages in network communication.

First, it significantly reduces the number of collisions compared to earlier protocols like ALOHA.

Second, it improves the efficient use of the communication channel.

Third, it allows multiple devices to share the same network medium while maintaining organized communication.

Fourth, it is relatively simple to implement in Ethernet networks.

Because of these advantages, CSMA/CD became widely used in early Ethernet technologies.

Limitations of CSMA/CD

Although CSMA/CD improves network efficiency, it also has some limitations.

One limitation is that collisions can still occur if two devices detect the channel as free at the same time.

Another limitation is that CSMA/CD works best in small to medium-sized networks. As the number of devices increases, the probability of collisions may increase.

Additionally, modern high-speed Ethernet networks often use switches instead of shared media, which eliminates the need for collision detection.

Because of this, CSMA/CD is less common in modern switched networks.

Real-World Example

Consider a situation where several computers are connected to the same Ethernet network.

If one computer wants to send data, it first checks whether the network cable is currently in use.

If another computer is already transmitting data, the first computer waits.

If the cable is free, the computer begins transmitting.

If two computers accidentally start transmitting at the same time, the collision is detected, the transmission stops, and both devices wait for a random period before trying again.

This process ensures that the network operates efficiently.

Summary

The CSMA/CD protocol is a network communication method used in Ethernet networks to control access to a shared communication medium.

It works by allowing devices to listen to the channel before transmitting, detect collisions during transmission, and retransmit data after waiting for a random time.

By using carrier sensing and collision detection, CSMA/CD significantly improves communication efficiency compared to earlier protocols such as ALOHA and Slotted ALOHA.

Although modern networks often use switching technology that reduces collisions, understanding CSMA/CD remains important for learning the fundamentals of network communication.

Ethernet LAN

Ethernet is one of the most widely used technologies for Local Area Networks (LANs). It provides a standard method for connecting computers and other devices within a network so that they can communicate and share data.

Ethernet was originally developed in the 1970s by Robert Metcalfe and his colleagues at Xerox PARC. Over time, Ethernet became the most popular networking technology used in homes, offices, schools, and organizations.

An Ethernet LAN is a network in which multiple devices such as computers, printers, and servers are connected using Ethernet technology to exchange data.

Ethernet networks typically use twisted pair cables, coaxial cables, or fiber optic cables as transmission media.

Ethernet LAN showing multiple computers connected through a switch

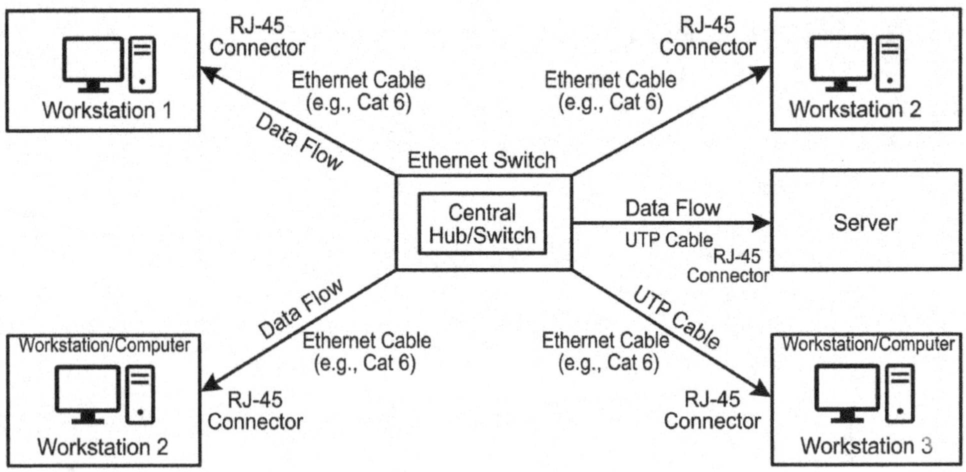

Because of its reliability, simplicity, and low cost, Ethernet has become the standard technology for building local area networks.

Basic Concept of Ethernet

Ethernet allows devices in a network to communicate by transmitting data frames through a communication medium.

In early Ethernet networks, devices were connected using a shared communication cable. Because multiple devices used the same cable, there was a possibility that two devices might attempt to send data at the same time.

To handle this situation, Ethernet originally used the CSMA/CD protocol, which allowed devices to detect collisions and retransmit data when necessary.

Modern Ethernet networks usually use switches, which reduce collisions and improve network performance.

Traditional Ethernet Bus Network vs Modern Switched Ethernet

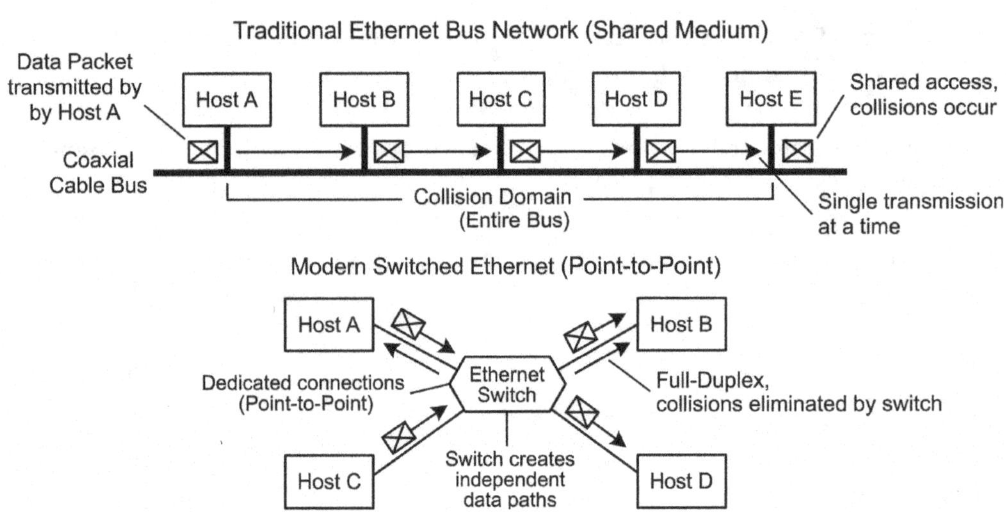

Ethernet Frame

In Ethernet communication, data is transmitted in the form of frames.

An Ethernet frame is a structured packet of data that contains important information needed for communication between devices.

An Ethernet frame includes several fields that help identify the sender, the receiver, and the type of data being transmitted.

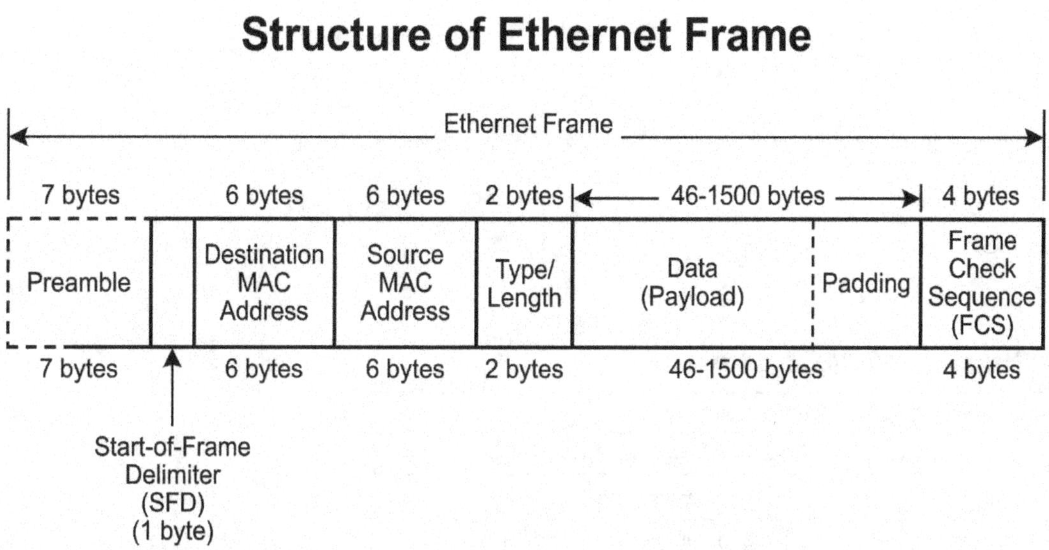

Fields of an Ethernet Frame

The Ethernet frame contains the following main components.

Preamble

The preamble is a sequence of bits used to synchronize communication between the sender and receiver. It allows the receiving device to prepare for incoming data.

Destination Address

This field contains the MAC address of the receiving device. The MAC address uniquely identifies each device in the network.

Source Address

This field contains the MAC address of the device sending the frame.

Type or Length Field

This field indicates the type of protocol or data contained in the frame.

Data Field
The data field contains the actual message or payload being transmitted.

Frame Check Sequence (FCS)
The Frame Check Sequence is used for error detection. It helps the receiver determine whether the data frame was transmitted correctly.

Ethernet Addressing
Ethernet networks use MAC addresses to identify devices.

A MAC address (Media Access Control address) is a unique hardware address assigned to a network interface card (NIC).

A MAC address typically consists of 48 bits and is usually written in hexadecimal form.

Example of a MAC address:

00:1A:2B:3C:4D:5E

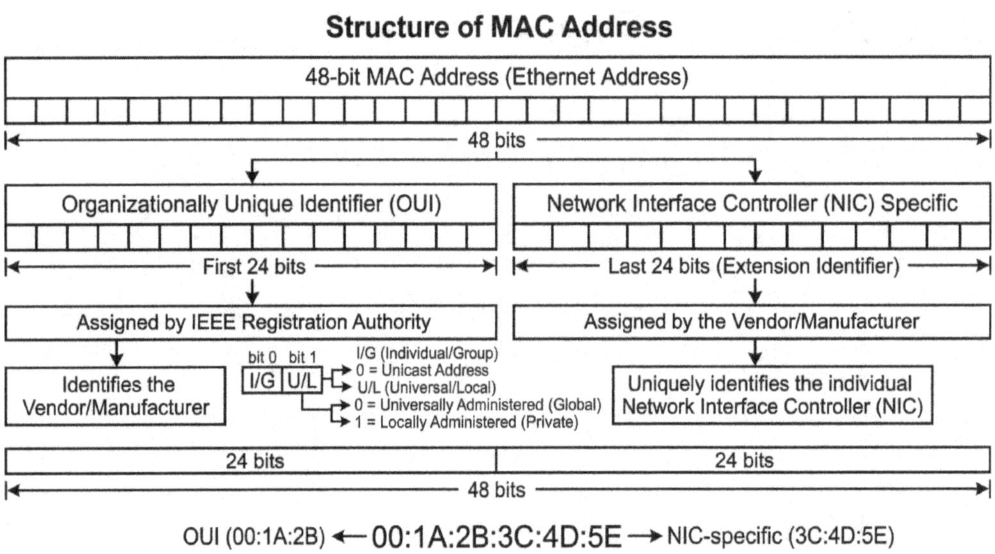

Because each device has a unique MAC address, Ethernet networks can correctly deliver data frames to the intended destination.

Types of Ethernet

Over time, Ethernet technology has evolved and several versions have been developed to support faster communication speeds.

Some common types of Ethernet include:

Standard Ethernet
This early version of Ethernet provided speeds of 10 Mbps.

Fast Ethernet

Fast Ethernet improved communication speed to 100 Mbps, making networks faster and more efficient.

Gigabit Ethernet

Gigabit Ethernet provides speeds of 1000 Mbps (1 Gbps) and is widely used in modern networks.

10 Gigabit Ethernet

This version supports speeds of 10 Gbps and is commonly used in data centers and large enterprise networks.

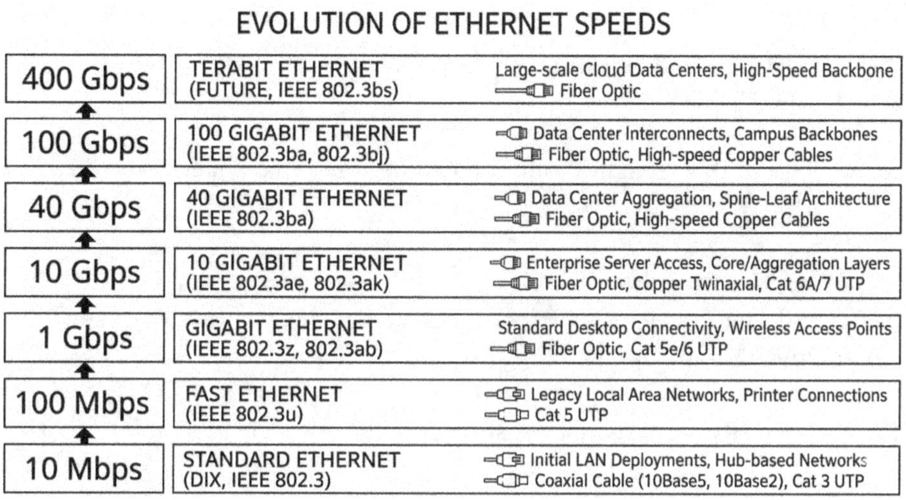

Advantages of Ethernet

Ethernet provides many benefits that make it suitable for networking.

First, Ethernet is simple and easy to implement.

Second, it provides high data transmission speeds.

Third, Ethernet technology is cost-effective, making it widely accessible.

Fourth, it supports both wired and fiber-based communication.

Because of these advantages, Ethernet has become the dominant LAN technology worldwide.

Limitations of Ethernet

Although Ethernet is widely used, it also has some limitations.

In earlier Ethernet networks that used shared communication media, collisions could occur frequently, which reduced network performance.

Another limitation is that Ethernet communication typically works within limited geographical areas, which is why it is mainly used in Local Area Networks.

However, modern Ethernet networks using switches have significantly improved performance and reduced these limitations.

Real-World Example

Ethernet is used in many everyday networking environments.

For example, in an office network, computers are connected to a switch using Ethernet cables. When one computer sends data, the switch forwards the data frame to the correct destination device.

Similarly, in homes, devices such as desktop computers, gaming consoles, and smart TVs often connect to routers using Ethernet cables for stable and high-speed Internet access.

These examples show how Ethernet technology enables reliable communication between devices.

Summary

Ethernet is a widely used technology for building Local Area Networks. It allows devices to communicate by transmitting data frames through wired communication media.

Ethernet networks use MAC addresses to identify devices and ensure that data is delivered to the correct destination.

Over time, Ethernet technology has evolved to support faster communication speeds such as Fast Ethernet, Gigabit Ethernet, and 10 Gigabit Ethernet.

Because of its simplicity, reliability, and efficiency, Ethernet remains one of the most important technologies used in modern computer networks.

Connecting LANs

In a small network, only a few computers may be connected together. However, in larger organizations such as offices, universities, or companies, there may be many Local Area Networks (LANs) that need to communicate with each other.

To allow communication between multiple LANs, special networking devices are used. These devices help connect different networks and ensure that data can travel from one network to another.

The process of connecting multiple Local Area Networks is known as LAN interconnection.

Different types of networking devices are used to perform this task. Each device performs a specific function in managing network communication.

Some commonly used devices for connecting LANs include:

Repeaters.
Hubs.

Switches.
Bridges.
Routers.
Gateways.

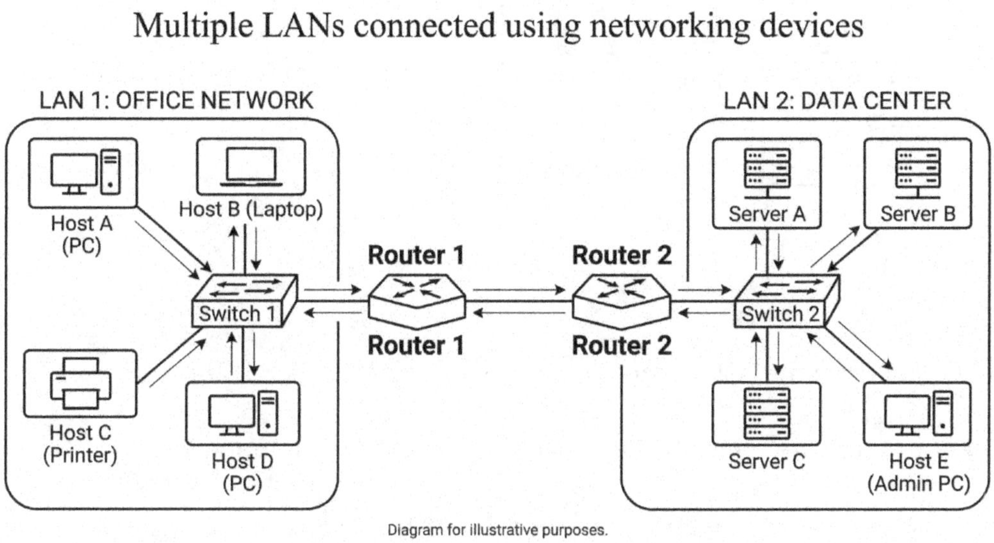

These devices help improve network communication, increase coverage area, and manage data transmission efficiently.

Repeaters

A repeater is a networking device used to extend the distance of a network.

When signals travel through a communication cable, their strength gradually decreases. This weakening of signals is called attenuation.

If the signal becomes too weak, the receiving device may not be able to interpret the data correctly. To solve this problem, repeaters are used.

A repeater receives a weak signal, regenerates it, and then retransmits the signal with its original strength.

Repeater regenerating weak signal between two network segments.

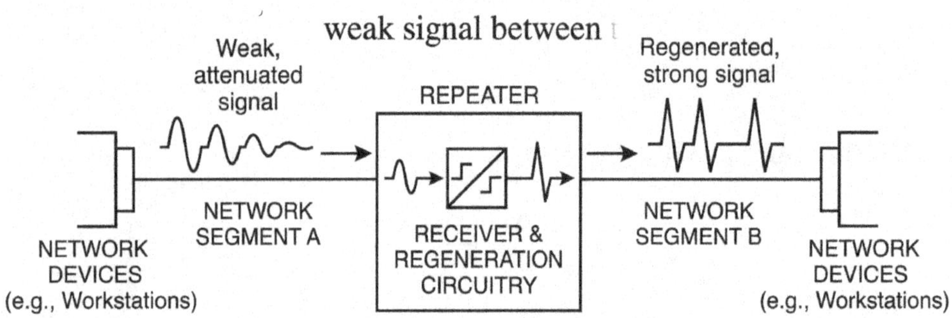

Repeaters operate at the Physical Layer of the OSI model.

They do not examine the content of the data; they simply strengthen the signal and transmit it again.

Because of this function, repeaters help extend the maximum distance of a network.

Hubs

A hub is a networking device used to connect multiple computers within a network.

A hub works like a central connection point where several devices are connected using cables.

When a device sends data to the hub, the hub broadcasts the data to all connected devices, regardless of the intended destination.

Hub broadcasting data to all connected devices.

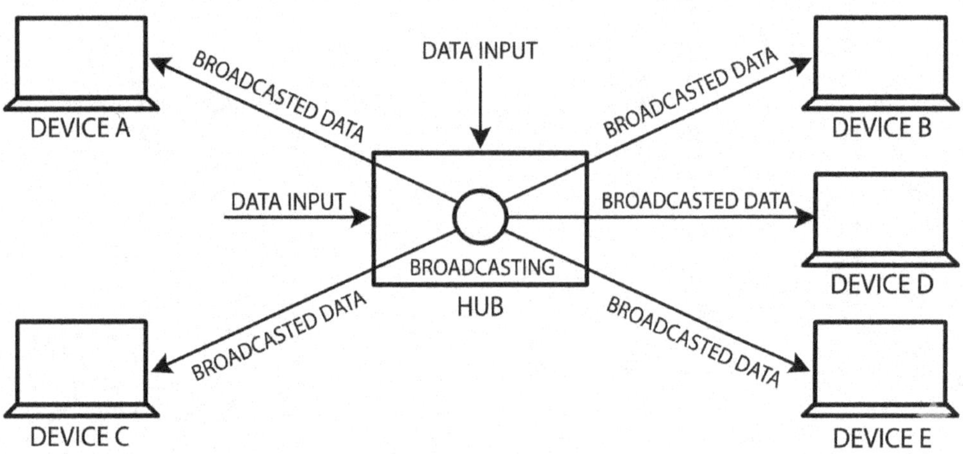

Because hubs broadcast data to all devices, they are considered less efficient compared to modern networking devices such as switches.

Hubs also operate at the Physical Layer of the OSI model.

Due to their limitations, hubs are rarely used in modern networks.

Switches

A switch is an advanced networking device used to connect multiple devices in a Local Area Network.

Unlike hubs, switches do not broadcast data to all devices. Instead, they use MAC addresses to identify the correct destination device.

When a switch receives a data frame, it examines the destination MAC address and forwards the frame only to the intended device.

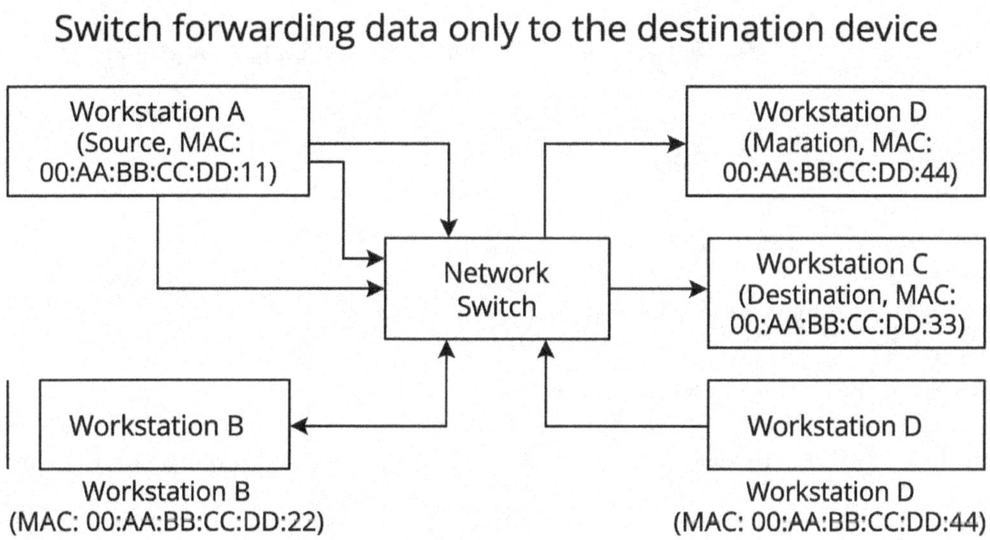

This method improves network efficiency and reduces unnecessary data traffic.

Switches operate at the Data Link Layer of the OSI model.

Because of their efficiency and reliability, switches are widely used in modern computer networks.

Bridges

A bridge is a networking device used to connect two or more LAN segments.

Bridges analyze the MAC addresses of data frames and decide whether the data should be forwarded to another network segment.

If the destination device is located in the same segment, the bridge blocks the transmission. If the destination device is located in another segment, the bridge forwards the data.

Bridge connecting two LAN segments

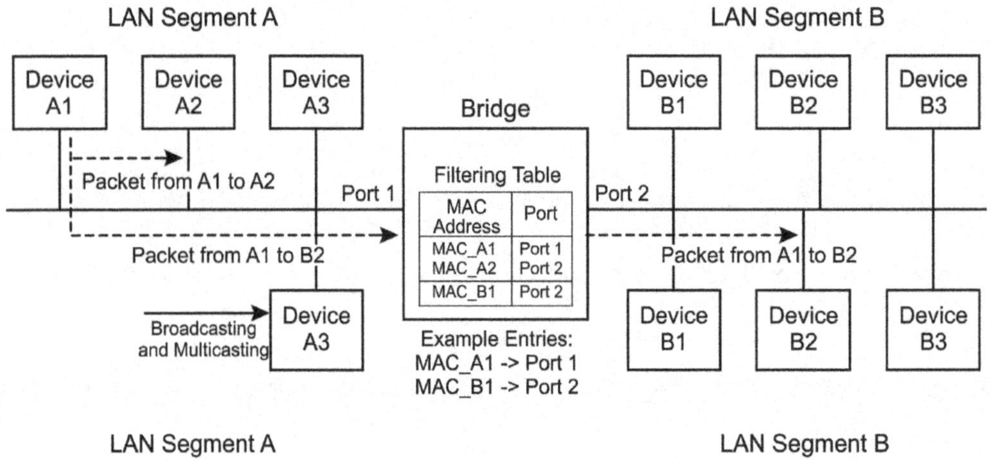

Bridges help reduce unnecessary traffic and improve network performance by dividing a large network into smaller segments.

Bridges operate at the Data Link Layer of the OSI model.

Routers

A router is a networking device used to connect different networks together.

Routers operate at the Network Layer of the OSI model.

Unlike switches and bridges, routers use IP addresses instead of MAC addresses to determine the path for data transmission.

Routers examine the destination IP address of a data packet and determine the best route for delivering the packet to its destination.

Router connecting multiple networks and directing packets.

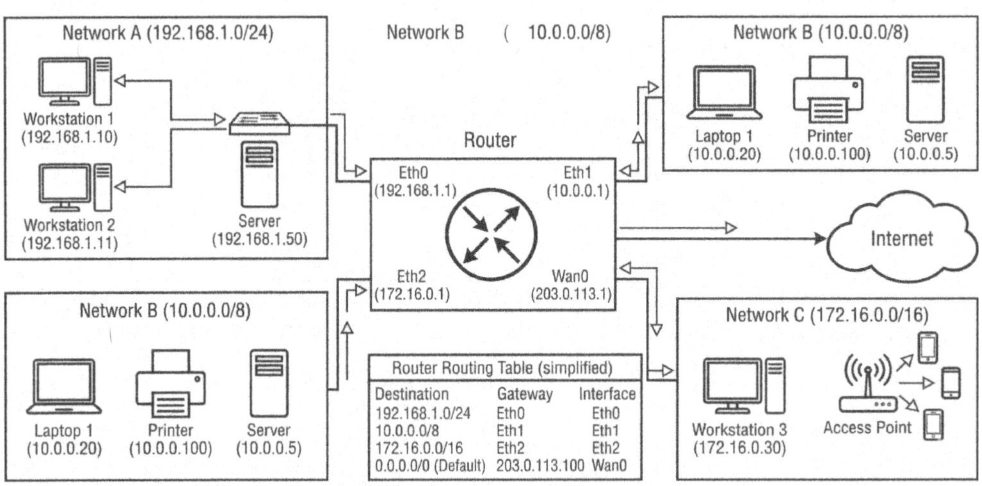

Routers are widely used in Internet communication. For example, the router in a home network connects the local network to the Internet.

Routers also maintain routing tables, which help determine the best path for transmitting data.

Gateways

A gateway is a networking device that connects two networks that use different communication protocols or technologies.

Gateways act as translators between networks so that devices using different communication systems can understand each other.

For example, one network may use one protocol while another network uses a different protocol. The gateway converts the data so that both networks can communicate successfully.

Diagram Title: Gateway translating communication between two different networks.

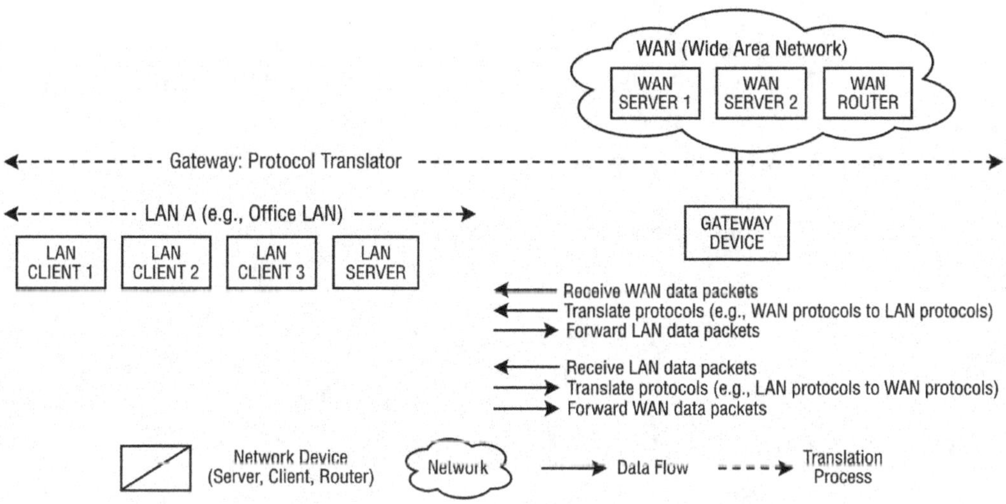

Gateways operate at multiple layers of the OSI model, often including the Application Layer.

Because of their ability to translate communication protocols, gateways play an important role in large and complex networks.

Importance of LAN Interconnection Devices

LAN interconnection devices play a crucial role in modern networking systems.

They allow networks to grow and expand while maintaining efficient communication between devices.

Repeaters help extend the distance of communication, hubs and switches connect multiple devices within a network, bridges divide networks into segments, routers connect different networks, and gateways enable communication between different technologies.

These devices work together to create reliable and scalable network infrastructure.

Real-World Example

In a large office building, different departments may have their own Local Area Networks.

These networks may be connected using switches and routers so that employees from different departments can share information.

A router may connect the office network to the Internet, while switches connect individual computers within the office.

This interconnected network allows employees to access shared resources such as printers, servers, and Internet services.

Summary

Connecting LANs is an important aspect of network design. Several networking devices are used to interconnect networks and manage communication.

Repeaters extend network distance, hubs connect multiple devices, switches intelligently forward data frames, bridges connect network segments, routers direct packets between networks, and gateways enable communication between networks using different protocols.

Together, these devices ensure that modern computer networks function efficiently and reliably.

CHAPTER NINE

Error Control and Flow Control

Error Detection Techniques

In a computer network, data travels from one device to another through communication channels such as cables, wireless signals, or fiber optic links. During transmission, there is always a possibility that the data may become corrupted or altered because of noise, interference, or hardware problems.

When such errors occur, the received data may not match the original data that was sent by the sender. Therefore, computer networks must include mechanisms to detect errors and ensure reliable communication.

This is where error detection techniques become important.

Error detection techniques are methods used in communication systems to identify whether the transmitted data has been received correctly or has been corrupted during transmission.

Once an error is detected, the system can take appropriate actions, such as requesting the sender to retransmit the data.

Data transmission showing correct data and corrupted data due to noise.

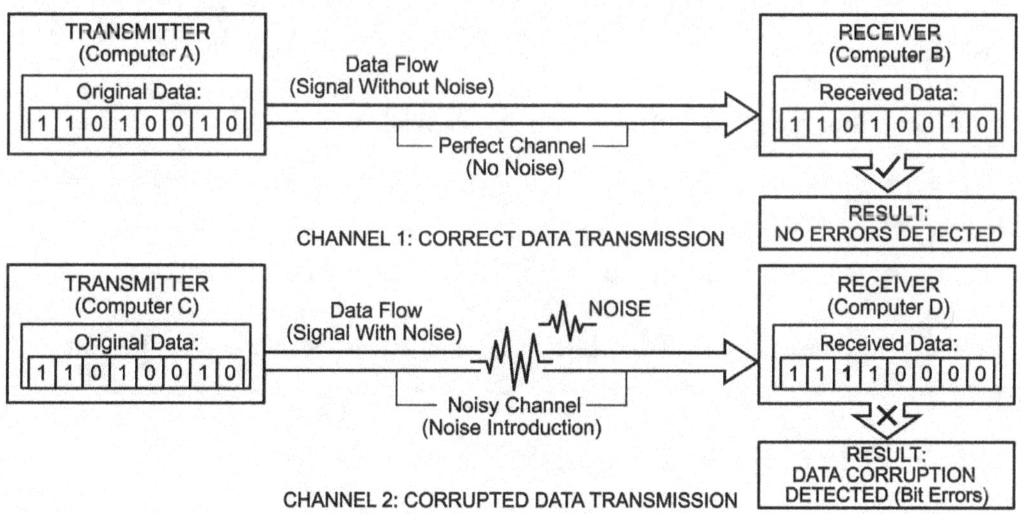

Error detection plays a critical role in ensuring data reliability and communication accuracy in networking systems.

Causes of Transmission Errors

Errors in data communication can occur for several reasons.

One common cause is electrical noise, which can interfere with signals traveling through communication cables.

Another cause is signal attenuation, where the signal strength becomes weaker as it travels over long distances.

Hardware failures, network congestion, or environmental conditions can also introduce errors during data transmission.

Because of these factors, communication systems must include mechanisms to detect and correct errors.

Importance of Error Detection

Error detection is important for maintaining the integrity and reliability of data communication.

If errors are not detected, incorrect information may be delivered to the receiving device. This can cause serious problems, especially in applications such as financial transactions, medical systems, or critical data processing.

By detecting errors, the communication system can ensure that data is retransmitted until it is received correctly.

Error detection therefore plays a vital role in maintaining the accuracy of digital communication.

Types of Error Detection Techniques

Several techniques are used in computer networks to detect transmission errors.

Two commonly used methods are:

Checksum
Cyclic Redundancy Check (CRC)

Each method uses a different mathematical approach to detect errors in transmitted data.

Checksum Method

The checksum method is one of the simplest techniques used for error detection in computer networks.

In this method, the sender divides the message into fixed-size data blocks and calculates a value called the checksum.

The checksum is generated by adding the binary values of the data blocks together.

This checksum value is then transmitted along with the data.

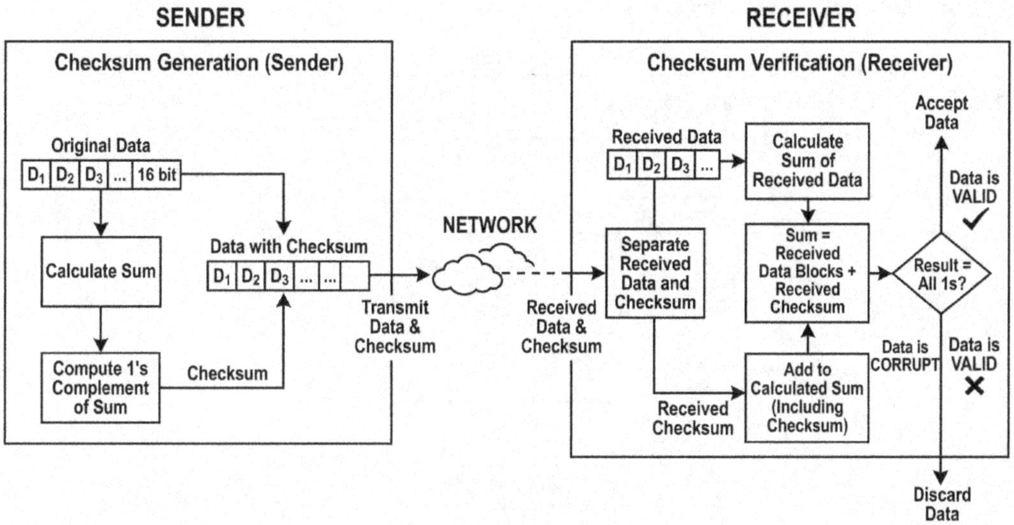

Working of Checksum

The operation of the checksum technique can be explained in several steps.

First, the sender divides the data into equal-sized blocks.

Second, the sender adds these blocks together using binary addition.

Third, the result of this addition is converted into a checksum value.

Fourth, the checksum is transmitted along with the data.

When the receiver receives the data, it performs the same calculation on the received data blocks.

If the calculated checksum at the receiver matches the transmitted checksum, the data is considered correct.

If the values do not match, the receiver concludes that an error has occurred during transmission.

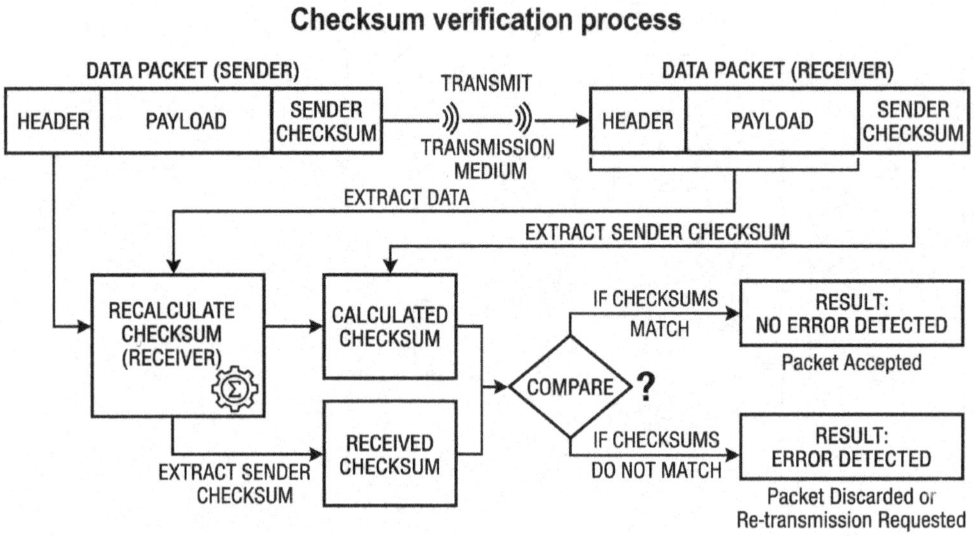

Advantages of Checksum

The checksum method has several advantages.

It is simple to implement and requires very little computational power.

Because of its simplicity, it is commonly used in many communication protocols.

Checksum techniques are often used in protocols such as UDP (User Datagram Protocol) to detect transmission errors.

Limitations of Checksum

Although the checksum method is simple, it is not always able to detect all types of errors.

Some complex error patterns may still go undetected.

Because of this limitation, more powerful error detection techniques such as Cyclic Redundancy Check (CRC) are often used in modern communication systems.

Cyclic Redundancy Check (CRC)

The Cyclic Redundancy Check (CRC) is one of the most reliable and widely used error detection techniques in computer networks.

CRC uses mathematical division of binary data to generate a special code that helps detect transmission errors.

Before transmitting the data, the sender performs a mathematical calculation using a predetermined binary number known as a generator polynomial.

The result of this calculation is called the CRC code.

This CRC code is appended to the data before transmission.

CRC generation using generator polynomial.

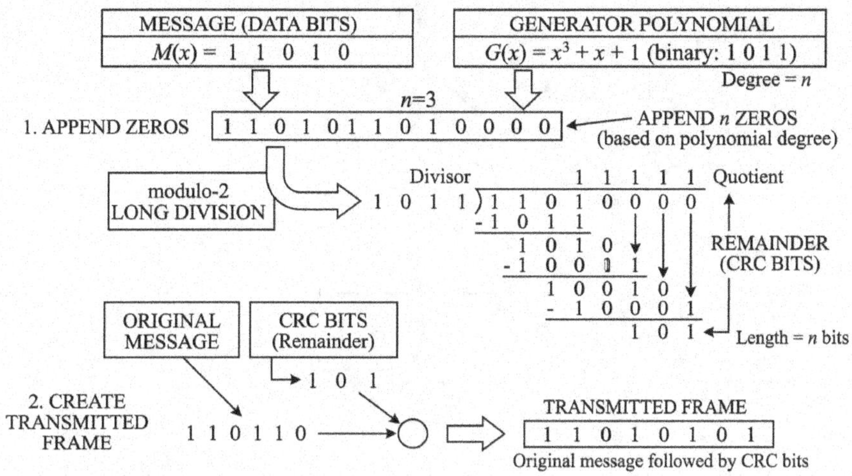

Working of CRC

The working of the CRC method involves several steps.

First, the sender selects a generator polynomial.

Second, the data is extended by adding extra zero bits.

Third, the data is divided by the generator polynomial using binary division.

Fourth, the remainder obtained from this division becomes the CRC value.

This CRC value is attached to the data frame before transmission.

When the receiver receives the data, it performs the same division operation using the same generator polynomial.

If the remainder obtained at the receiver is zero, the data is considered correct.

If the remainder is non-zero, it indicates that an error occurred during transmission.

CRC verification process at receiver

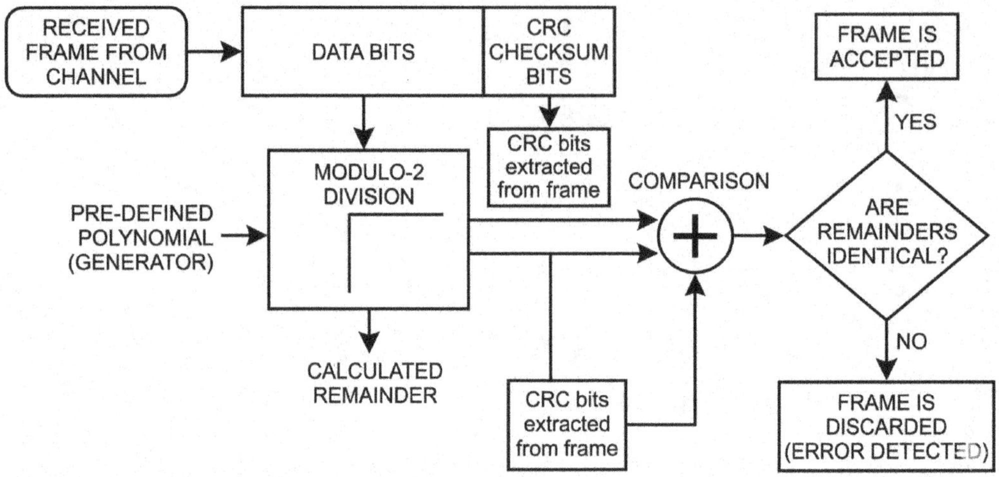

Advantages of CRC

The CRC technique offers several advantages.

First, it provides very high error detection capability.

Second, it can detect common types of errors such as single-bit errors, burst errors, and multiple-bit errors.

Third, CRC is widely used in many communication technologies such as Ethernet networks and storage devices.

Because of its accuracy and reliability, CRC is considered one of the most effective error detection methods.

Real-World Example

Error detection techniques are used in many everyday technologies.

For example, when a file is downloaded from the Internet, the system may use error detection methods to ensure that the downloaded file matches the original file.

Similarly, when data is transmitted through network cables, CRC checks help ensure that the data has not been corrupted during transmission.

These mechanisms help maintain the reliability and integrity of communication systems.

Summary

Error detection techniques are essential for maintaining reliable communication in computer networks.

These techniques help identify whether the transmitted data has been corrupted during transmission.

Two common error detection methods are the checksum technique and the Cyclic Redundancy Check (CRC).

The checksum method is simple and easy to implement, while CRC provides stronger error detection capability.

By detecting transmission errors, communication systems can request retransmission and ensure that data is delivered accurately.

Flow Control Protocols

In computer networks, data is transmitted from a sender to a receiver through communication channels. Sometimes the sender may transmit data faster than the receiver can process it. If this happens, the receiver's buffer (temporary storage area) may become overloaded, which can lead to data loss or communication errors.

To prevent such situations, communication systems use mechanisms called flow control protocols.

Flow control refers to techniques used to control the rate of data transmission between the sender and receiver so that the receiver can process the incoming data without being overwhelmed.

Flow control ensures that the sender does not transmit data faster than the receiver can handle.

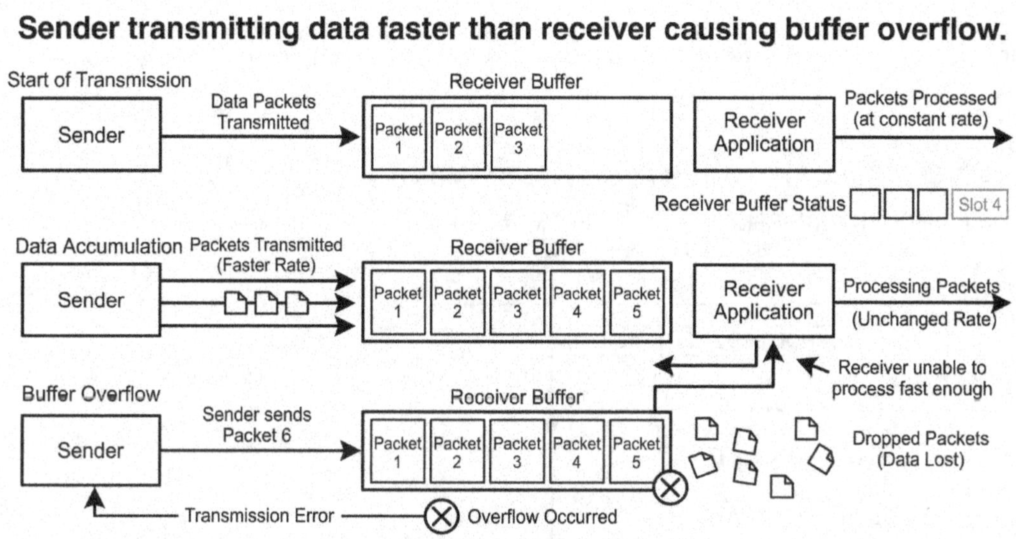

Diagram illustrating flow control issue

By regulating the speed of transmission, flow control helps maintain reliable and efficient communication in computer networks.

Importance of Flow Control

Flow control is important for maintaining the stability and reliability of communication systems.

If a sender continuously sends data at high speed without considering the receiver's capacity, the receiver may not be able to process the data in time. This can lead to packet loss, retransmissions, and reduced network performance.

Flow control ensures that data is transmitted in a controlled manner so that the receiver can process each frame properly.

It also helps maintain efficient use of network resources.

Types of Flow Control Protocols

Several protocols have been developed to implement flow control in communication systems. Some commonly used protocols include:

Stop and Wait ARQ
Sliding Window Protocol
Go-Back-N Protocol
Selective Repeat Protocol

Each protocol uses a different method to regulate the transmission of data frames between the sender and receiver.

Stop and Wait ARQ Protocol

The Stop and Wait Automatic Repeat Request (ARQ) protocol is one of the simplest flow control mechanisms used in computer networks.

In this protocol, the sender transmits one data frame at a time and then waits for an acknowledgment from the receiver before sending the next frame.

STOP AND WAIT ARQ SHOWING SENDER WAITING FOR ACKNOWLEDGMENT

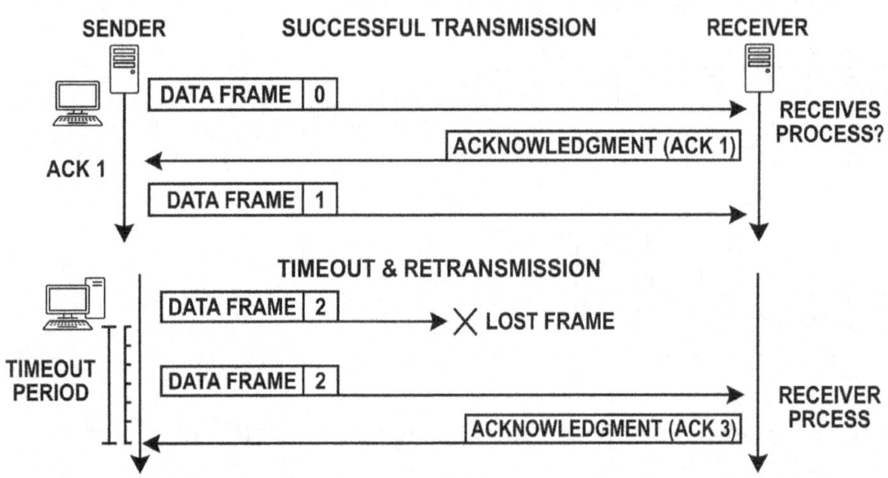

Working of Stop and Wait ARQ

The operation of the Stop and Wait ARQ protocol can be explained through the following steps.

First, the sender transmits a data frame to the receiver.

Second, the sender stops transmission and waits for an acknowledgment message from the receiver.

If the receiver receives the frame correctly, it sends an ACK (acknowledgment) back to the sender.

Once the sender receives the acknowledgment, it transmits the next frame.

If the acknowledgment is not received within a certain time, the sender assumes that the frame was lost or corrupted and retransmits the frame.

RETRANSMISSION OF FRAME WHEN ACKNOWLEDGMENT IS NOT RECEIVED

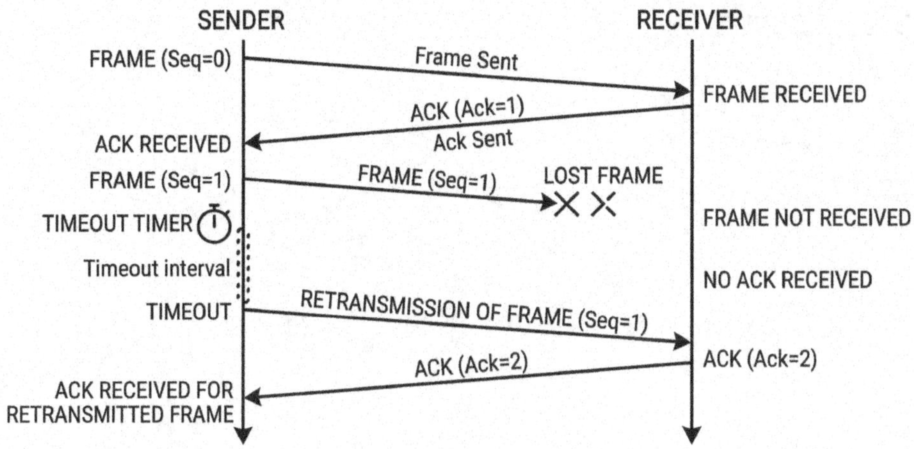

Advantages of Stop and Wait ARQ

The Stop and Wait ARQ protocol is simple and easy to implement.

Because the sender waits for acknowledgment after each frame, the system ensures reliable communication.

It also provides good error detection and correction by retransmitting lost frames.

Limitations of Stop and Wait ARQ

Although Stop and Wait ARQ is simple, it is not very efficient.

The sender remains idle while waiting for acknowledgment, which leads to wasted communication time.

This inefficiency becomes more noticeable in networks with long transmission delays.

To overcome this limitation, more advanced protocols such as the Sliding Window Protocol were developed.

Sliding Window Protocol

The Sliding Window Protocol is a more efficient flow control mechanism that allows the sender to transmit multiple frames before receiving acknowledgments.

Instead of sending only one frame at a time, the sender can send several frames within a defined window size.

Sliding window showing multiple frames in transmission.

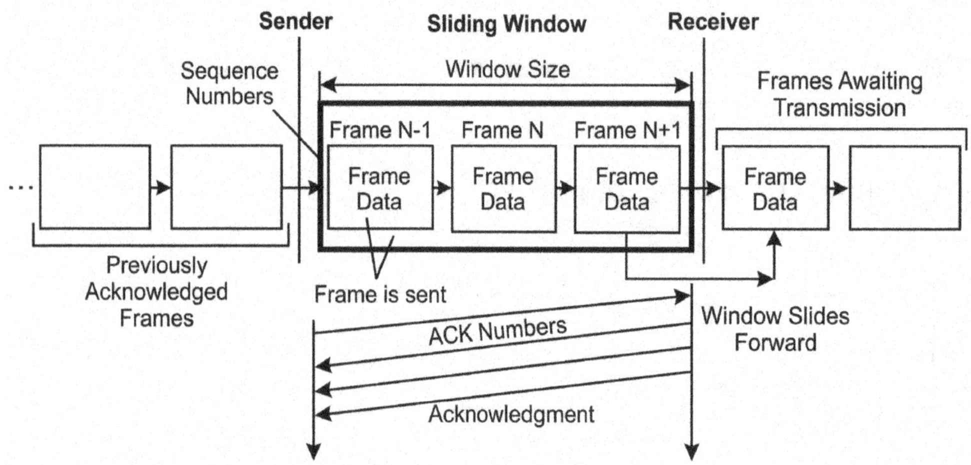

This improves network efficiency because the sender does not have to wait after sending every frame.

Working of Sliding Window Protocol

In this protocol, the sender maintains a window that represents the number of frames that can be transmitted before receiving acknowledgments.

The sender can send all frames within this window without waiting.

As the receiver acknowledges frames, the window moves forward, allowing the sender to transmit additional frames.

This movement of the transmission window is called the sliding window mechanism.

Window sliding forward as acknowledgments are received.

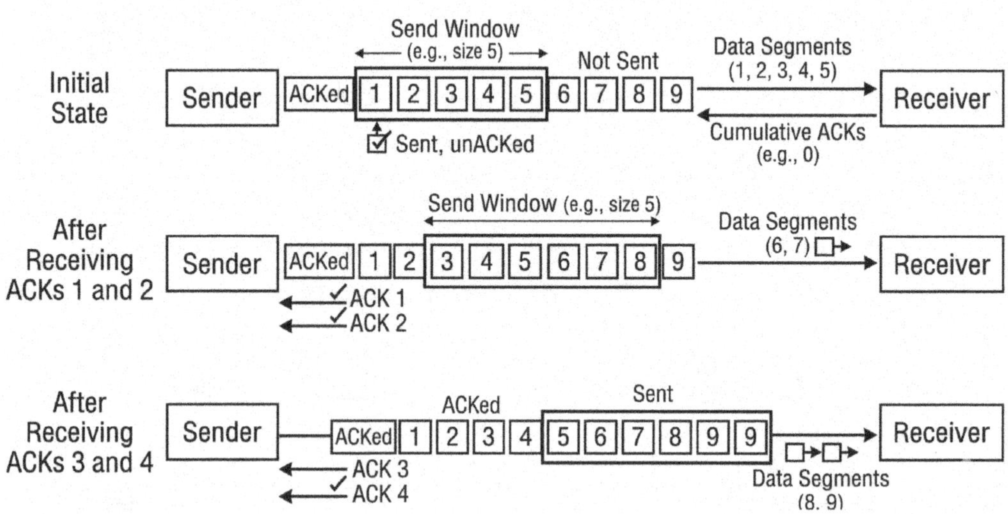

Go-Back-N Protocol

The Go-Back-N protocol is an extension of the sliding window protocol.

In this protocol, the sender can transmit multiple frames continuously. However, if an error occurs in one frame, the receiver discards that frame and all subsequent frames.

The sender must then retransmit the erroneous frame and all frames that follow it.

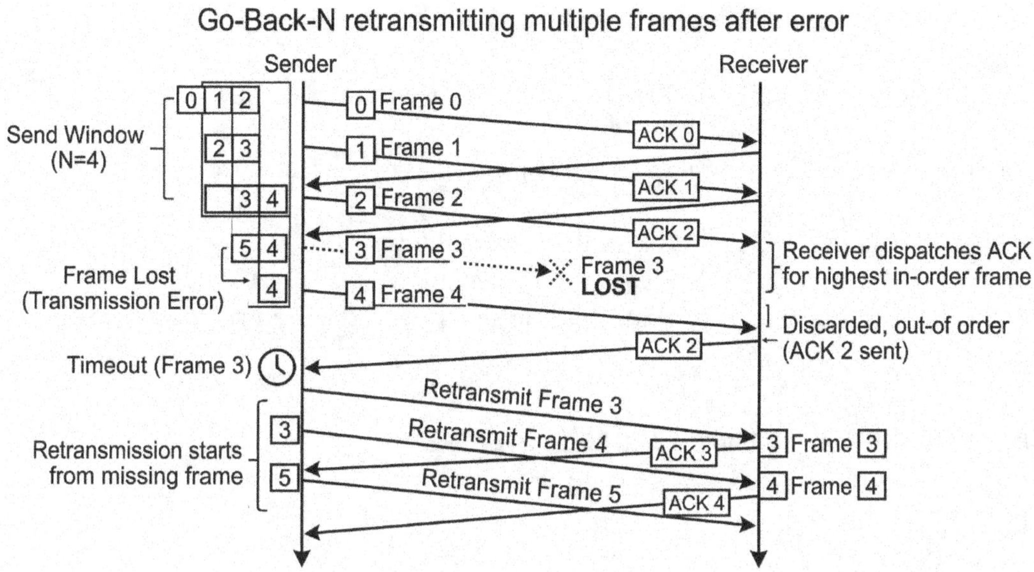

Although this method ensures reliable communication, it may cause unnecessary retransmissions.

Selective Repeat Protocol

The Selective Repeat Protocol improves the efficiency of Go-Back-N.

In this protocol, the receiver only requests retransmission of the specific frames that were lost or corrupted.

Correctly received frames are stored temporarily until the missing frames are retransmitted.

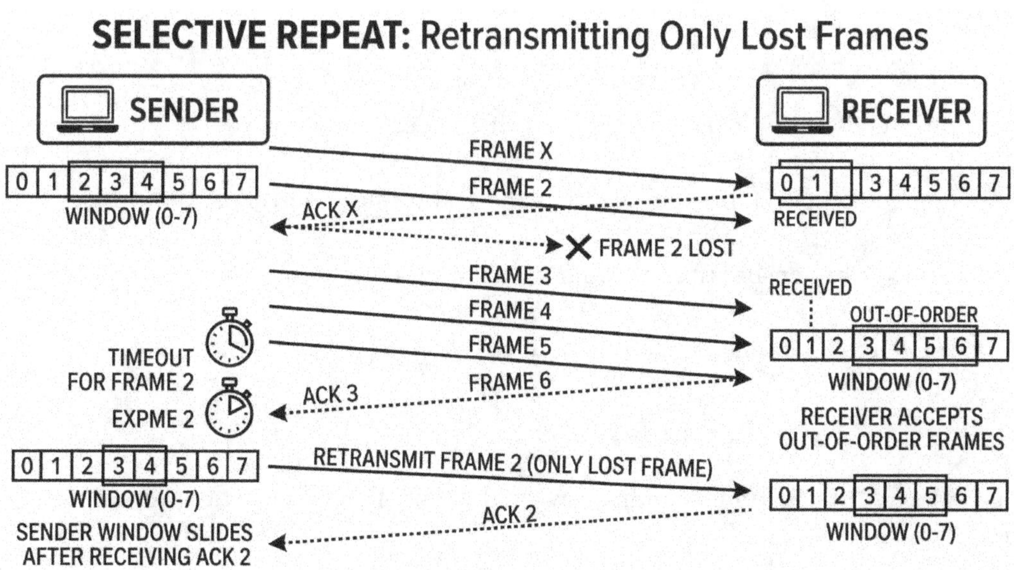

Because only the erroneous frames are retransmitted, this method improves network efficiency and reduces unnecessary data transmission.

Comparison of Flow Control Methods

Different flow control protocols offer different levels of efficiency.

The Stop and Wait protocol is simple but inefficient because it allows only one frame at a time.

The Sliding Window protocol improves efficiency by allowing multiple frames to be transmitted.

Go-Back-N simplifies error handling but may require retransmitting several frames.

Selective Repeat provides the highest efficiency because it retransmits only the frames that were lost or corrupted.

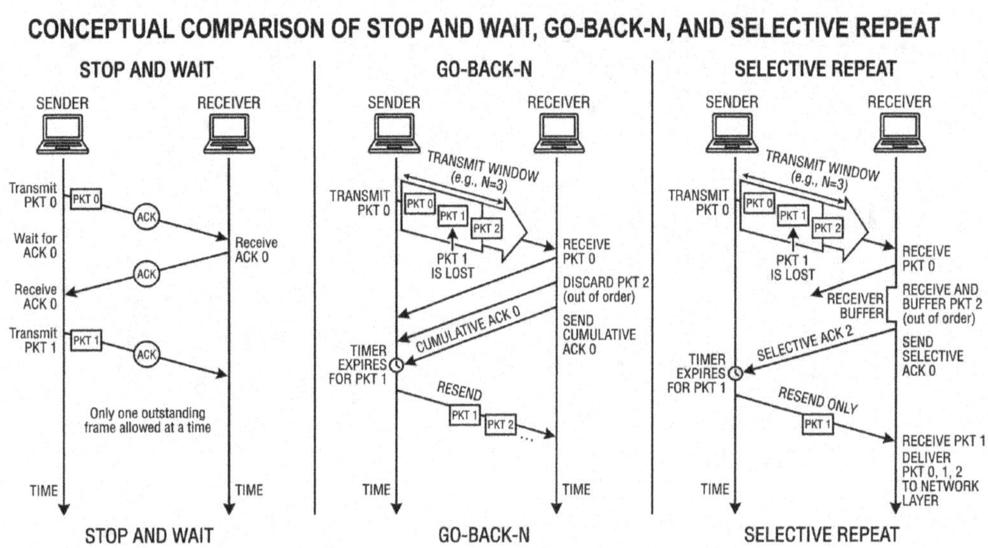

Real-World Example

Consider a situation where a server sends multiple data packets to a client over a network.

If the client can process only a limited number of packets at a time, the server must control its transmission rate.

Using flow control protocols, the server can ensure that it does not overwhelm the client.

This mechanism helps maintain smooth communication between devices in networks such as the Internet.

Summary

Flow control protocols regulate the rate of data transmission between the sender and receiver to prevent data loss and maintain efficient communication.

Several flow control techniques are used in computer networks, including Stop and Wait ARQ, Sliding Window Protocol, Go-Back-N Protocol, and Selective Repeat Protocol.

These protocols ensure that the receiver can process incoming data properly while maintaining reliable and efficient network communication.

HDLC Protocol
(High-Level Data Link Control)

In computer networks, reliable data communication is very important. When data travels from a sender to a receiver, it must arrive accurately and in the correct order. To achieve this reliability, communication protocols are used at different layers of the network.

One important protocol used at the Data Link Layer is called HDLC, which stands for High-Level Data Link Control.

HDLC is a bit-oriented data link layer protocol designed to provide reliable communication over point-to-point and multipoint links.

It was developed by the International Organization for Standardization (ISO) and is widely used in various communication systems.

HDLC provides features such as error detection, flow control, and reliable frame transmission.

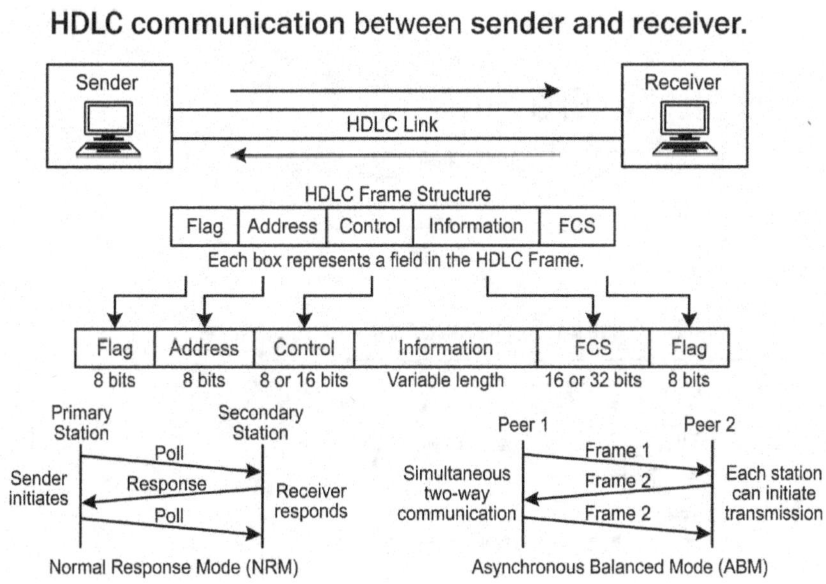

HDLC is considered a powerful protocol because it supports efficient and reliable data transmission between network devices.

Characteristics of HDLC

HDLC has several important characteristics that make it suitable for network communication.

First, it is a bit-oriented protocol, meaning it handles data as a stream of bits rather than characters.

Second, it provides error detection and flow control mechanisms to ensure reliable communication.

Third, HDLC supports point-to-point as well as multipoint communication.

Fourth, it uses a structured frame format to transmit data between devices.

Because of these features, HDLC is widely used in many communication technologies.

HDLC Frame Structure

Data in HDLC communication is transmitted in the form of frames.

Each frame contains specific fields that help control communication between the sender and receiver.

The HDLC frame structure includes the following components:

Flag Field.
Address Field.
Control Field.
Data Field.
Frame Check Sequence.
Ending Flag.

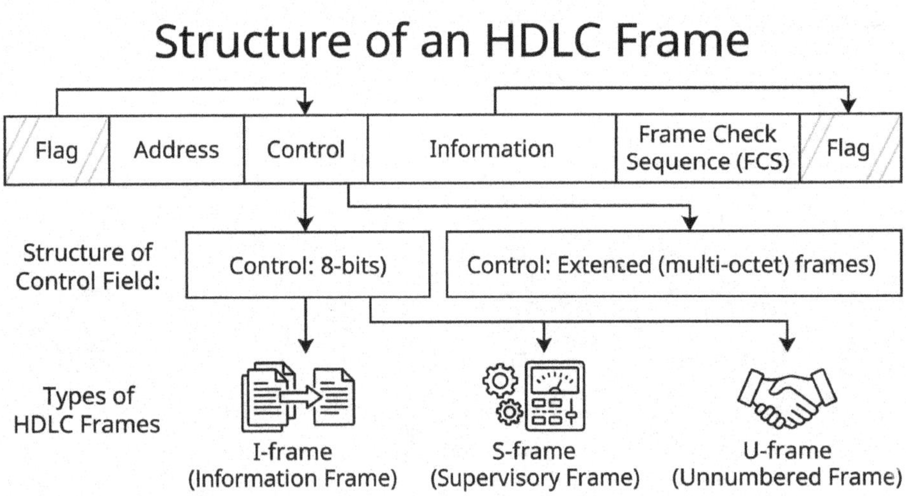

Each of these fields plays an important role in the communication process.

Flag Field

The flag field marks the beginning and end of a frame.

It is represented by a specific bit pattern that indicates where a frame starts and where it ends.

This helps the receiver identify the boundaries of each frame during data transmission.

Address Field

The address field identifies the destination device in the network.

In multipoint communication systems, this field helps determine which device should receive the frame.

Control Field

The control field manages communication between devices.

It includes information related to flow control, acknowledgments, and frame sequencing.

This field helps maintain the proper order of data transmission.

Data Field

The data field contains the actual information or message being transmitted.

The size of the data field may vary depending on the type of communication.

Frame Check Sequence (FCS)

The Frame Check Sequence is used for error detection.

It contains a value calculated using error detection methods such as Cyclic Redundancy Check (CRC).

When the receiver receives the frame, it verifies this value to determine whether the data has been transmitted correctly.

Types of HDLC Frames

HDLC defines three different types of frames used for communication.

These frames perform different functions in the data link layer.

Information Frames (I-Frames)
Information frames are used to carry user data from the sender to the receiver.
These frames also include control information used for sequencing and acknowledgment.

Information frame carrying data

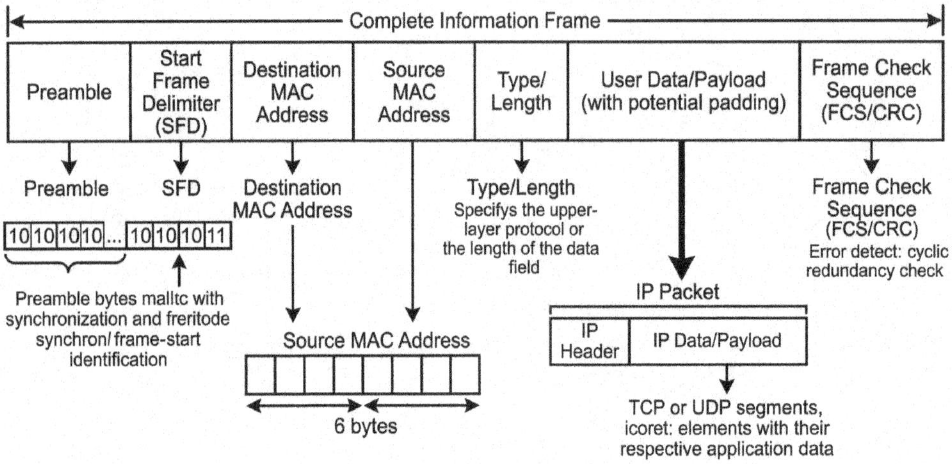

Supervisory Frames (S-Frames)

Supervisory frames are used for flow control and error control.
They do not carry user data but are used to manage communication between devices.
Examples include acknowledgment messages that confirm successful reception of frames.

Unnumbered Frames (U-Frames)

Unnumbered frames are used for control purposes, such as establishing and terminating communication sessions.
These frames help manage the connection between network devices.

Operation of HDLC

HDLC communication follows a structured process to ensure reliable transmission.

First, the sender creates a frame containing data and control information.

Second, the frame is transmitted over the communication channel.

Third, the receiver checks the frame using the Frame Check Sequence to verify whether any error has occurred.

If the frame is received correctly, the receiver sends an acknowledgment.

If an error is detected, the receiver may request retransmission of the frame.

HDLC FRAME TRANSMISSION AND ACKNOWLEDGMENT PROCESS

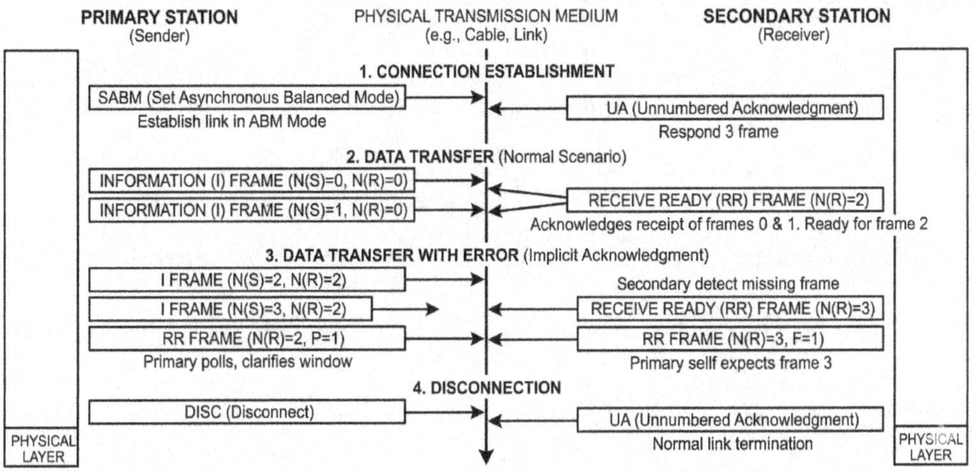

This process ensures that data is delivered accurately and in the correct sequence.

Advantages of HDLC

HDLC provides several advantages for network communication.

First, it offers reliable data transmission with built-in error detection.

Second, it supports efficient flow control, ensuring that the receiver is not overwhelmed with data.

Third, it supports both point-to-point and multipoint communication.

Fourth, it provides a flexible and structured frame format for transmitting data.

Because of these advantages, HDLC has been widely used in many communication systems.

Applications of HDLC

HDLC is used in several networking technologies and communication systems.

For example, HDLC has been used in wide area networks (WANs) and various telecommunications systems.

Many other communication protocols were also developed based on HDLC concepts.

One example is the Point-to-Point Protocol (PPP), which is commonly used for Internet communication.

Real-World Example

In long-distance communication networks, data may travel across multiple network devices and communication channels.

Protocols such as HDLC help ensure that the data is transmitted reliably between devices.

For example, when two routers communicate over a dedicated link, HDLC may be used to structure and control the communication process.

This helps ensure that data frames are delivered accurately and efficiently.

Summary

HDLC is a high-level data link control protocol used for reliable communication in computer networks.

It is a bit-oriented protocol that provides mechanisms for error detection, flow control, and frame management.

HDLC frames contain several fields, including flag fields, address fields, control fields, data fields, and frame check sequences.

By using these structured frames and communication mechanisms, HDLC ensures reliable and efficient data transmission between network devices.

Point-to-Point Protocol (PPP)

In computer networks, communication often takes place between two devices that are directly connected to each other through a communication link. This type of communication is known as point-to-point communication.

To manage reliable communication over such links, a protocol called Point-to-Point Protocol (PPP) is used.

The Point-to-Point Protocol (PPP) is a data link layer protocol used to establish a direct communication link between two network devices.

PPP is commonly used for communication between a computer and an Internet Service Provider (ISP), or between two routers connected through a dedicated communication link.

POINT-TO-POINT COMMUNICATION BETWEEN TWO DEVICES USING PPP

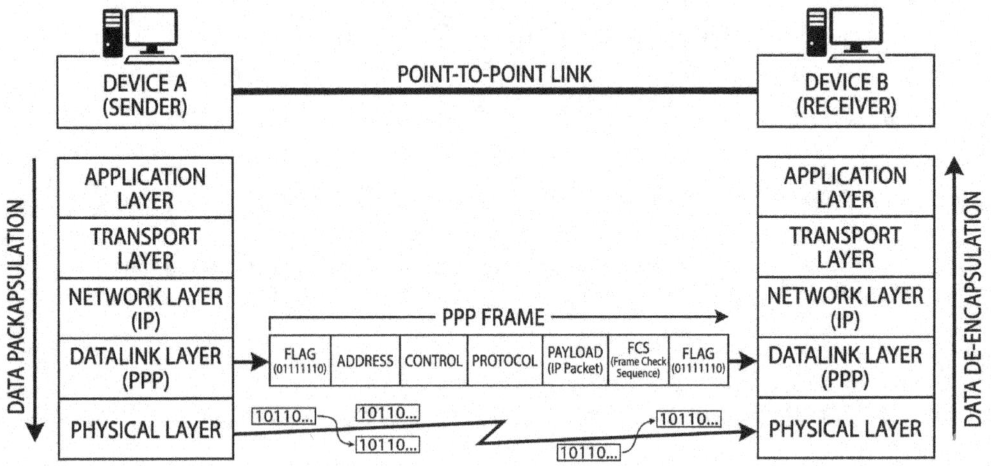

PPP provides several important features such as error detection, authentication, and data encapsulation, which help ensure secure and reliable communication.

Features of PPP

PPP has several features that make it suitable for point-to-point communication.

First, PPP provides data encapsulation, which allows network layer packets to be transmitted over the data link layer.

Second, PPP includes error detection mechanisms to ensure that corrupted data frames can be detected.

Third, PPP supports authentication, which helps verify the identity of devices participating in communication.

Fourth, PPP supports multiple network layer protocols, making it flexible for different types of network communication.

Because of these features, PPP has been widely used in many Internet communication systems.

PPP Frame Structure

Similar to other data link layer protocols, PPP transmits data in the form of frames.

The PPP frame contains several fields that help manage communication between devices.

The main fields of a PPP frame include:

Flag Field.
Address Field.
Control Field.
Protocol Field.
Data Field.
Frame Check Sequence.

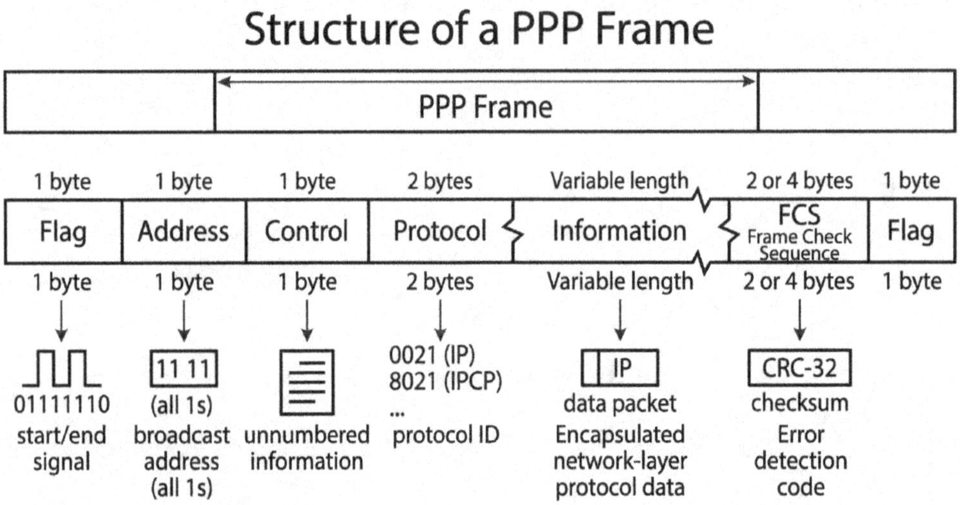

These fields help ensure that data is transmitted correctly and efficiently.

Flag Field

The flag field indicates the start and end of a frame. It helps the receiver identify the boundaries of each frame during transmission.

Address Field

The address field identifies the destination device in the communication link.

In point-to-point communication, this field usually contains a standard value because only two devices are involved.

Control Field

The control field manages communication between the sender and receiver.

It helps maintain proper sequencing and control of transmitted frames.

Protocol Field

The protocol field specifies the type of network layer protocol being used.

For example, it may indicate whether the transmitted data belongs to IP, IPX, or another protocol.

Data Field

The data field contains the actual information or message being transmitted.

This is the main part of the frame where the user data is stored.

Frame Check Sequence

The Frame Check Sequence (FCS) is used for error detection.

It allows the receiver to verify whether the frame was transmitted correctly.

Components of PPP

PPP includes several components that help manage communication between devices.

These components include:

Link Control Protocol (LCP)
Network Control Protocol (NCP)
Link Control Protocol (LCP)

The Link Control Protocol is responsible for establishing, configuring, and testing the communication link. LCP performs tasks such as negotiating link parameters and maintaining the connection between devices.
Network Control Protocol (NCP)

The Network Control Protocol allows PPP to support multiple network layer protocols.
It manages communication between the data link layer and network layer protocols such as IP.
This flexibility allows PPP to work with different types of network protocols.

PPP ARCHITECTURE SHOWING LCP AND NCP LAYERS

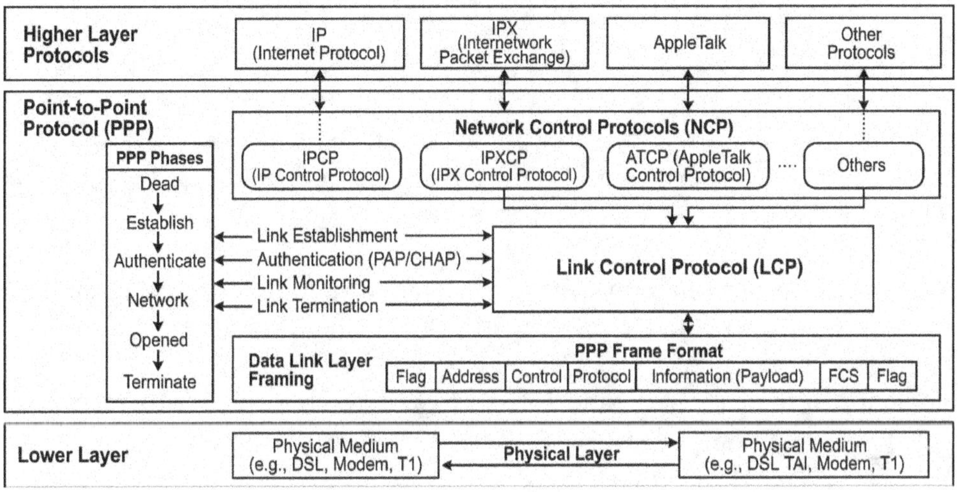

Advantages of PPP

PPP provides several advantages for network communication.

First, it provides reliable communication between two devices.

Second, it supports authentication mechanisms, which help ensure secure communication.

Third, it supports multiple network layer protocols, making it flexible for different communication systems.

Fourth, PPP provides efficient data encapsulation and error detection mechanisms.

Because of these advantages, PPP has been widely used in many communication technologies.

Applications of PPP

PPP has been used in several networking environments.

For example, PPP was widely used in dial-up Internet connections, where a computer connected to an Internet Service Provider through a modem.

PPP is also used in communication between routers over leased lines.

Even though modern broadband technologies are now widely used, PPP still plays an important role in many communication systems.

Real-World Example

In early Internet connections, users often connected to the Internet using a modem and a telephone line.

When the connection was established, PPP was used to create a communication link between the user's computer and the Internet Service Provider.

PPP ensured that data was transmitted reliably and that the user was properly authenticated before accessing the network.

Summary

The Point-to-Point Protocol (PPP) is a data link layer protocol used for direct communication between two network devices.

PPP provides several features such as data encapsulation, error detection, authentication, and support for multiple network protocols.

It uses components such as Link Control Protocol (LCP) and Network Control Protocol (NCP) to manage communication between devices.

Because of its reliability and flexibility, PPP has been widely used in Internet communication systems.

Channelization

In many communication systems, multiple users need to share the same communication medium. For example, in mobile networks, thousands of users may be communicating through the same wireless spectrum at the same time.

If all users try to transmit signals on the same channel without any control, it would lead to interference and communication errors. To solve this problem, communication systems use a technique called channelization.

Channelization is a method used to divide a single communication channel into multiple smaller channels so that multiple users can transmit data simultaneously without interfering with each other.

This technique is widely used in wireless communication systems, satellite communication, and mobile networks.

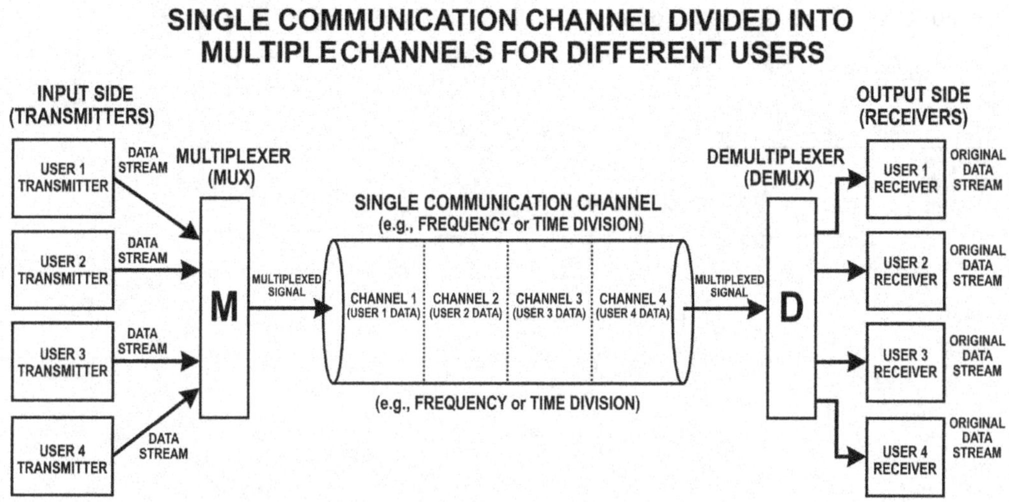

Channelization helps improve the efficient utilization of available bandwidth and allows multiple devices to communicate at the same time.

Types of Channelization

There are several methods used to divide a communication channel among multiple users.

Three commonly used channelization techniques are:

Frequency Division Multiple Access (FDMA)
Time Division Multiple Access (TDMA)
Code Division Multiple Access (CDMA)

Each technique divides the communication resources in a different way.

Frequency Division Multiple Access (FDMA)

Frequency Division Multiple Access (FDMA) is a channelization technique in which the available communication bandwidth is divided into multiple frequency bands.

Each user is assigned a separate frequency band for communication.

This means that multiple users can transmit data at the same time, but each user uses a different frequency range.

Frequency spectrum divided into multiple frequency bands for FDMA

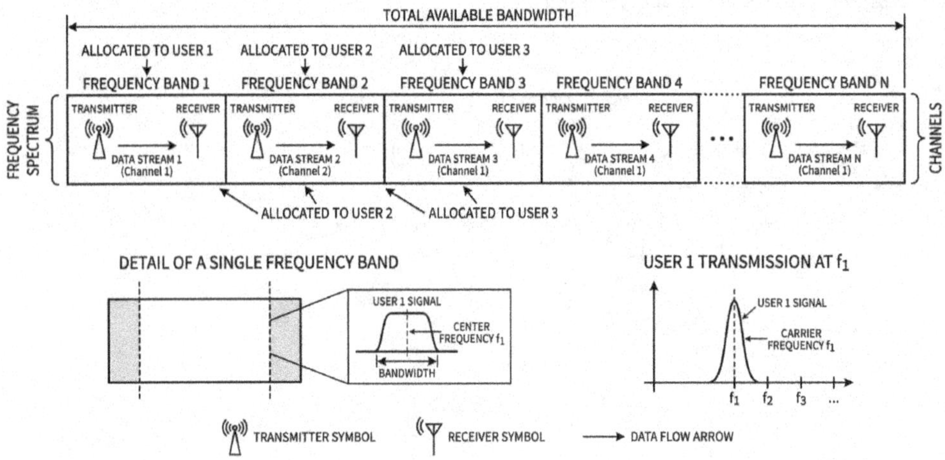

For example, in a wireless communication system, the available frequency range may be divided into several smaller bands, and each band is allocated to a different user.

Because each user operates on a different frequency, interference between users is minimized.

Characteristics of FDMA

FDMA has several characteristics.

Each user is assigned a fixed frequency band.

Communication can occur continuously because each user has a dedicated frequency channel.

Guard bands are often placed between frequency channels to prevent interference between adjacent channels.

FDMA was widely used in early analog communication systems and early mobile communication technologies.

Time Division Multiple Access (TDMA)

Time Division Multiple Access (TDMA) is another channelization technique used in communication systems.

Instead of dividing the communication channel by frequency, TDMA divides it by time.

In TDMA, multiple users share the same frequency channel but transmit data during different time slots.

Each user is assigned a specific time interval during which they can transmit data.

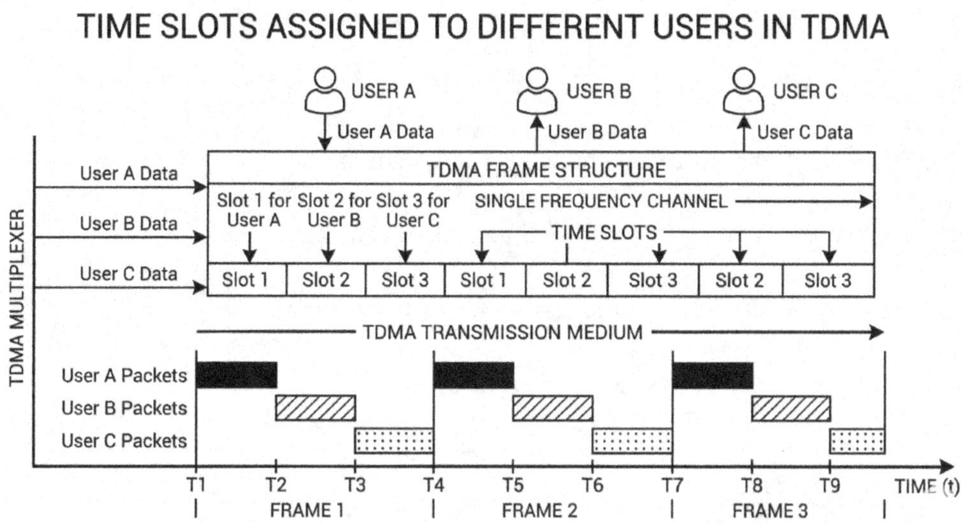

Because users transmit data at different times, they do not interfere with each other.

Working of TDMA

The working of TDMA can be explained through a simple concept.

The entire communication time is divided into small time intervals called time slots.

Each user is assigned a specific time slot for transmission.

When a user's time slot arrives, the user transmits data. After that, the next user transmits during the next time slot.

This process continues repeatedly in a cycle.

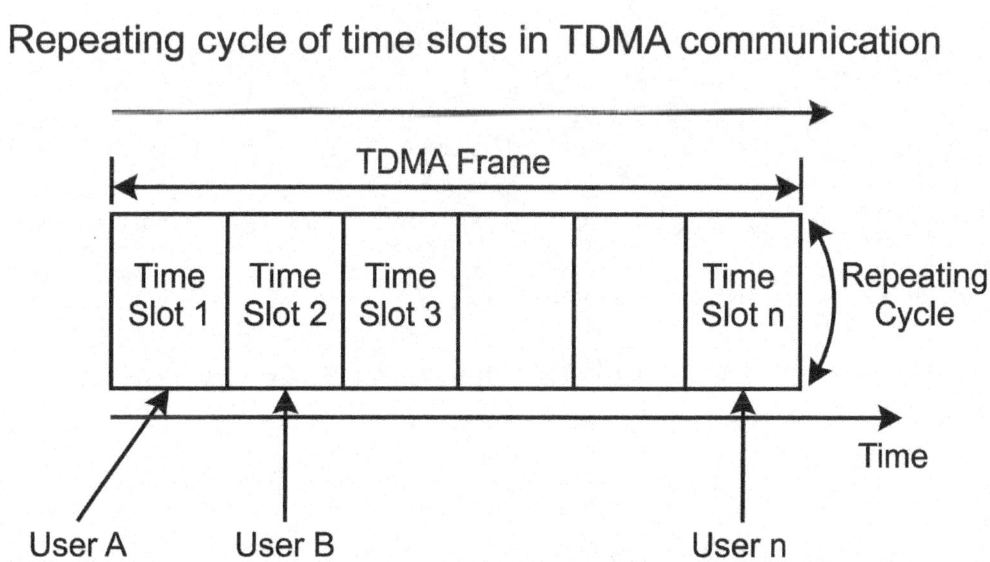

TDMA is widely used in many digital communication systems.

Code Division Multiple Access (CDMA)

Code Division Multiple Access (CDMA) is a more advanced channelization technique.

In CDMA, all users transmit data simultaneously over the same frequency band and time.

However, each user is assigned a unique code that distinguishes their signals from others.

These codes allow the receiver to separate signals belonging to different users.

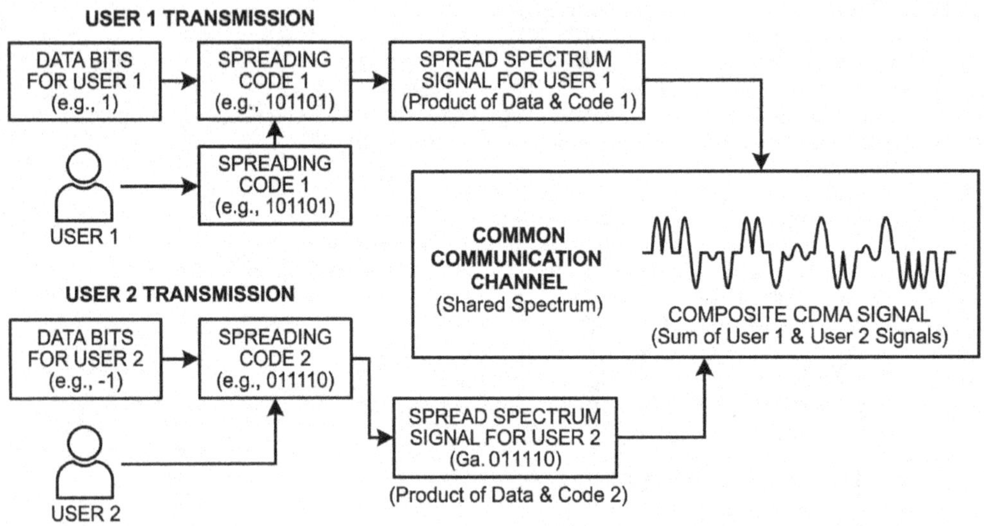

Because each signal is encoded with a unique code, the receiver can decode the desired signal while ignoring others.

Advantages of CDMA

CDMA provides several advantages over other channelization techniques.

It allows multiple users to transmit data simultaneously without requiring separate frequencies or time slots.

It provides better spectral efficiency, meaning more users can share the same communication channel.

CDMA also provides improved security and resistance to interference.

Because of these benefits, CDMA has been widely used in modern wireless communication systems, including earlier generations of mobile networks.

Comparison of Channelization Techniques

Each channelization technique has its own advantages and applications.

FDMA divides communication channels based on frequency.

TDMA divides communication channels based on time.

CDMA allows multiple users to transmit simultaneously using unique codes.

Comparison showing frequency division, time division, and code division.

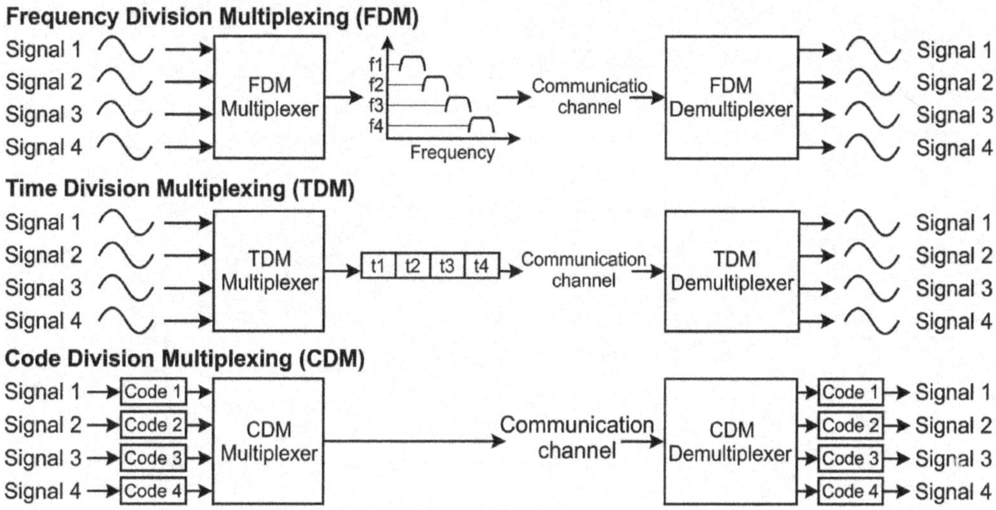

These techniques help communication systems efficiently share limited communication resources.

Real-World Example

Channelization techniques are widely used in mobile communication networks.

For example, when many users make phone calls or access the Internet through a mobile network, the communication system must allow all users to transmit data without interference.

Techniques such as FDMA, TDMA, and CDMA help manage this process by dividing the communication channel among multiple users.

This ensures efficient and reliable communication in large wireless networks.

Summary

Channelization is a technique used to divide a communication channel into multiple smaller channels so that multiple users can transmit data simultaneously.

Three important channelization methods are Frequency Division Multiple Access (FDMA), Time Division Multiple Access (TDMA), and Code Division Multiple Access (CDMA).

FDMA divides communication channels based on frequency, TDMA divides them based on time slots, and CDMA uses unique codes to allow multiple users to transmit simultaneously.

These techniques play an essential role in modern wireless communication systems.

CHAPTER TEN

Internet Protocols and Modern Networking

Logical Addressing

In computer networks, devices communicate with each other by sending data from one device to another. For successful communication, each device in the network must have a unique identification so that data can reach the correct destination.

At the physical level, devices are identified by physical addresses (MAC addresses). However, physical addresses are not suitable for communication across large networks such as the Internet. Therefore, networks use another type of addressing system known as logical addressing.

Logical addressing is a method used in computer networks to uniquely identify devices across different networks using addresses assigned by the network layer.

These addresses are used to ensure that data packets can travel from the source device to the correct destination device across multiple interconnected networks.

Data Packet Traveling Across Multiple Networks Using Logical Addresses

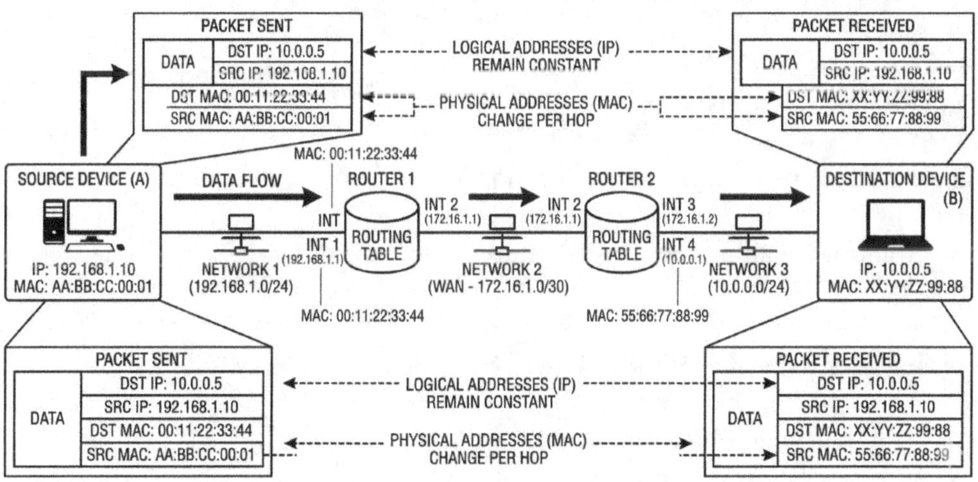

Logical addressing plays a very important role in the Internet and large computer networks, because it allows devices to communicate even when they are located in different geographic locations.

Need for Logical Addressing

In small networks, communication between devices may occur directly using physical addresses. However, when networks become large and interconnected, physical addresses alone cannot efficiently handle communication.

For example, when a computer in one city sends data to a server located in another country, the data must pass through many intermediate routers and networks before reaching its destination.

In such situations, logical addressing helps identify both the source network and the destination network, making it easier for routers to forward the data.

Packet tr aveling through multiple routers using logical addressing.

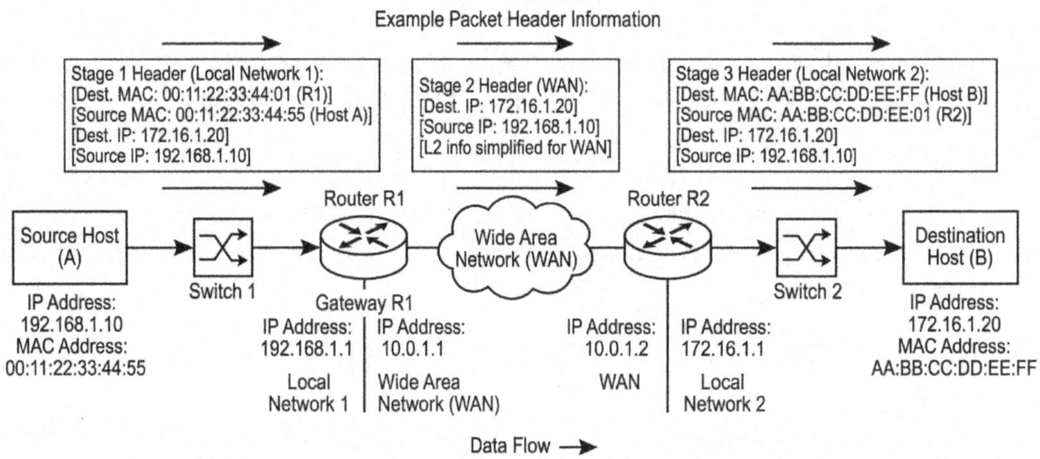

Packet traveling through multiple routers using logical addressing.

Without logical addressing, routing data across the Internet would be extremely difficult.

Characteristics of Logical Addressing

Logical addressing has several important characteristics.

First, logical addresses are assigned at the network layer of the OSI model.

Second, logical addresses are hierarchical, meaning they contain information about the network as well as the specific device within that network.

Third, logical addresses can be changed or reassigned if the device moves to a different network.

Fourth, logical addressing supports routing, which allows data packets to travel across multiple networks.

These characteristics make logical addressing suitable for communication across the Internet.

Role of Logical Addressing in Packet Delivery

When a device sends data across a network, the data is divided into small units called packets.

Each packet contains important information such as:

Source address.
Destination address.
Control information.
Actual data.

The logical address is included in the packet so that routers can determine where the packet should be forwarded.

Structure of a packet showing source and destination logical addresses.

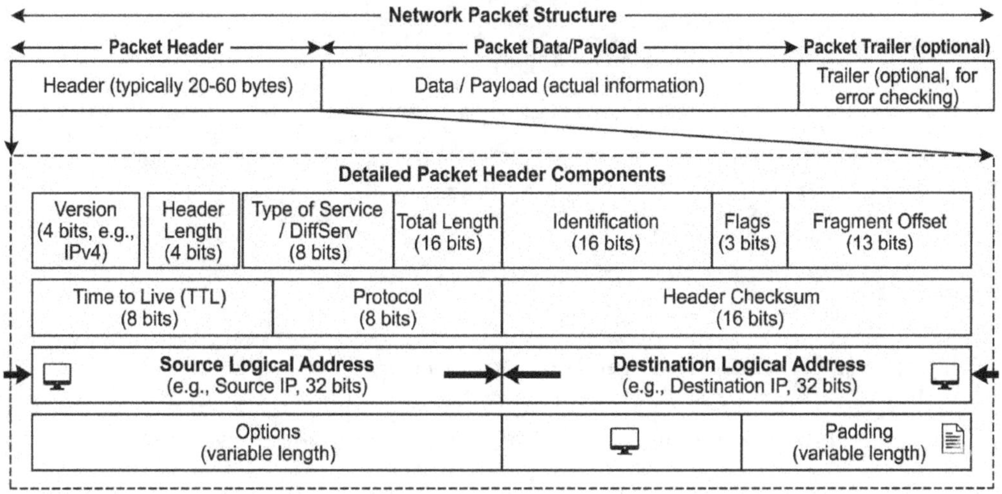

As the packet travels through different routers, each router examines the destination logical address and forwards the packet toward the appropriate network.

This process continues until the packet finally reaches the destination device.

Example of Logical Addressing

Consider a simple example where a student sends an email from a laptop to a web server located on the Internet.

The laptop first sends the data to a router in the local network. The router then forwards the packet through several other routers until it reaches the destination server.

Throughout this process, routers use the logical address of the destination device to determine the best path for the packet.

This allows communication to occur across long distances and multiple networks.

Communication between laptop and server through routers using logical addressing

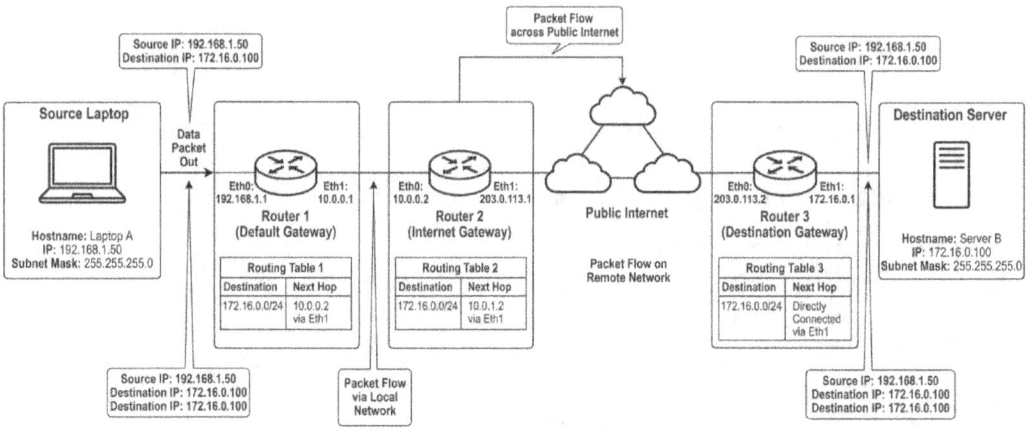

Logical Addressing in the Internet

In the Internet, logical addressing is implemented using the Internet Protocol (IP).

The Internet Protocol assigns a unique IP address to each device connected to the network.

These IP addresses help identify the source and destination devices involved in communication.

There are two main versions of Internet Protocol used today:

IPv4
IPv6

These protocols define the structure and format of logical addresses used on the Internet.

The next sections will explain these addressing systems in detail.

Difference Between Logical Address and Physical Address

To better understand logical addressing, it is useful to compare it with physical addressing.

A physical address (also known as a MAC address) identifies a device within a local network.

A logical address, on the other hand, identifies a device across multiple interconnected networks.

Physical addresses are assigned by the device manufacturer and usually remain fixed.

Logical addresses are assigned by the network and can change depending on the network configuration.

Difference between MAC address communication and IP address communication

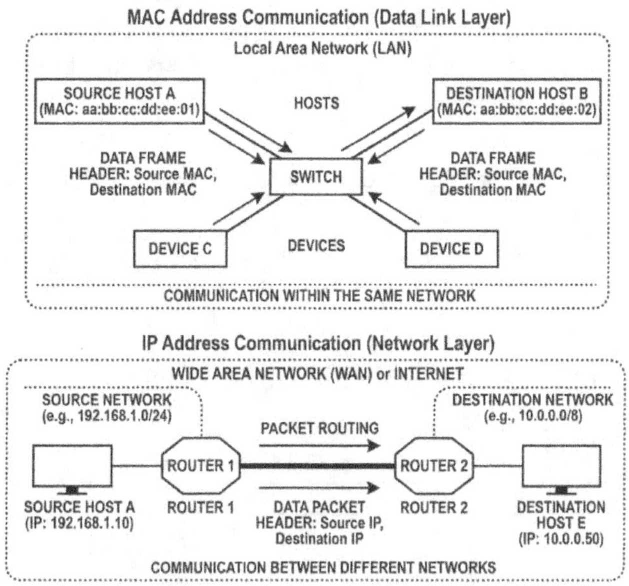

Real-World Example

Logical addressing can be compared to a postal address system.

When you send a letter through the postal service, you include the complete address of the recipient, including the city, state, and country.

Similarly, in computer networks, logical addresses help identify the location of devices so that data packets can reach the correct destination.

Just as postal workers use addresses to deliver letters, routers use logical addresses to forward data packets across networks.

Summary

Logical addressing is a method used in computer networks to uniquely identify devices across interconnected networks.

It is implemented at the network layer and allows routers to forward packets from the source to the destination device.

Logical addressing plays a crucial role in Internet communication because it enables devices located in different networks to communicate with each other efficiently.

The most common logical addressing systems used in the Internet are IPv4 and IPv6, which will be discussed in the next sections.

IPv4 Addressing

In computer networks, every device connected to the Internet must have a unique address so that data can be delivered to the correct destination. This addressing system is provided by the Internet Protocol (IP).

One of the earliest and most widely used versions of the Internet Protocol is called IPv4, which stands for Internet Protocol Version 4.

IPv4 provides a system of logical addressing that allows devices to communicate across the Internet.

An IPv4 address is a 32-bit numeric address assigned to every device connected to a network that uses the Internet Protocol.

STRUCTURE OF A 32-BIT IPv4 ADDRESS DIVIDED INTO FOUR PARTS

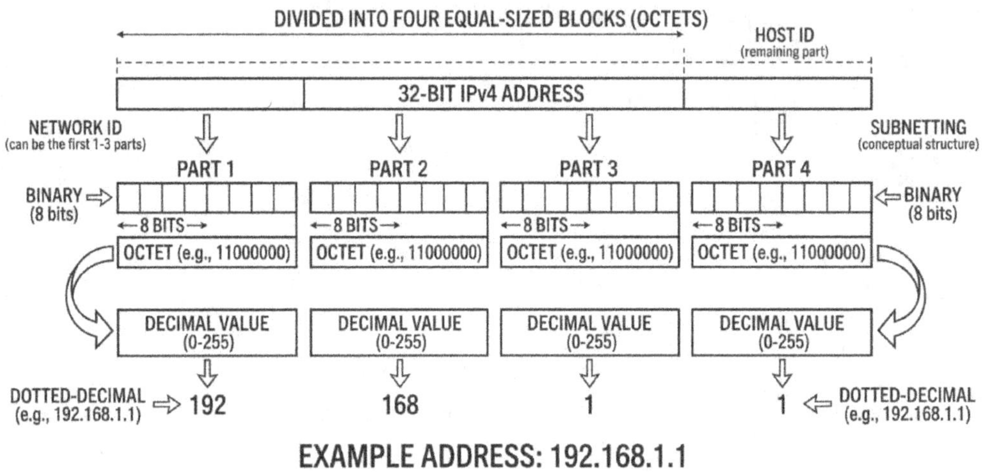

The IPv4 address is usually written in a format called dotted decimal notation, where the 32-bit address is divided into four 8-bit sections called octets.

Each octet is represented as a decimal number separated by dots.

For example:

192.168.1.1

In this example, the IPv4 address is divided into four parts:

192
168
1
1

Each of these numbers represents 8 bits of the 32-bit address.

Structure of an IPv4 Address

As mentioned earlier, an IPv4 address consists of 32 bits. These bits are divided into two main parts:

- Network Portion
- Host Portion

Diagram Title: IPv4 address showing network portion and host portion.

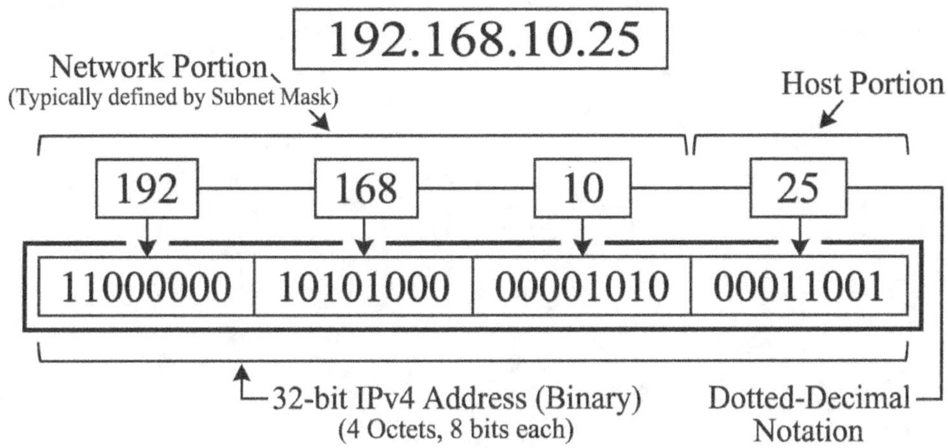

The network portion identifies the specific network to which the device belongs.

The host portion identifies the specific device within that network.

This structure helps routers determine how to deliver data packets to the correct network and device.

Network Portion

The network portion of the IPv4 address represents the network identifier.

All devices within the same network share the same network portion of the address.

For example, consider the following IPv4 addresses:

192.168.1.10
192.168.1.20
192.168.1.35

In this case, the network portion is 192.168.1, which indicates that all these devices belong to the same network.

The last number identifies the specific device.

Host Portion

The host portion identifies the specific device within the network.

Each device connected to a network must have a unique host address.

If two devices have the same host address in the same network, it will create a conflict, and communication problems may occur.

Therefore, network administrators must ensure that every device has a unique host address.

Multiple devices in a network with unique host addresses.

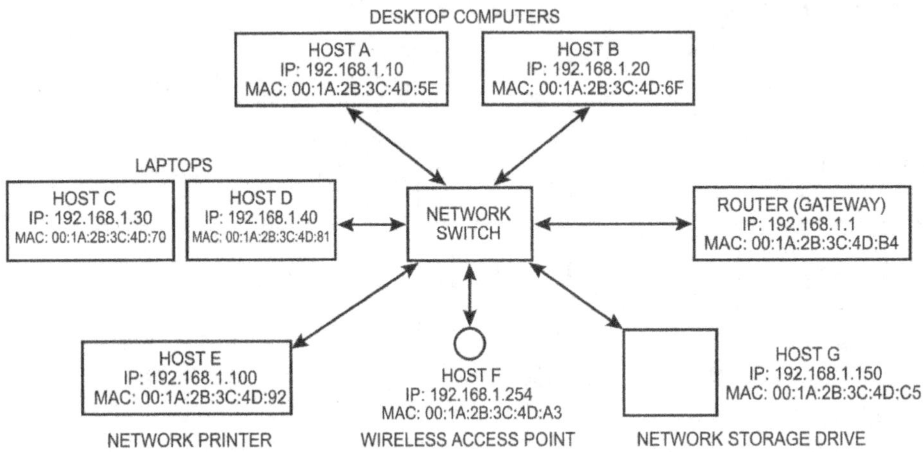

Range of IPv4 Addresses

Because IPv4 addresses use 32 bits, the total number of possible addresses is:

2^32

This means there are approximately 4.3 billion unique IPv4 addresses available.

At the time when IPv4 was created, this number seemed very large. However, with the rapid growth of the Internet, the number of connected devices increased significantly.

Today, billions of devices such as computers, smartphones, servers, and IoT devices are connected to the Internet.

As a result, IPv4 addresses are gradually becoming insufficient for modern networking needs.

This limitation led to the development of a new addressing system called IPv6, which will be discussed later.

Classes of IPv4 Addresses

To organize the allocation of addresses, IPv4 addresses were originally divided into different classes.

These classes helped define how the network and host portions were structured.

The main IPv4 address classes are:

- Class A
- Class B
- Class C

- Class D
- Class E

Each class is designed for different types of networks.

IPv4 address classes showing different ranges

Class	First Octet Range (Binary)	Decimal Range (First Octet)	Default Subnet Mask	Number of Networks	Number of Hosts per Network	Primary Use / Description
Class A	0xxxxxxx (0 to 127)	1.0.0.0 – 126.255.255.255 (excluding 0 and 127)	255.0.0.0	126 (2^7-2)	16,777,214 (2^24-2)	Large organizations, few networks, many hosts.
Class B	10xxxxxx (128 to 191)	128.0.0.0 – 191.255.255.255	255.255.0.0	16,384 (2^14)	65,534 (2^16-2)	Medium-sized organizations, moderate hosts.
Class C	110xxxxx (192 to 223)	192.0.0.0 – 223.255.255.255	255.255.255.0	2,097,152 (2^21)	254 (2^8-2)	Small organizations, many networks, few hosts.
Class D	1110xxxx (224 to 239)	224.0.0.0 – 239.255.255.255	N/A	N/A	N/A	Multicast addressing (groups).
Class E	1111xxxx (240 to 255)	240.0.0.0 – 255.255.255.255	N/A	N/A	N/A	Experimental and future use.

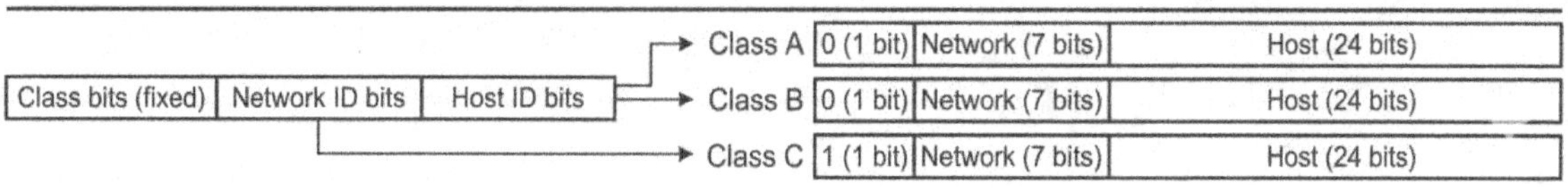

Class A Addresses

Class A addresses are used for very large networks.

In Class A addresses, the first octet represents the network portion, and the remaining three octets represent the host portion.

This allows a single network to support a very large number of devices.

Class A addresses typically start with numbers between 1 and 126.

These addresses were historically used by large organizations and Internet service providers.

Class B Addresses

Class B addresses are designed for medium-sized networks.

In Class B addresses, the first two octets represent the network portion, and the remaining two octets represent the host portion.

This structure allows organizations to support thousands of devices within a network.

Class B addresses usually start with numbers between 128 and 191.

Class C Addresses

Class C addresses are used for smaller networks.

In this class, the first three octets represent the network portion, and the last octet represents the host portion.

This allows networks to support up to 254 devices.

Class C addresses typically start with numbers between 192 and 223.

These addresses are commonly used in local area networks (LANs).

Class D Addresses

Class D addresses are used for multicast communication.

Multicast allows data to be transmitted to multiple devices simultaneously.

These addresses start with numbers between 224 and 239.

Class E Addresses

Class E addresses are reserved for experimental and research purposes.

These addresses are not used for regular communication.

They usually start with numbers between 240 and 255.

Limitations of IPv4

Although IPv4 has been widely used for many years, it has some limitations.

The biggest limitation is the limited number of available addresses.

With the rapid growth of the Internet and the increasing number of connected devices, the IPv4 address space is becoming exhausted.

To overcome this limitation, a new addressing system called IPv6 was developed.

IPv6 provides a much larger address space and several improvements over IPv4.

The next section will explain IPv6 addressing in detail.

Real-World Example

When you connect your laptop or smartphone to the Internet, your device is assigned an IP address.

This address allows websites and servers to identify your device and send the requested data back to you.

For example, when you open a website in your browser, your device sends a request to the web server using its IP address.

The server then sends the webpage data back to your device using the same addressing system.

This entire communication process depends on IP addressing.

Summary

IPv4 is the fourth version of the Internet Protocol used for logical addressing in computer networks.

It uses 32-bit addresses written in dotted decimal notation and divides the address into network and host portions.

IPv4 addresses are categorized into different classes such as Class A, Class B, and Class C to support networks of different sizes.

Although IPv4 has been widely used, the limited number of available addresses has led to the development of IPv6, which provides a larger address space.

IPv6 Addressing

As discussed in the previous section, IPv4 uses a 32-bit addressing system, which allows approximately 4.3 billion unique addresses. When IPv4 was designed, this number seemed more than enough. However, with the rapid growth of the Internet, billions of devices such as smartphones, computers, smart TVs, IoT devices, and servers are now connected to networks.

Because of this rapid growth, the available IPv4 addresses began to run out. To solve this problem, a new version of the Internet Protocol was developed called IPv6, which stands for Internet Protocol Version 6.

IPv6 is the latest version of the Internet Protocol, designed to provide a much larger address space and improved network performance.

An IPv6 address uses 128 bits, which provides an extremely large number of unique addresses compared to IPv4.

IPv6 128-bit address structure divided into eight groups.

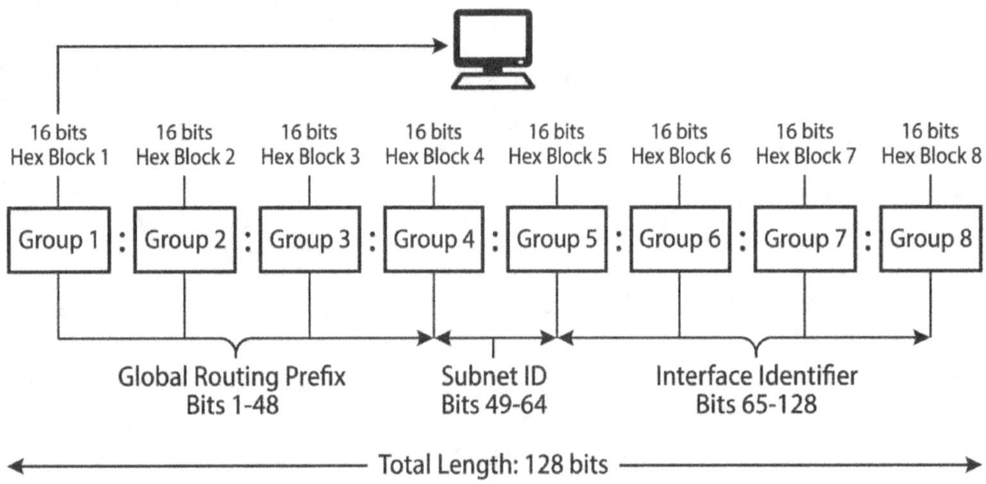

This large address space allows IPv6 to support trillions of devices, making it suitable for the future growth of the Internet.

Structure of an IPv6 Address

An IPv6 address consists of 128 bits, which are divided into eight groups of 16 bits each.

Each group is written in hexadecimal format, and the groups are separated by colons.

A typical IPv6 address looks like this:

2001:0db8:85a3:0000:0000:8a2e:0370:7334

Each section represents 16 bits of the total 128-bit address.

Because hexadecimal notation is used, IPv6 addresses appear longer and more complex than IPv4 addresses.

Example of IPv6 address divided into eight blocks

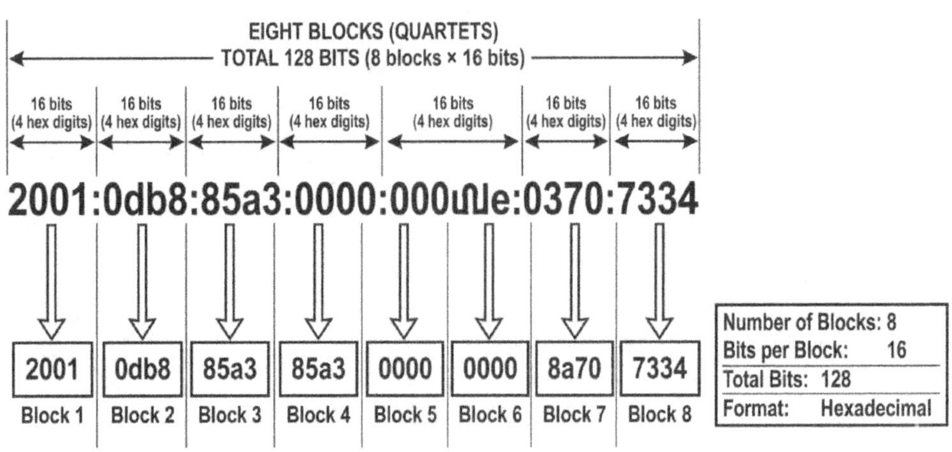

Simplified Representation of IPv6

To make IPv6 addresses easier to read and write, certain simplification rules are used.

One common rule is that leading zeros in each block can be removed.

For example:

2001:0db8:0000:0000:0000:0000:1428:57ab can be written as 2001:db8:0:0:0:0:1428:57ab

Another rule allows consecutive blocks of zeros to be replaced with double colon (::).

For example:

2001:db8:0:0:0:0:1428:57ab can be written as 2001:db8::1428:57ab

Simplification of IPv6 address using zero compression

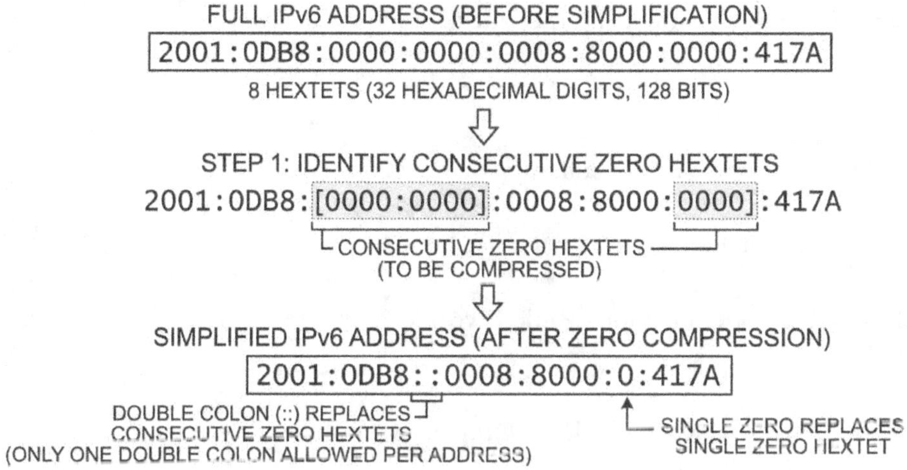

This makes IPv6 addresses easier to manage.

Advantages of IPv6

IPv6 provides several advantages compared to IPv4.

One of the most important advantages is the huge address space. Because IPv6 uses 128 bits, it provides an enormous number of possible addresses.

Another advantage is improved network efficiency. IPv6 simplifies packet headers, which improves routing performance.

IPv6 also provides better security features. It includes built-in support for security protocols such as IPSec, which helps protect data during transmission.

Another benefit is automatic configuration. Devices connected to a network can automatically obtain IPv6 addresses without requiring manual configuration.

IPv6 AUTO-CONFIGURATION PROCESS

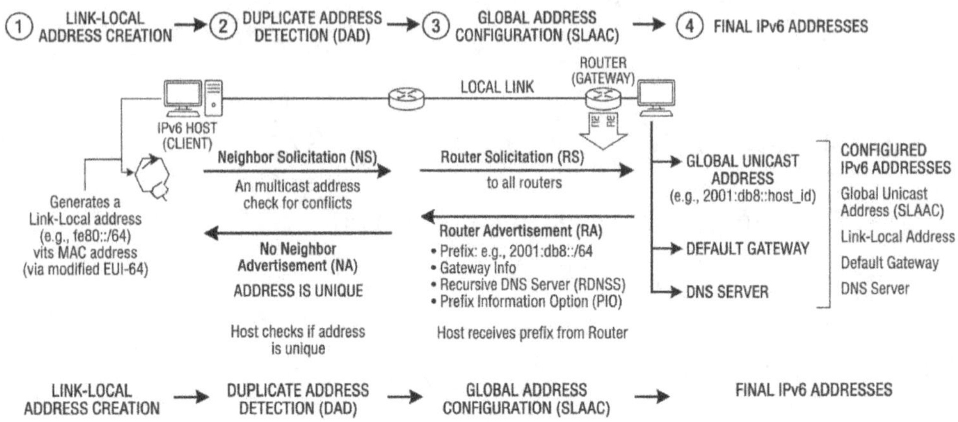

Because of these advantages, IPv6 is considered the future of Internet addressing.

Differences Between IPv4 and IPv6

Although IPv4 and IPv6 serve the same purpose, there are several important differences between them.

IPv4 uses 32-bit addresses, while IPv6 uses 128-bit addresses.

IPv4 addresses are written in decimal format separated by dots, while IPv6 addresses are written in hexadecimal format separated by colons.

IPv4 provides limited address space, while IPv6 provides a very large number of addresses.

IPv6 also improves network security and efficiency compared to IPv4.

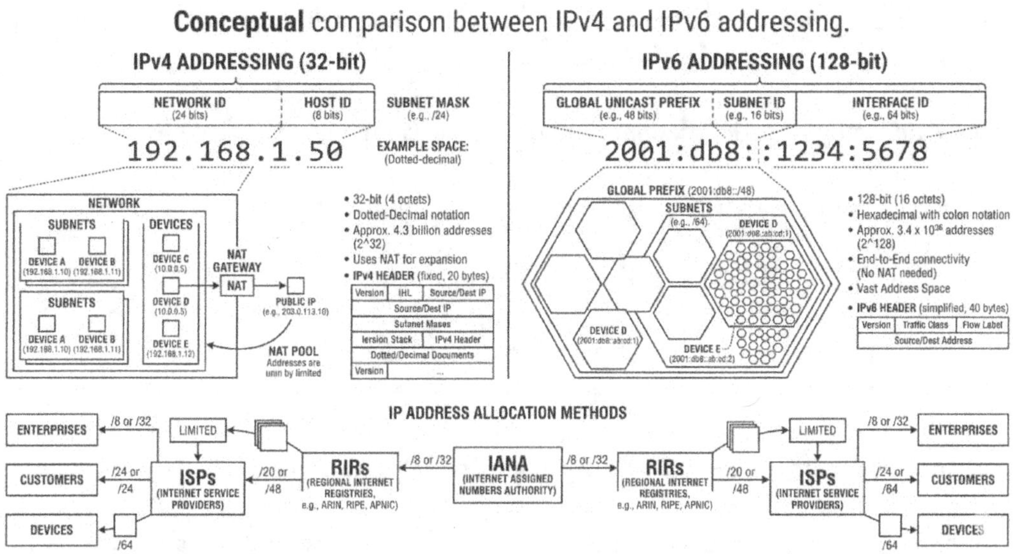

Transition from IPv4 to IPv6

Even though IPv6 has many advantages, the transition from IPv4 to IPv6 is gradual.

Many existing networks still use IPv4 because it has been widely implemented for many years.

To support this transition, several techniques are used, such as:

Dual stack implementation.
Tunneling mechanisms.
Translation techniques.

These methods allow IPv4 and IPv6 networks to work together during the transition period.

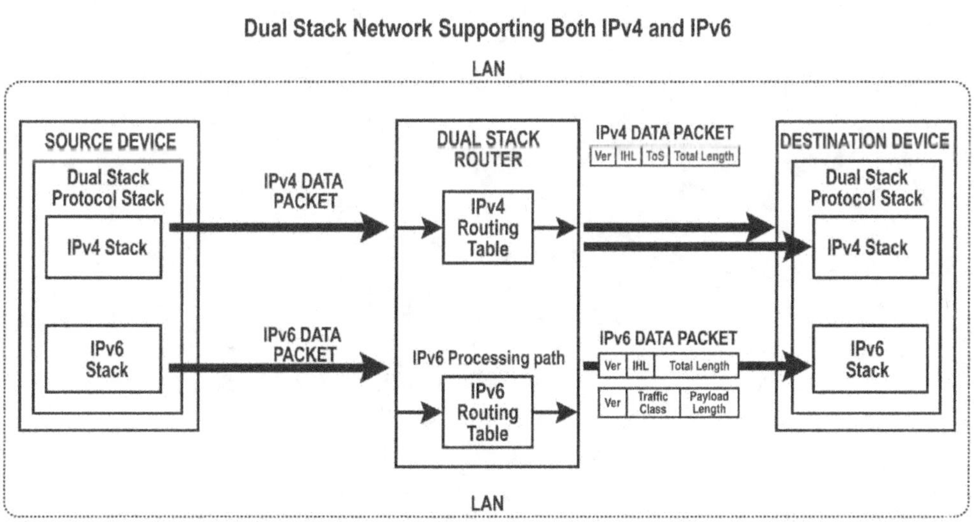

Real-World Example

Today, many modern devices such as smartphones, smart home devices, and IoT sensors require Internet connectivity.

With the increasing number of devices, IPv4 addresses alone cannot support all devices.

IPv6 allows each device to have its own unique address, which simplifies communication across the Internet.

For example, in a smart home environment, devices such as smart lights, security cameras, thermostats, and appliances can all communicate using IPv6 addresses.

Summary

IPv6 is the latest version of the Internet Protocol designed to overcome the limitations of IPv4.

It uses 128-bit addresses written in hexadecimal format, which provide a much larger address space than IPv4.

IPv6 also offers improved security, better network performance, and automatic address configuration.

Because of these advantages, IPv6 is gradually replacing IPv4 and is expected to support the future growth of the Internet.

Routing Concepts

In computer networks, data often needs to travel from one network to another before reaching its final destination. For example, when a user sends an email, opens a website, or streams a video, the data must travel through many intermediate networks before reaching the destination device.

The process that determines how data packets travel from the source network to the destination network is called routing.

Routing is the process of selecting the best path for data packets to travel across interconnected networks.

This process is mainly performed by special networking devices called routers.

Data packets traveling from source network to destination network through multiple routers.

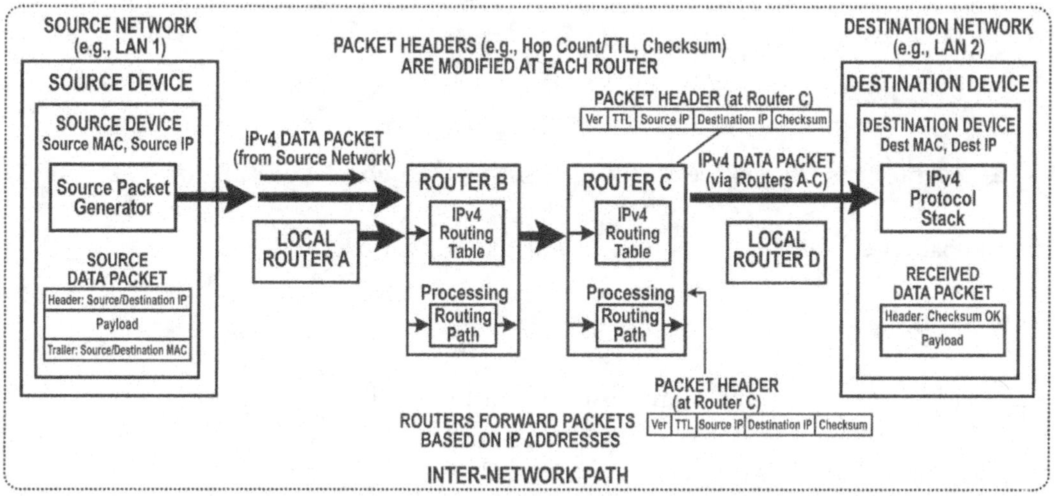

Routing is essential for communication over large networks such as the Internet, where millions of networks are interconnected.

Role of Routers in Networking

A router is a network device that connects multiple networks and forwards data packets between them.

Routers operate mainly at the Network Layer (Layer 3) of the OSI model.

The primary function of a router is to examine the destination IP address of a data packet and determine the best path for delivering that packet.

Router connecting multiple networks

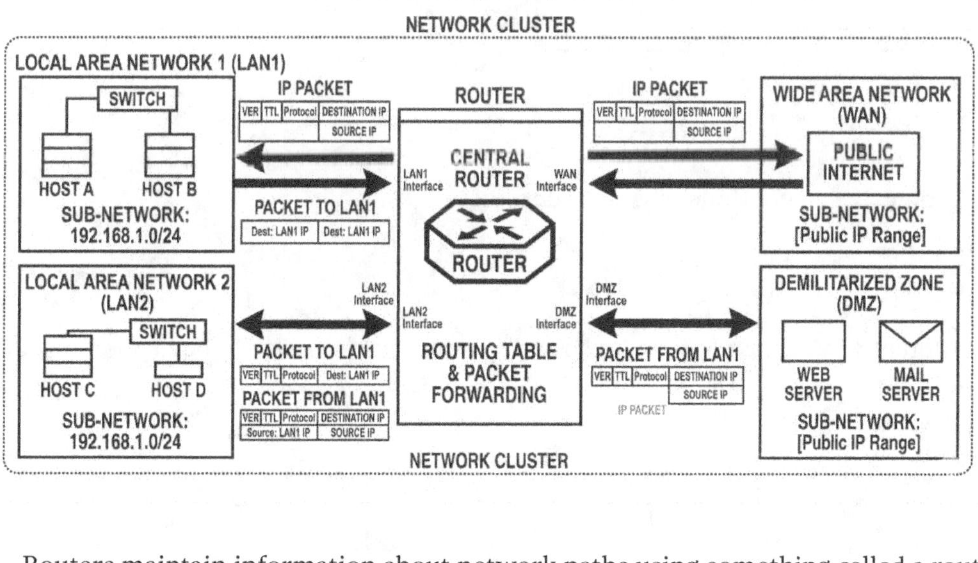

Routers maintain information about network paths using something called a routing table.

A routing table contains information about available networks and the best routes to reach them.

When a router receives a packet, it checks the routing table and forwards the packet to the next appropriate router or network.

Routing Process

The routing process involves several steps that ensure data packets reach their correct destination.

First, the sender creates a data packet containing the source IP address and destination IP address.

Second, the packet is sent to the local router.

Third, the router checks its routing table to determine the best path for forwarding the packet.

Fourth, the packet is forwarded through a series of routers until it reaches the destination network.

Finally, the packet is delivered to the destination device.

DIAGRAM TITLE: Step-by-step packet routing through multiple routers.

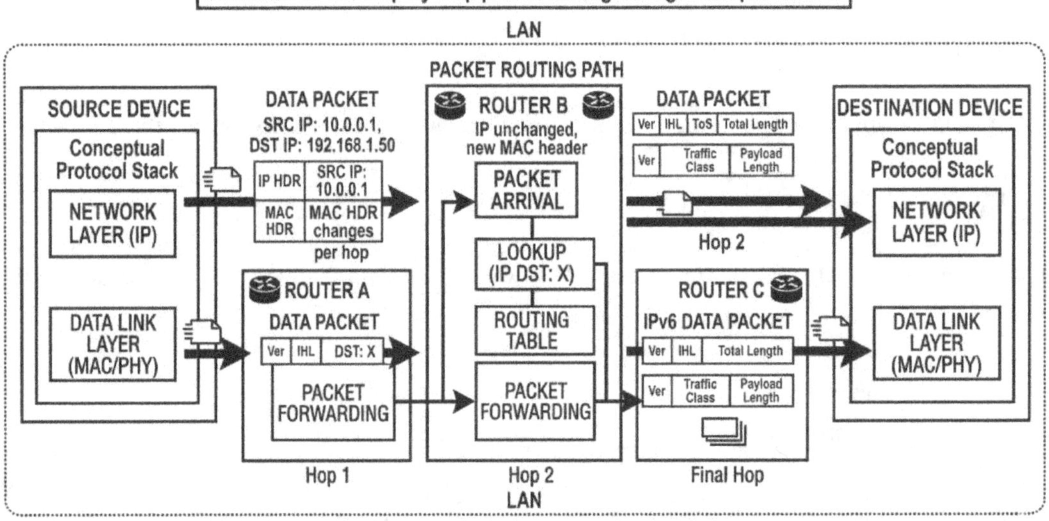

This process happens extremely quickly and continuously in modern networks.

Types of Routing

Routing can be performed in different ways depending on how routing information is maintained and updated.

The two main types of routing are:

- Static Routing
- Dynamic Routing

Static Routing

In static routing, network administrators manually configure routing paths in the router.

This means the router will always follow the same predefined path to send data packets.

Static routing is simple and easy to implement in small networks.

However, it has limitations because the routes do not change automatically if a network failure occurs.

Static Routing Showing Fixed Path Between Networks

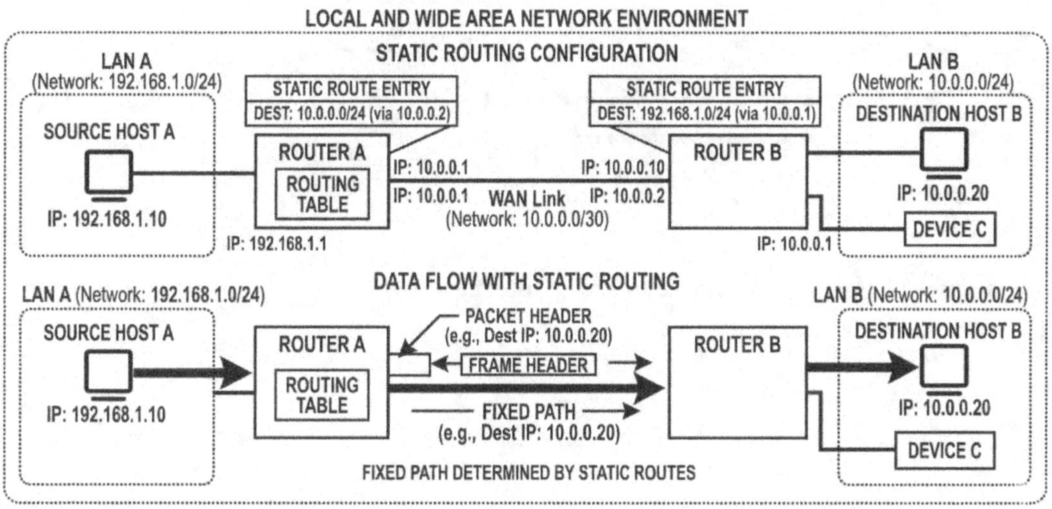

Because of these limitations, static routing is usually used in small networks or simple network environments.

Dynamic Routing

In dynamic routing, routers automatically learn and update routing information using special routing protocols.

These protocols allow routers to exchange information about network paths and update their routing tables automatically.

If a network path becomes unavailable, dynamic routing protocols can automatically find an alternative path.

Dynamic Routing Showing Routers Exchanging Routing Information

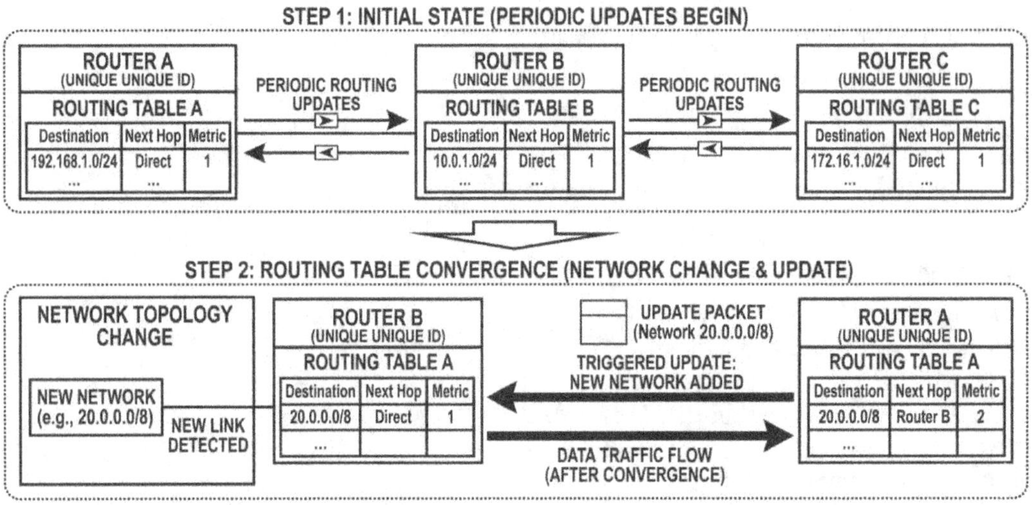

Dynamic routing is commonly used in large networks such as the Internet.

Routing Protocols

Routing protocols are used by routers to communicate with each other and share routing information.

Some commonly used routing protocols include:

- RIP (Routing Information Protocol)
- OSPF (Open Shortest Path First)
- BGP (Border Gateway Protocol)

These protocols help routers determine the most efficient path for data packets.

Routers exchanging routing updates using routing protocols.

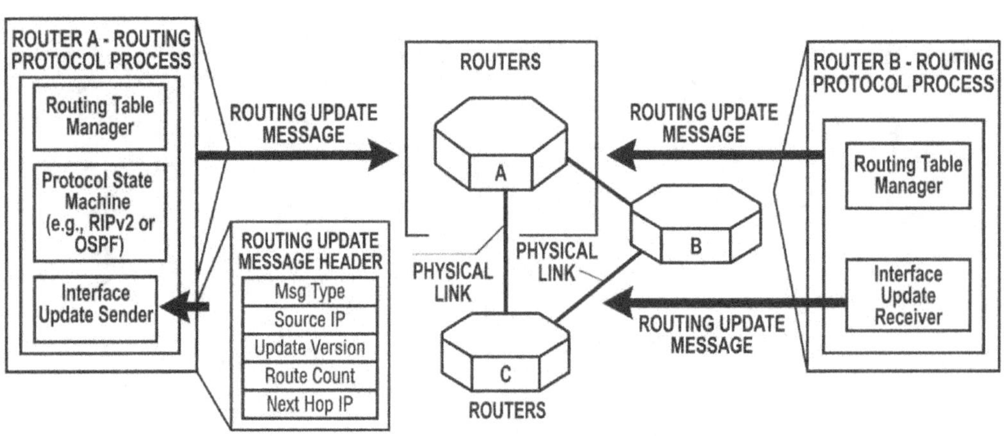

Importance of Routing in Modern Networks

Routing plays a crucial role in modern networking systems.

Without routing, communication between different networks would not be possible.

Routing allows networks across different locations, cities, and even countries to communicate with each other.

It also ensures that data packets travel through the most efficient path, reducing network congestion and improving communication speed.

Real-World Example

When a user opens a website in a browser, the request is sent from the user's device to a nearby router.

The router then forwards the request through several other routers across the Internet until it reaches the web server hosting the website.

The server sends the response back using a similar routing process.

Even though this communication may involve many routers, the entire process happens within a fraction of a second.

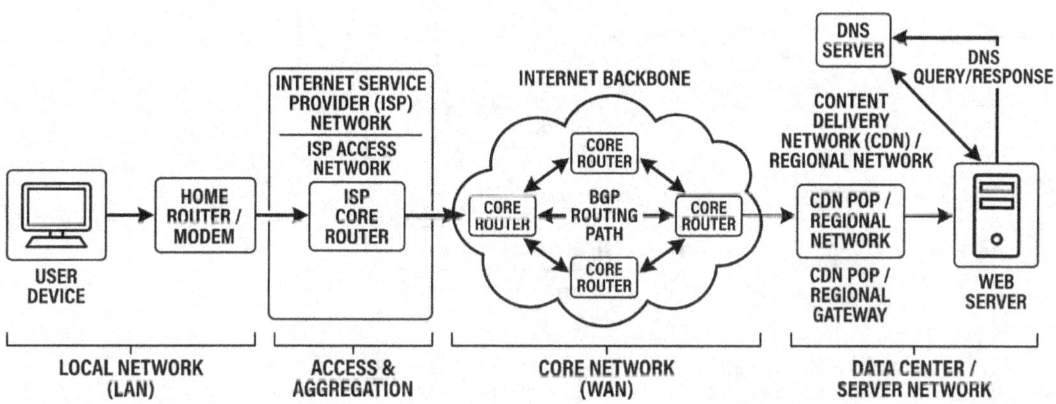

Summary

Routing is the process of determining the best path for data packets to travel between different networks.

Routers perform this function by examining destination IP addresses and forwarding packets accordingly.

Routing can be performed using static routing or dynamic routing, depending on how routing information is managed.

Routing protocols such as RIP, OSPF, and BGP help routers exchange information and maintain efficient communication across networks.

Routing is a fundamental concept that enables communication across the Internet and other large networks.

Transport Layer Protocols

In computer networks, once data has been routed to the correct network using IP addresses, it still needs to be delivered reliably to the correct application on the destination device.

This responsibility is handled by the Transport Layer of the OSI model.

The transport layer ensures that data is delivered correctly, efficiently, and in the proper order between the sender and receiver.

It also manages tasks such as:

Data segmentation.
Flow control.
Error control.
End-to-end communication.

Communication between two applications using the transport layer.

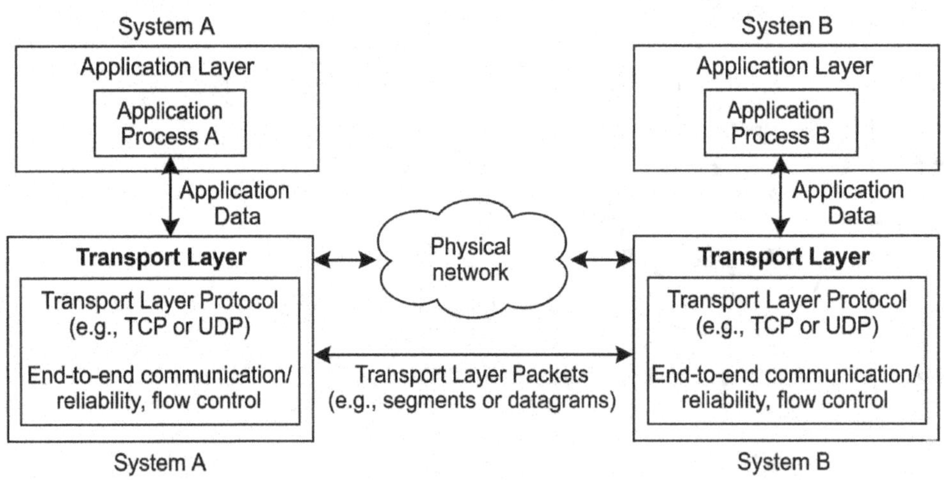

To perform these tasks, the transport layer uses special communication protocols known as Transport Layer Protocols.

The two most important transport layer protocols used on the Internet are:
Transmission Control Protocol (TCP)

User Datagram Protocol (UDP)

Each of these protocols is designed for different types of communication.

Transmission Control Protocol (TCP)

The Transmission Control Protocol (TCP) is a connection-oriented transport protocol used for reliable communication.

Connection-oriented means that a connection must be established between the sender and receiver before data transmission begins.

TCP ensures that data is delivered accurately, completely, and in the correct order.

Because of this reliability, TCP is widely used in applications where data accuracy is very important.

Examples include:

Web browsing
Email communication
File transfers

Working of TCP

TCP communication follows a structured process.

First, a connection is established between the sender and receiver using a process called the three-way handshake.

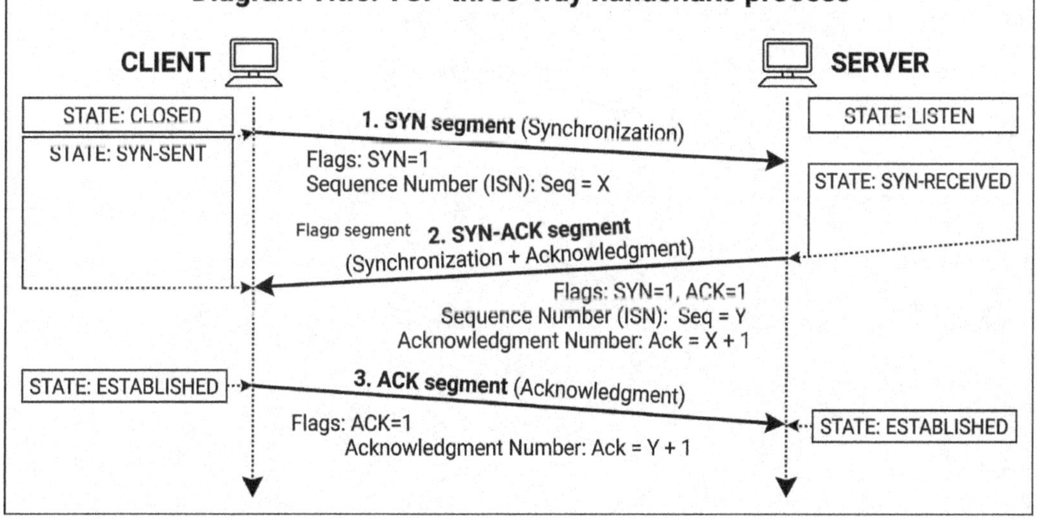

Diagram Title: TCP three-way handshake process

The three steps of this handshake are:

The sender sends a SYN (synchronize) message to the receiver.
The receiver replies with a SYN-ACK (synchronize acknowledgment) message.
The sender sends an ACK (acknowledgment) message.

After this process, the connection is established and data transmission begins.

Features of TCP

TCP provides several important features that make communication reliable.

One important feature is error detection and correction. If any data segment is lost or corrupted during transmission, TCP can detect the error and request retransmission.

Another feature is flow control, which ensures that the sender does not transmit data faster than the receiver can handle.

TCP also provides sequence numbering, which ensures that data segments are reassembled in the correct order at the destination.

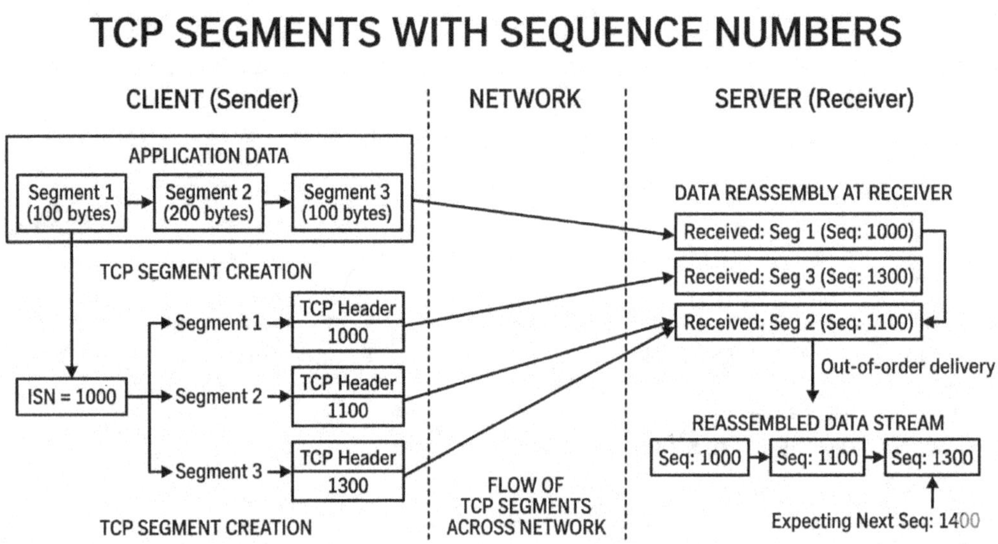

Because of these features, TCP is considered a reliable communication protocol.

Applications of TCP

TCP is used in many Internet applications that require reliable data transmission.

Some examples include:

HTTP – used for web browsing.
FTP – used for file transfer.
SMTP – used for sending emails.

In these applications, it is very important that all data arrives correctly and completely.

User Datagram Protocol (UDP)

The User Datagram Protocol (UDP) is another transport layer protocol used in computer networks.

Unlike TCP, UDP is a connectionless protocol, which means that data can be sent without establishing a connection first.

UDP sends data in the form of datagrams.

Because UDP does not establish a connection or perform extensive error checking, it is faster but less reliable than TCP.

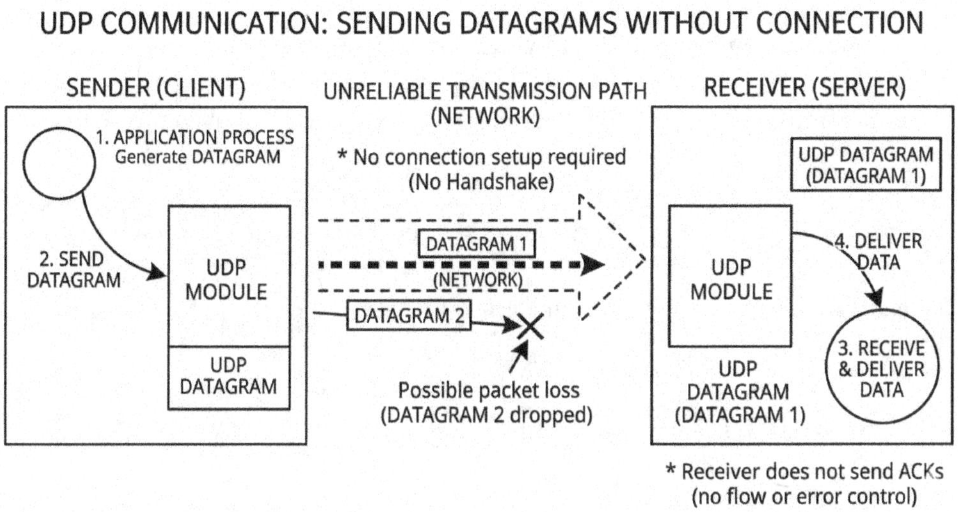

Characteristics of UDP

UDP has several characteristics that distinguish it from TCP.

First, UDP provides faster data transmission because it does not require connection establishment.

Second, UDP does not guarantee reliable delivery of data packets.

Third, UDP does not provide sequencing or retransmission mechanisms.

However, because UDP has very little overhead, it is suitable for applications where speed is more important than reliability.

Applications of UDP

UDP is commonly used in applications that require real-time communication.

Examples include:

Video streaming.
Online gaming.
Voice over Internet Protocol (VoIP).
Live broadcasting.

In these applications, receiving data quickly is more important than retransmitting lost packets.

For example, in a live video stream, losing a few packets may not significantly affect the viewing experience, but delays caused by retransmission could disrupt the stream.

Difference Between TCP and UDP

Although both TCP and UDP are transport layer protocols, they serve different purposes.

TCP provides reliable and ordered communication, while UDP provides fast and lightweight communication.

TCP establishes a connection before transmitting data, while UDP sends data immediately without establishing a connection.

Because of these differences, different applications choose the protocol that best suits their requirements.

Comparison of Reliable TCP Communication and Faster UDP Communication

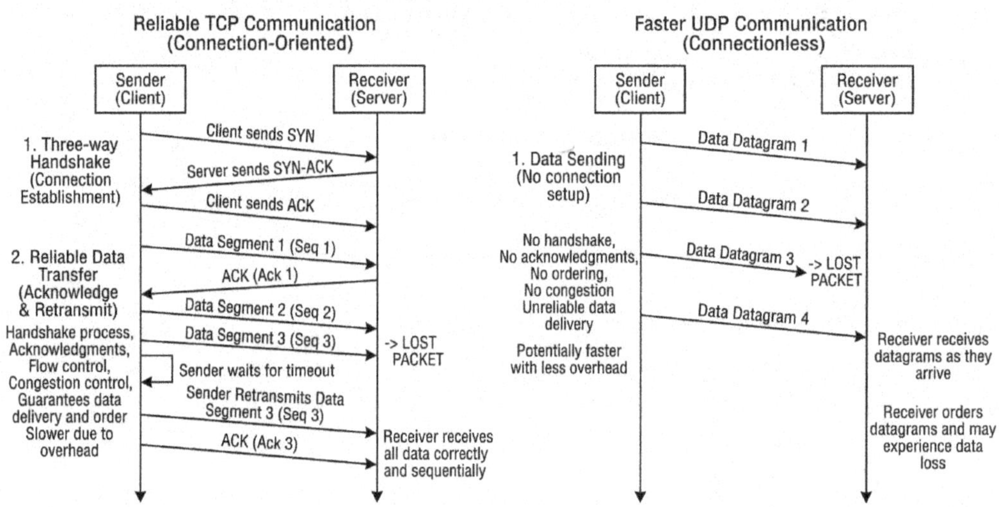

Real-World Example

Consider the example of watching a live sports match online.

If the video streaming service used TCP, any lost packet would require retransmission, which might cause delays and buffering.

Instead, many streaming services use UDP because it allows continuous streaming even if some packets are lost.

On the other hand, when downloading a file from the Internet, TCP is used to ensure that the entire file is received correctly.

Summary

The transport layer plays a crucial role in ensuring reliable communication between applications on different devices.

Two major transport layer protocols used in computer networks are TCP and UDP.

TCP is a connection-oriented protocol that provides reliable data transmission with error detection and flow control.

UDP is a connectionless protocol that provides faster communication but does not guarantee reliable delivery.

Both protocols are widely used in modern networking depending on the requirements of the application.

Application Layer Protocols

In computer networks, users interact with network services through applications such as web browsers, email clients, and file transfer programs. These applications require specific rules and standards to communicate with servers across the Internet.

These rules are defined by Application Layer Protocols.

The Application Layer is the topmost layer of the OSI model. It provides an interface between the user and the network services. Application layer protocols define how applications communicate over the network.

These protocols allow services such as:

Web browsing.
Email communication.
File transfer.
Domain name resolution.

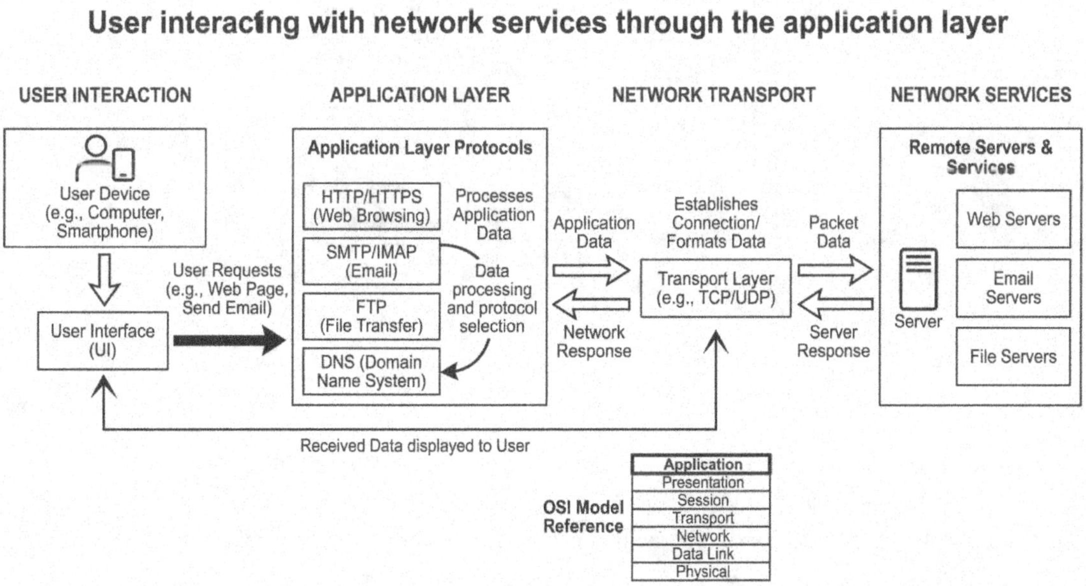

Some of the most important application layer protocols include:

DNS
HTTP
SMTP
POP
FTP
URL and WWW

Each of these protocols performs a specific function in Internet communication.

DNS (Domain Name System)

The Domain Name System (DNS) is a protocol used to translate human-readable domain names into IP addresses.

Computers and networking devices communicate using IP addresses, but it is difficult for humans to remember numerical addresses. Instead, people use domain names such as:

www.google.com
www.amazon.com
www.wikipedia.org

DNS converts these domain names into the corresponding IP addresses.

DNS resolving domain name into IP address.

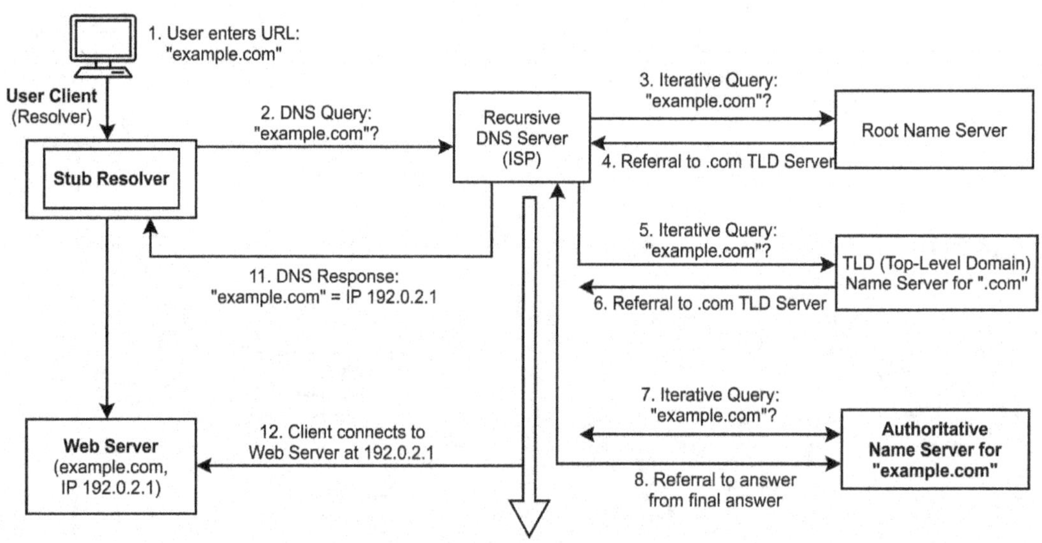

Working of DNS

When a user enters a website address in a browser, the browser sends a request to a DNS server.

The DNS server looks up the domain name in its database and returns the corresponding IP address.

Once the IP address is obtained, the browser can establish communication with the web server hosting the website.

DIAGRAM: DNS REQUEST AND RESPONSE PROCESS

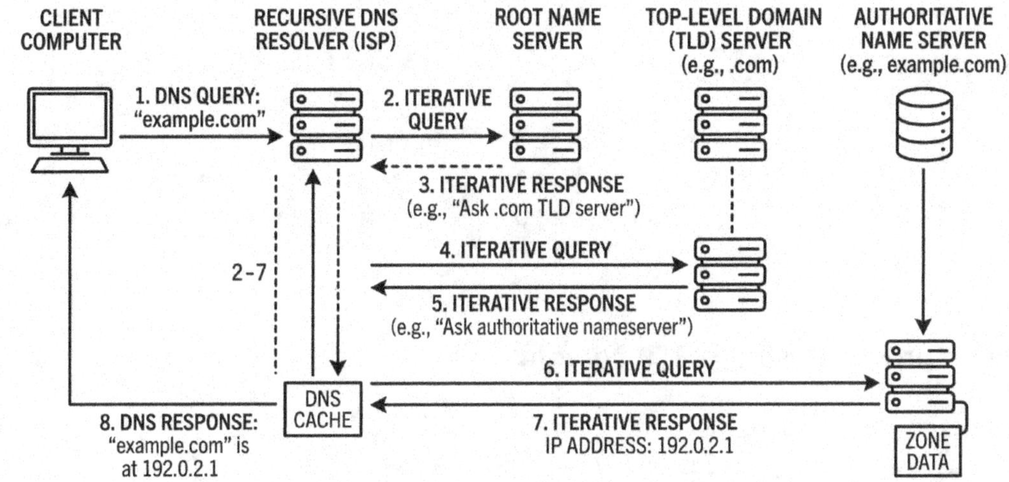

Without DNS, users would have to remember IP addresses for every website they want to visit.

HTTP (Hypertext Transfer Protocol)

The Hypertext Transfer Protocol (HTTP) is the protocol used for communication between web browsers and web servers.

Whenever a user opens a website in a browser, HTTP is used to request the webpage from the server and deliver it to the user.

HTTP COMMUNICATION BETWEEN BROWSER AND WEB SERVER

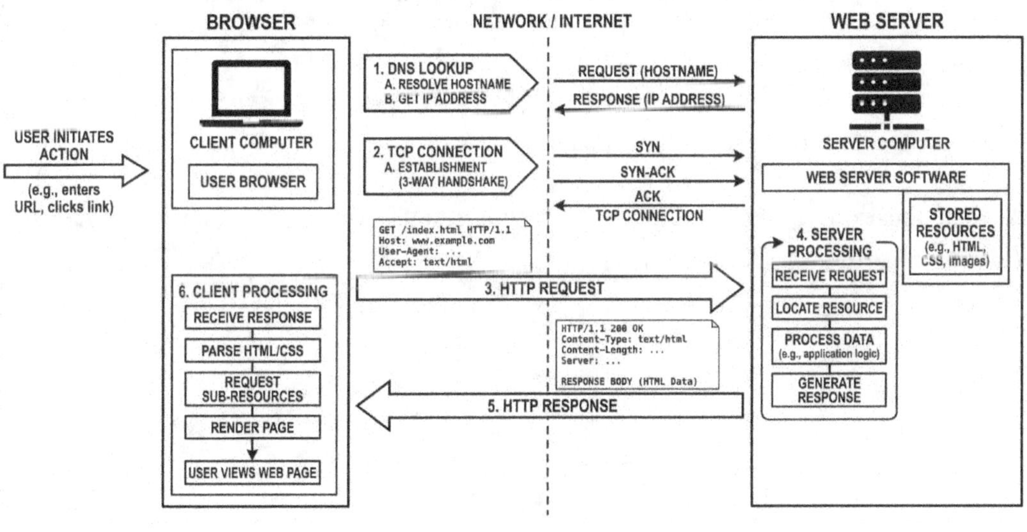

HTTP follows a request-response model.

First, the browser sends a request to the server.

Then, the server processes the request and sends the webpage data back to the browser.

This data may include text, images, videos, and other multimedia content.

SMTP (Simple Mail Transfer Protocol)

The Simple Mail Transfer Protocol (SMTP) is used to send emails over the Internet.

When a user sends an email, SMTP is responsible for transferring the message from the sender's mail server to the recipient's mail server.

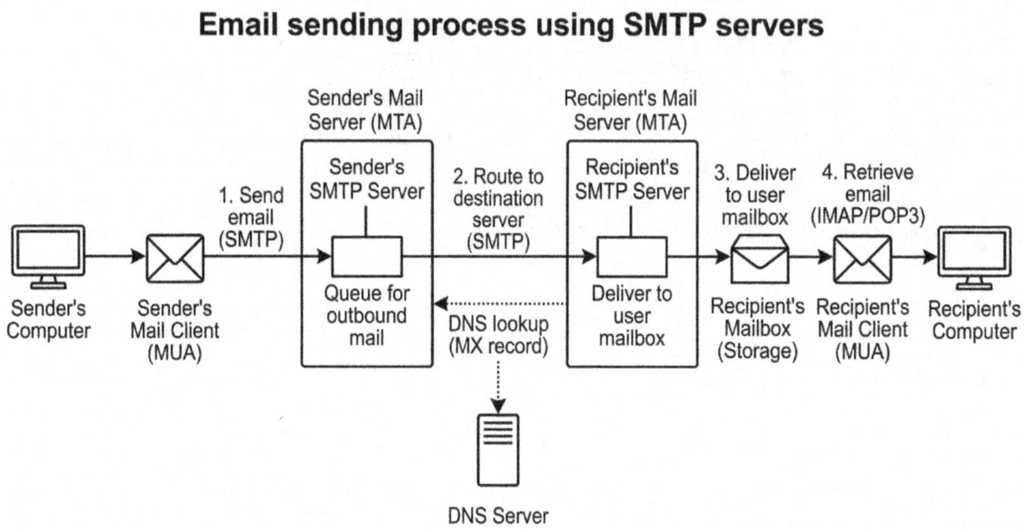

SMTP works in cooperation with other protocols such as POP and IMAP, which are used to retrieve emails.

POP (Post Office Protocol)

The Post Office Protocol (POP) is used to retrieve emails from a mail server.

When a user opens their email application, the POP protocol downloads emails from the mail server to the user's device.

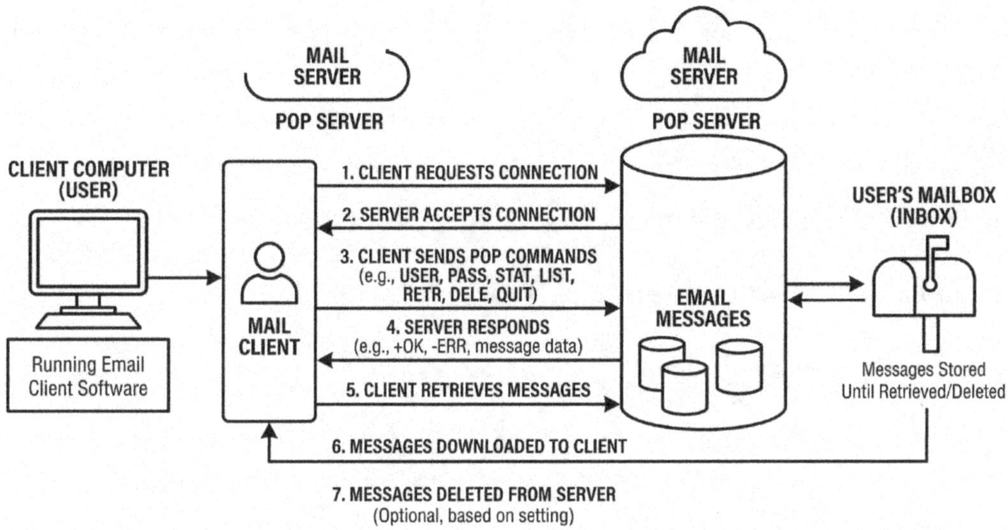

After downloading, the emails may be stored locally on the user's device.

POP is commonly used in traditional email systems.

FTP (File Transfer Protocol)

The File Transfer Protocol (FTP) is used for transferring files between computers over a network.

FTP allows users to upload and download files between a client device and a server.

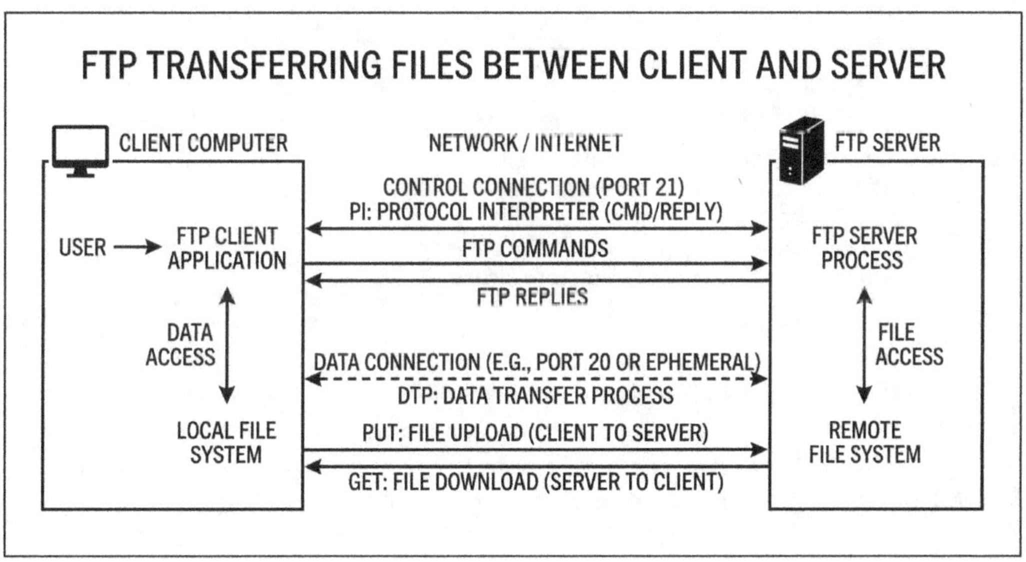

FTP is commonly used for tasks such as:

Uploading files to web servers.
Downloading software from servers.
Managing website content.

Although FTP is widely used, secure versions such as SFTP and FTPS are often preferred today because they provide better security.

URL (Uniform Resource Locator)

A URL is the address used to locate a resource on the Internet.

Every webpage, image, video, or file available on the Internet has a unique URL.

A typical URL consists of several components, including:

Protocol (such as HTTP or HTTPS)

Domain name.
Path to the resource.

For example:
https://www.example.com/index.html

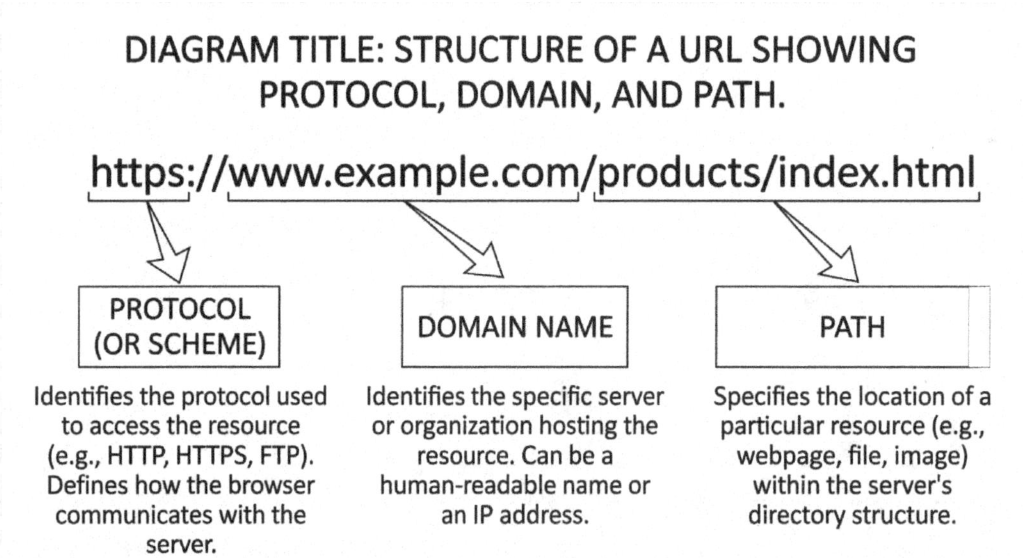

The URL helps the browser locate and retrieve the requested resource from the web server.
WWW (World Wide Web)

The World Wide Web (WWW) is a system of interconnected web pages that can be accessed through the Internet.

The Web is built using technologies such as:

HTTP
HTML
Web browsers
Web servers

Users access the World Wide Web using browsers such as Chrome, Firefox, or Edge.

World Wide Web connecting users to web servers.

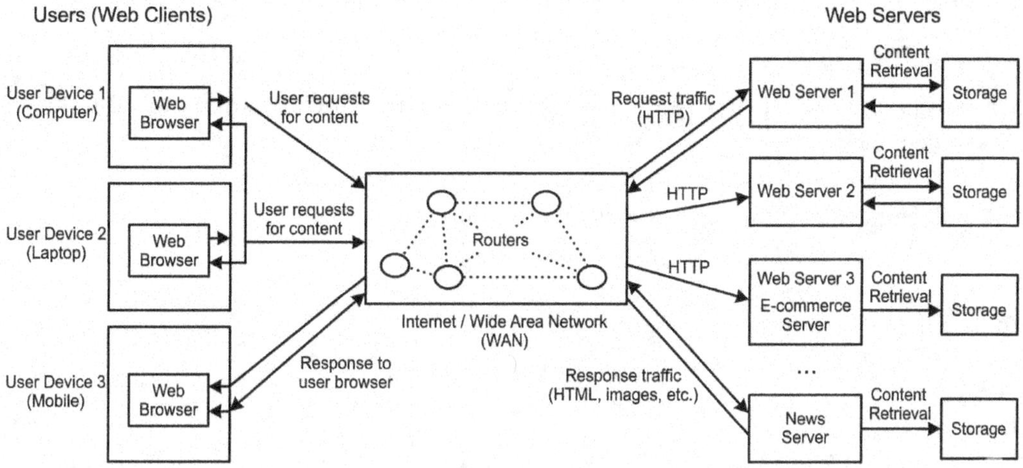

The web allows users to access information, communicate, watch videos, read articles, and perform many online activities.

Real-World Example

When a user opens a website in a browser, several application layer protocols work together.

First, the browser uses DNS to convert the domain name into an IP address.

Next, HTTP is used to request the webpage from the web server.

If the user sends an email through a webmail service, SMTP is used to send the message.

If files are uploaded or downloaded from a server, FTP may be used.

This collaboration of protocols enables smooth communication across the Internet.

Summary

Application layer protocols allow users and applications to interact with network services.

Protocols such as DNS, HTTP, SMTP, POP, and FTP perform specific tasks such as domain name resolution, web communication, email transfer, and file transfer.

The URL provides a unique address for resources on the Internet, and the World Wide Web connects billions of web pages and services across the globe.

Together, these protocols form the foundation of modern Internet communication.

Modern Networking Technologies

Computer networking technology has evolved significantly over the years. Earlier networks were limited to simple wired connections between computers. Today, modern networking technologies allow people and devices to communicate from almost anywhere in the world.

Modern networks support a wide range of services such as wireless communication, cloud computing, smart devices, and high-speed mobile connectivity.

Some of the most important modern networking technologies include:

Wi-Fi (IEEE 802.11)
Mobile Networks (4G and 5G)
Cloud Networking
Internet of Things (IoT)

These technologies play a crucial role in today's digital world and enable new applications in communication, business, education, healthcare, and entertainment.

Overview of modern networking technologies connecting multiple devices

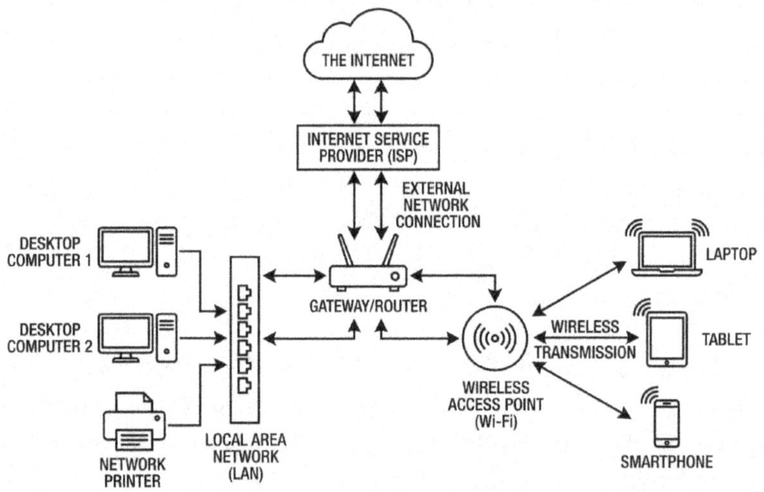

Wi-Fi (IEEE 802.11)

Wi-Fi is one of the most widely used wireless networking technologies in the world. It allows devices such as laptops, smartphones, tablets, and smart TVs to connect to a network without using physical cables.

Wi-Fi is based on a set of standards developed by the Institute of Electrical and Electronics Engineers (IEEE) known as IEEE 802.11.

These standards define how wireless communication should occur between devices and wireless access points.

Wi-Fi network with access point and multiple devices

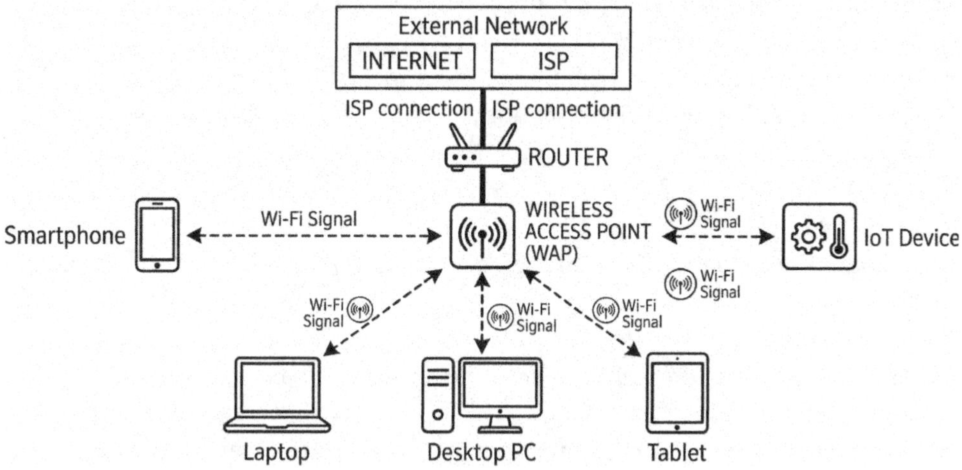

Working of Wi-Fi

A Wi-Fi network usually consists of a device called a wireless access point (AP) or wireless router.

The access point is connected to the Internet through a wired network connection.

Wireless devices communicate with the access point using radio signals.

The access point then forwards the data to the Internet or to other devices on the network.

Wi-Fi communication between devices and router.

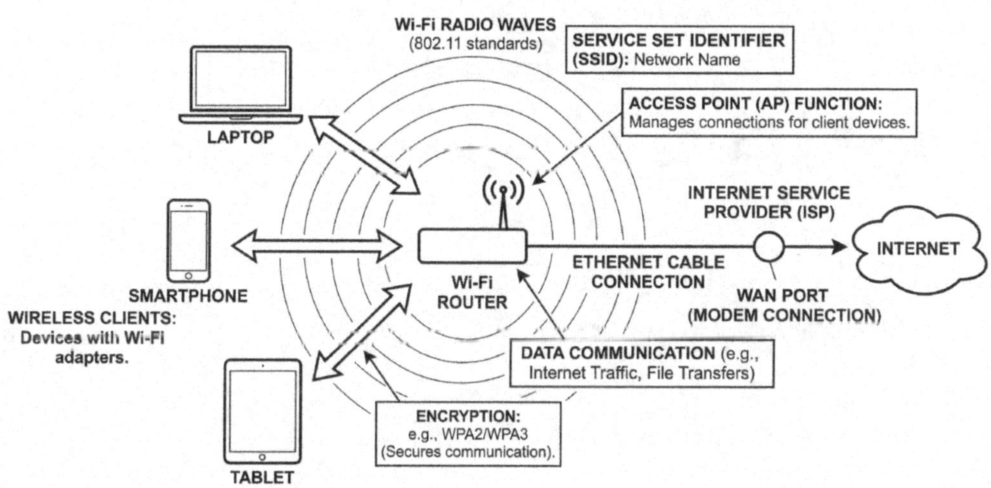

Advantages of Wi-Fi

Wi-Fi provides several advantages for users.

First, it allows mobility, meaning users can move around within the coverage area while remaining connected to the network.

Second, it eliminates the need for cables, which simplifies installation and reduces infrastructure costs.

Third, Wi-Fi supports high data speeds, making it suitable for applications such as video streaming, online gaming, and file sharing.

Because of these benefits, Wi-Fi is widely used in homes, offices, schools, airports, and public spaces.

Mobile Networks (4G and 5G)

Mobile networks allow users to access communication services through cellular devices such as smartphones and tablets.

These networks use a system of cell towers that provide wireless coverage over large geographic areas.

Modern mobile networks use technologies such as 4G (Fourth Generation) and 5G (Fifth Generation).

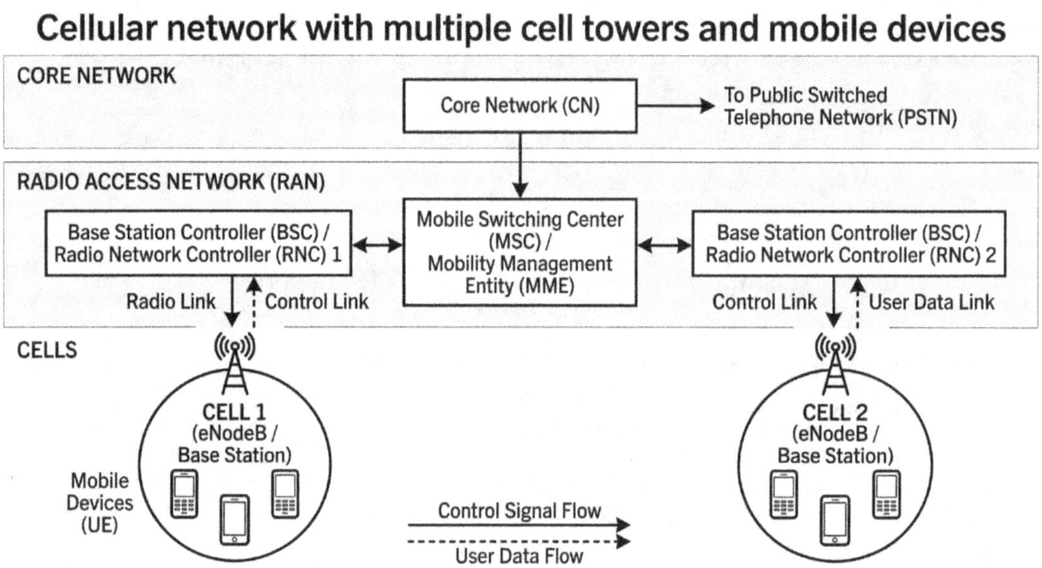

4G Networks

4G networks provide high-speed mobile Internet connectivity.

They support services such as:

Video streaming
Online gaming
Video calls
Mobile applications

4G networks provide faster speeds and better performance compared to earlier technologies such as 2G and 3G.

5G Networks

5G networks represent the next generation of mobile communication technology.

They provide extremely high data speeds, lower latency, and the ability to support a large number of connected devices.

5G networks enable new applications such as:

Smart cities
Autonomous vehicles
Remote surgery
Advanced IoT systems

High-speed 5G communication connecting many smart devices.

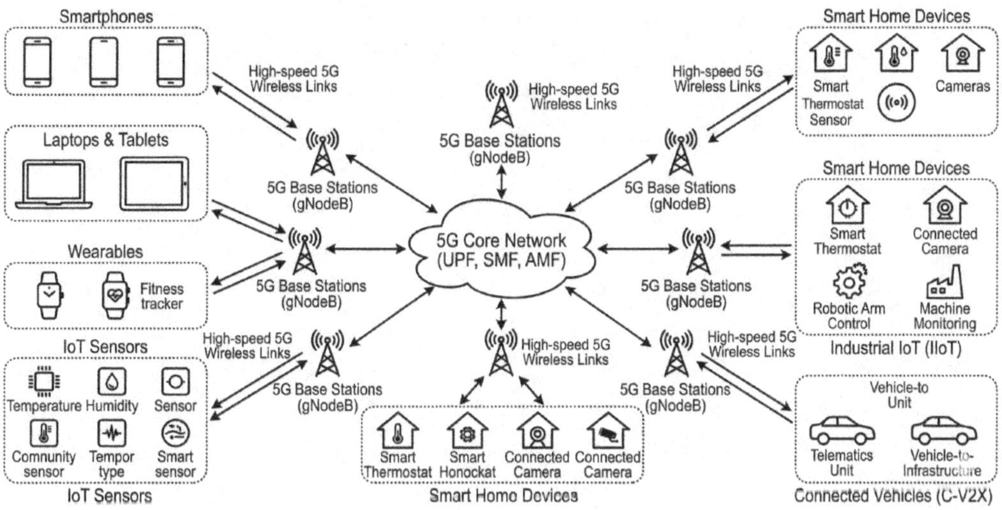

Because of these capabilities, 5G is expected to transform many industries.

Cloud Networking

Cloud networking refers to the use of cloud computing infrastructure to deliver networking services.

Instead of relying entirely on local servers and hardware, organizations can store data and run applications on remote cloud servers.

These cloud servers are accessible through the Internet.

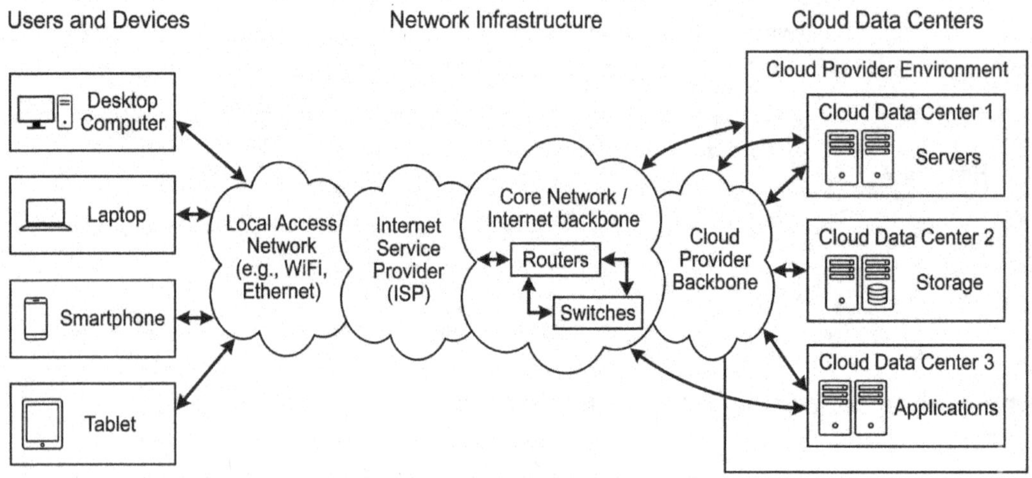

Advantages of Cloud Networking

Cloud networking provides several benefits.

First, it allows organizations to access data and applications from anywhere.

Second, it reduces the need for expensive hardware and maintenance.

Third, cloud services can easily scale up or down depending on demand.

For example, companies can increase server capacity during peak usage periods and reduce it when demand decreases.

Cloud networking is widely used in services such as:

Online storage systems
Web applications
Software-as-a-Service (SaaS) platforms

Internet of Things (IoT)

The Internet of Things (IoT) refers to a network of physical devices that are connected to the Internet and can communicate with each other.

These devices may include:

Smart home appliances
Security cameras
Smart watches
Sensors
Industrial machines

IoT devices collect data from their environment and transmit it to other devices or cloud systems for processing.

IoT ecosystem connecting smart devices, sensors, and cloud servers

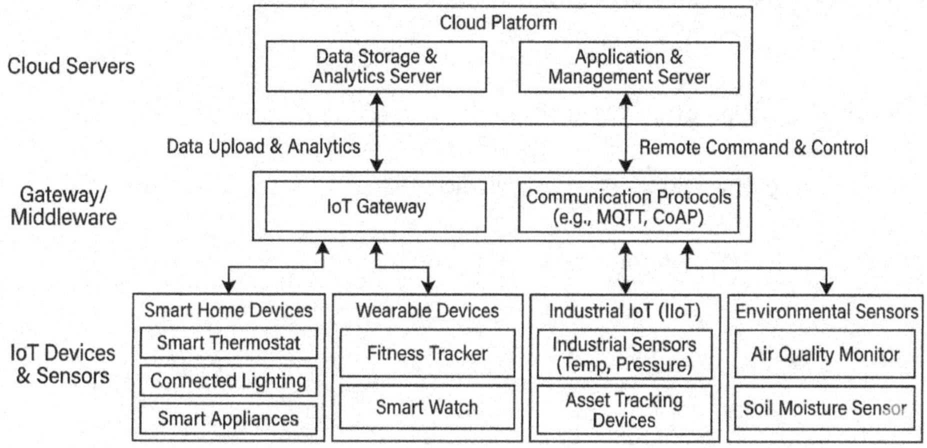

Applications of IoT

IoT technology is used in many areas of modern life.

In smart homes, IoT devices allow users to control lights, thermostats, and security systems remotely.

In healthcare, IoT devices monitor patient health and transmit medical data to doctors.

In industrial environments, IoT sensors help monitor equipment performance and detect potential failures.

These applications improve efficiency, automation, and convenience.

Future of Networking Technologies

Modern networking technologies continue to evolve rapidly.

Advances in wireless communication, cloud computing, and IoT are transforming the way devices interact with each other.

Future networking systems are expected to provide:

Higher data speeds
Lower latency
Greater reliability
Support for billions of connected devices

These developments will enable new technologies such as smart cities, autonomous transportation systems, and advanced artificial intelligence applications.

Real-World Example

Consider a smart home environment.

In a smart home, devices such as smart lights, security cameras, thermostats, and voice assistants are connected through Wi-Fi and IoT technologies.

These devices communicate with cloud servers and mobile applications.

Users can control their home devices remotely using a smartphone application.

This integration of Wi-Fi, cloud networking, and IoT demonstrates how modern networking technologies work together in everyday life.

Summary

Modern networking technologies have transformed the way devices communicate and share information.

Technologies such as Wi-Fi, mobile networks (4G and 5G), cloud networking, and IoT enable fast, flexible, and scalable communication systems.

These technologies support a wide range of applications, from everyday Internet use to advanced smart systems.

As networking technology continues to evolve, it will play an even greater role in shaping the future of communication and digital innovation.

www.ingramcontent.com/pod-product-compliance
Lightning Source LLC
LaVergne TN
LVHW080037210926
848481LV00011B/3213
* 9 7 9 8 9 0 2 6 9 6 5 9 9 *